THE BEAT GENERATION WRITERS

The Beats' enthusiasm for new voices and new ways of expression distinguishes them as one of the most democratic group of writers that America has ever produced. This intelligently focused collection – especially the chapters on race and gender issues – helps to locate the Beat writers in the social and cultural context of their times. It is a very welcome and useful supplement to their work.

Ann Charters

At last, an intelligent and peerless compendium of critical essays on the Beat Literacy Movement, tackling prickly issues of language, gender, race, feminism, anarchy, subjectivity. This is a much needed guide and recondite reading of these controversial writers and cultural icons. I recommend *The Beat Generation Writers* to serious scholars, students and fans of the historic Beat canon.

Anne Waldman, Director,
The Jack Kerouac School of Disembodied Poetics,
The Naropa Institute, Boulder, Colorado

The Beat Generation Writers

Edited by
A. Robert Lee

Pluto AP Press
London • East Haven, Connecticut

First published 1996 by Pluto Press
345 Archway Road, London N6 5AA
and 140 Commerce Street, East Haven
Connecticut 06512, USA

British Library Cataloguing in Publication Data
A catalogue record for this book is available from the British Library

ISBN 0 7453 0660 8 hbk

Library of Congress Cataloging in Publication Data
The beat generation writers/edited by A. Robert Lee
    p.   cm.
  Includes index.
  ISBN 0–7453–0660–8. — ISBN 0–7453–0661–6 (pbk.)
  1. American literature—20th century—History and criticism.
  2. Beat generation. I. Lee, A. Robert
  PS228.B6B425   1996
  810.9'0054—dc20   95–7723
                                                        CIP

Designed and produced for Pluto Press by
Chase Production Services, Chipping Norton, OX7 5QR
Typeset from disk by Stanford DTP Services, Milton Keynes
Printed in the EC by WSOY, Finland

Contents

Acknowledgements

The Beat Generation Writers began under the editorship of Brian Docherty. For private reasons he had to withdraw from the project and other essays were then commissioned by Pluto Press. My role as Editor has thus been recent and grew out of being one of the initial essay-contributors. I need to thank all the essayists involved, and Anne Beech and Robert Webb of Pluto Press, for their helpfulness in working with this slight change of masthead.

A. Robert Lee, University of Kent at Canterbury

Introduction

A. Robert Lee

The Beat Generation is altogether too vigorous, too intent, too inde-
fatigable, too curious to suit its elders. Nothing seems to satisfy or
interest it but extremes, which if they have included the criminality
of narcotics, have also included the sanctity of monasteries. Everywhere
the Beat Generation seems occupied with the feverish production of
answers – some of them frightening, some of them foolish – to a single
question: how are we to live?

John Clellon Holmes, 'The Philosophy of
the Beat Generation' (1958)[1]

The word 'beat' originally meant poor, down and out, dead-beat, on
the bum, sad, sleeping in subways. Now that the word is belonging
officially it is being made to stretch to include people who do not
sleep in subways but have a new gesture, or attitude, which I can only
describe as a new *more*. 'Beat Generation' has simply become the slogan
or label for a revolution in manners in America.

Jack Kerouac, 'The Origins of The Beat Generation' (1959)[2]

The Beat Generation is filled with divinations, it has stiff hair, large
bones, firm and robust limbs, short muscular neck, firm and erect,
the head and breast high, the forehead short, hard, and peaked, with
bristly hair, large feet, rather thick than broad, a harsh unequal voice,
a voice of divinity, a new voice, conqueror eater voice, parasite of the
old dead voice.

Gregory Corso, 'Variations On A Generation' (1959)[3]

For a readership now closer to the incoming new century than to the
Second World War the 'Beat Generation' might well give the impression
of having arisen out of an immediate postwar world if not wholly
passed from view then fast-receding. The America of the late 1940s and
1950s which supplies a begetting context for the Beats – its pre-eminent
names those of Jack Kerouac, Allen Ginsberg, Lawrence Ferlinghetti,

Gregory Corso, John Clellon Holmes, Gary Snyder, Michael McClure, Phil Walen and John Wieners – increasingly takes on datedness, a historic pastness.

At home the writ had become one of the suburbs, consumer durables, autos, TVs, corporations, and eventually Eisenhower's 'military–industrial complex' and McCarthyism. Abroad it meant Cold War anti-Sovietism, isolationism and Korea. Nor, for all the greyness, could it ever be denied that America at mid-century was not also an age of anxiety, even paranoia. However risky any account of history by decades, especially one rife in contradiction and which runs over into a 1960s whose own turbulence marks both a continuance and a leave-taking, the era begins to seem of a kind with the Jazz Age or the Depression as yet another fabled American time-when.

If the signs were there of a new dispensation in the person of John F. Kennedy, with soon to follow The White House as Camelot, the Space Age as a literal 'New Frontier' and, more darkly, the Cuban Missile Crisis as a first global crisis, so, the Beats, too, dissident, countercultural, harbingers of their own kind of newness, play a matching part. 'Woe unto those who don't realize that America must, will, is changing now, for the better I say' announced Jack Kerouac in playful, mock-prophetic mode in 1959.[4] 'America ... Are you going to let your emotional life be run by Time magazine?' asked an even more tongue-in-cheek Allen Ginsberg in his poem 'America'.[5]

For in keeping with fellow Beats and at whatever risk of grandiosity theirs was the self-appointed task of both unmaking and making America. Middle-American conformity represented a citadel to be stormed, youth an energy to be liberated, the official politics of Corporation and Pentagon a ruse to be exposed, and sexual repressions a burden in need of challenge and release. Life, if it were to matter, would be lived existentially at the edge; confrontation, shock-tactic obscenity when needed, a non-ideological politics of drop-out or commune, sex or marijuana virtually on demand, endless readings, love-ins, happenings, changes of fashion and talk, these would all be the means of assault and change. Notice, it could hardly go unremarked, had been served on mid-cult, as it became known, the latest Babbittry of organisation-man and the grey-flannelled suit.

Poetry and fiction, accordingly, would be de-academised, visionary, performative, a 'bop prosody' in Jack Kerouac's memorial phrase and given over to a language able to refract, and help usher in, the new 'beatitude'. The page was more to be spoken, or heard, anything but to be studied in the academies, and offering a 'measure' whose origins were to be found in the American line-cadences of Walt Whitman, Carl Sandburg, Hart Crane and William Carlos Williams, in the incantation of Bible and Torah, in the blues. Ephemera notwithstanding, and without taking them unreservedly at their own value, does not so open and accessible an aesthetic in part help explain why the Beats continue to arouse interest, Kerouac, Ginsberg and the rest as perennial figures of stimulus and rediscovery?

East to West Coast America, South of the Border to North Africa, Tibet to Amsterdam, India to London, may all have supplied staging-posts for Beat gatherings (the 'International Poetry Incarnation', held at the Royal Albert Hall in June 1965, with its publicity as 'World declaration hot peace shower!' and 'Spontaneous planet-chant Carnival!' holds a special place in British annals). Pot, later LSD (though not heroin), booze to an extent, Transcendental Meditation, every manner of sexual per-mutation, and 'kicks' in general, may all been part of the publicity and baggage. Yet for all their vaunted populism (redskins as against palefaces in Philip Rahv's celebrated opposition), their writings from the start carried the impress of antecedent literary presences and influences.[6] How bookish they were, to be sure bookish in their own way, has been one of the important features to emerge in any number of revisionary accounts of their place in American literature.

Despite, too, the in-reference, the 'boy-gang' or 'fellahin' ethos as it became known, and all the fame and notoriety which came with it, they themselves were anything but the only players. The missing, and still only gradually emerging signatures, point to a generation of 'Beat women' beyond 'the chicks', the supposed virgin–whores or sainted mothers – chief among the latter a Naomi Ginsberg or 'Mémère' Kerouac. Only in the aftermath of the movement's hey-day has their witness duly begun to emerge: poets, anthologists, and latterday memoirists, whose ranks include Diane Di Prima, Anne Waldman, Joanna Kyger, Joyce Johnson, Carolyn Cassady, Eileen Kaufman, Hettie Jones, Jan Kerouac and Ann Charters.

The other great imput derives from an African–American gathering, the LeRoi Jones still to transpose into the black-nationalist Imamu Amiri Baraka, the virtuoso 'street' Californian black–Jewish writer Bob Kaufman, and the 'talking blues', international performance-poet Ted Joans. If Afro-America, its jazz, argots, street savvy, risk, are all enseamed in Beat writing, then these, and especially black musicians like Archie Shepp or Miles Davis to whom they were drawn (and who were drawn to them), constitute a literary citizenry from source, their blackness lived at, and written from, first hand.

Around them, too, were yet other co-presences often of an eventually near-mythic kind. Few were to achieve greater notoriety than William Burroughs, *el hombre invisible* as became his soubriquet, whose *Naked Lunch* (1952) at once startled and exhilarated by its Swiftian, laconic, drug-originated 'cut-up' of a world hooked into supplier-user images of power. Neal Cassady, hipster princeling and Jack Kerouac's model for Dean Moriarty in *On The Road* (1956) and his successor Cody Pomeray in *Visions of Cody* (1972), equally features, a memorialisation further augmented by his death in 1968.

John Clellon Holmes, who helped define the 'Beat movement' after Kerouac's founding use of the term himself contributed two landmark novels, the pre-Beat, 'hip', anything-for-kicks *Go* (1952) and the jazz-centred *The Horn* (1958). Herbert Huncke, Times Square existentalist-thief whose Jean Genet-like autobiography, *Guilty of Everything*, would wait until 1990 for publication, seemed the very spirit of American Dostoevskianism, a literal figure of shadow and underground. Ken Kesey, on the other hand, whose debts to the Beat ethos in *One Flew Over the Cuckoo's Nest* (1962) and his 'on the road' LSD and other prankster antics he readily acknowledges in his essay-collection *Demon Box* (1986), suggested a figure of life, Beat as affirmation, energy, beatitude. Of a slightly older vintage is Chandler Brossard whose novel, *Who Walk in Darkness* (1952), New York down-and-out bohemianism with a Beat overlay, anticipates much of the movement's style and concerns.

One key interested party, himself celebrated as a celebrant of hipsterism, has to be Norman Mailer. His essay-pamphlet, 'The White Negro' (1957), with its talk of 'a new breed of adventurers, who drifted out at night looking for adventures with a black man's code to fit their facts' offers a key marker, a hymn to Beat life as a style of redemptive and enmas-culinising daring.[7] Kenneth Rexroth, the veteran West Coast poet-polemicist of American letters ('an old warhorse of the revolution of the word' he calls himself) would supply an important genealogy for the Beats in his 'Disengagement: The Art of The Beat Generation' (1957), not to say a rallying-cry in his conclusion – 'The avant garde has not only not ceased to exist. It's jumping all over the place.'[8] William Carlos Williams, imagist, author of so ranking a modernist American poem-epic as *Paterson* (1946–51), notably enters the fray in his 'Introduction' to Allen Ginsberg's *Howl and Other Poems* (1956) with its admiring talk of experience witnessed 'to the hilt' and made over into the 'effrontery' of a poetry to take its reader 'though hell'.

Given the range, the virtuosity, on offer, however, the continuance of interest in the Beat movement's best-known names often still tends to settle on two presiding texts, virtual Books of Genesis, Allen Ginsberg's *Howl and Other Poems* (1956), with its title-poem 'Howl' as centrepiece, and Jack Kerouac's *On The Road* (1956). Here, if anywhere, were the anthems of a counter-America, spontaneous, itinerary, sexual in one or another degree, in all nothing if not conceived in the spirit of

Whitman's 'Song of Myself' (1855) with its call for 'a new identity' and pluralist insistence on 'all truths in all things'.

One easily enough forgets the impact of the Beat movement's particular 'shock of the new', and the ensuing cries of outraged parenthood and different High School, college, church and military authorities. Sex, drugs, though not quite yet the full blast of rock 'n' roll, all of it often subsumed under the label Beat or Beatnik, had come to threaten the American Way, an 'unwashed' and simultaneous danger to youth, decorum, right-thinking, the Bible, 'proper' speech, and even (if *Time*, *Newsweek* and like mass-weeklies were to be believed) the very history which had 'made' the ship of state.

Applauded by some, feared and attacked by others, Beats, Beatniks, so became the focus for a popular culture which would include James Dean, Elvis Presley and Bob Dylan, reawaken mainstream America to the 'blackness' of jazz and blues and rock, cause fear as to what or what not might be soon to appear on TV or at the movie-houses and drive-ins, and reflect the growing discontent of women with their predestination as American moms and nice-girls. In Kerouac, Ginsberg, Ferlinghetti and the rest the eddies and summonings of a new writer-dissident generation were to be celebrated or resisted. From readings (or bannings) of 'Howl' and other Beat offerings to flower-power hippiedom, from Ginsberg publicly naked to the seizures of City Lights stock or *The Naked Lunch*, the times indeed were a-changing.

The higher punditry, too, in the universities and top literary magazines, spoke for the most part of a fearsome drop in standards, the barbarians – holy as they may have deemed themselves – truly at the gates. Writing in 1958, Norman Podhoretz, symptomatically, had no trouble in sub-stituting 'Know-Nothing Bohemians' for 'Holy Barbarians'.[9] Meantime the mass read-ins (often enough with accompanying haze of pot-smoke and the expectation that something untoward might happen or at least be said), the counterculture happenings (Ginsberg, say, with Ed Sanders' performance-group, 'The Fugs', or in company with Burroughs, Genet and Terry Southern at 'The Siege of Chicago' riots of 1968), the ever-present fandangoes over obscenity and/or irreligion (notably the 'Not guilty' decision by Judge Clayton Horn in the prosecution of Lawrence Ferlinghetti for publication of *Howl and Other Poems*), kept the fevers continuing and high. Each implied a generation no longer cosily at suburban rest; rather the will to 'bop' or 'cool', to a first-hand experience of the senses, had beckoned and found a wholly ready younger-generation response.

Locales, too, might shift, whether Greenwich Village, a 'drop-out' Manhattan to the edges of Columbia University, Denver (with the Naropa Institute's School of Disembodied Poetics to follow in Boulder in 1974), San Francisco, Wichita, Kansas, Harlem, Rutherford, New Jersey, or Mexico from Yucatán to Chiapas, or, quite as frequently, a freight train boxcar or hitched truck. But Beat energies were still to be called upon, lived out, pitched towards new self-possibility. Clock and calendar time, argued poets and followers alike, mattered less than inner time. Space, equally, lay as much within as outside, the Poe to Rimbaud *moi intérieur* as much as some 'normative' social existence. Coterist, subterranean, priapic voyager, or Buddhist as may be, the 'Beat', the 'Beatnik' (the suffix a Yiddish diminutive), would lead a life in which one's existential all was unreservedly demanded; or so, if any one ethos prevailed in so diverse a gallery, ran the banner philosophy.

What, then, mainstream editorials had good reason to ask, *was* happening? Whether as a poetry and fiction, or as styles of talk and dress (the ubiquitous use of 'cool' and 'man', the wearing of 'shades' and long hair), or as youth/student habits of dropping-out, freightcar-riding, sleeping-around, could Beatdom actually be contesting an America still residually if not actually under the benign residual aegis of Ike and Mamie? What had become of the much vaunted community values of Main Street, or of the High School and campus as training-ground for a life of respectable business or the professions, or the Book-of-The Month-Club and the *Reader's Digest* literary standards?

Who, in other words, were these mouthers of dissent with their resolutely male, if at the same time often androgynous and pan-sexual, insistence on America's 'other' cultural seams: blues, jazz, orgasm, Buddhism and Eastern philosophy in general, negritude, Blake- and/or pot-inspired visions, *wanderlust*, even the American language itself as iconoclastically defied and thereby freed of all previous gentility and restraint?

If there now seems something more than a touch hysterical, comic-farcical, in the way certain Beat habits made an impact, that might be no more than the chaff to be sorted out from the wheat. On the other hand nor is it to take all the various Beat manifestos and pronounce-ments wholly and always at their own plentiful word. Among camp-followers, especially, there was no shortage of self-publicity, paper-wars, easy millenialism.

None of which is to underplay a real core of seriousness as born out in Donald Allen's seminal Grove Press anthology, *The New American Poetry 1945–1960*, originally issued in 1960.[10] Apart from the poetry, Allen had the good sense to offer with the other literary poetics a selection of Beat pronouncements – prime among them Jack Kerouac on 'an endless one-line poem called prose', Allen Ginsberg on 'Hebraic-Melvillian bardic breath' (the organising measure of 'Howl' and his other longer poems) and Lawrence Ferlinghetti with his now well-known proposition that 'Only the dead are disengaged'. Seen again from the present time a number of linked and overlapping questions emerge into ever sharper focus. Their import underwrites much of this essay-collection.

Did the Beats, their writings and other doings, in fact yield a usable political-cultural legacy as Vietnam, Watergate, and through to the 1980s, even Reaganism, came into the frame? What, in truth, was the relationship in the Beat phenomenon between art and politics, the power of the word and the power of the deed? How are we to read the 'gender' dimension of Beat life and art, the hardly edifying treatment of women both by the men involved and often by the women themselves or the phallocentrism straight and gay? Is it, can it ever be, fair to think that Beatdom, whether as a literary current spanning New York's Greenwich Village to San Francisco's City Lights Bookshop or as an American postwar call to a life beyond suburbia and conformism, should have provided some kind of *realpolitik* rather than a prompt to individual awakening and self-awareness?

The immediate issue, however, lies in what, and what writing in particular, gives ground for the continuing hold of the Beats. It is with this end in mind that the present collection has been commissioned, a reassessment (and in some case a re-excavation) of Beat legacy and achievement. Yet another Beat sympathiser, Henry Miller, himself often the shock-horror figure of American letters, offered more than a passing clue as to why the Beats made their impact and, most of all, why their custodial spirit was to be found in Jack Kerouac. Writing in 1959, and with an invocation of Allen Ginsberg's praise of Kerouac as a 'gentle, intelligent, suffering prose saint', he very persuasively suggests the qualities which made the Beat generation's founder-stylist so immediate and potent an American luminary:

> Everything Kerouac writes about – those weird, hauntingly ubiquitous characters whose names may be read backwards or upside down, those lovely, nostalgic, intimate-grandiose stereopticon views of America, those nightmarish, ventilated joy-rides in gondolas and hot rods – plus the language he uses (à la Gautier in reverse) to describe his 'earthly-heavenly visions,' surely even the readers of *Time* and *Life*, of the Digests and the Comics, cannot fail to discern such a rapport between these hypergonic extravaganzas and such perennial blooms as the *Golden Ass*, the *Satyricon*, and *Pantagruel*.[11]

It is, nonetheless, with Allen Ginsberg that *The Beat Generation Writers* opens, whose *Howl and Other Poems* would be seized by both the US Customs and San Francisco Police. For has not the opening line of 'Howl' – 'I saw the best minds of my generation destroyed by madness, starving hysterical naked' – become a *locus classicus* of Beat idiom, a bearing of witness and a call to 'beatitude' in a time of anti-life 'Moloch'?

John Muckle begins proceedings with an account running from the Ginsberg who first gave his name to *Howl and Other Poems* as a mainstay in the City Lights 'Pocket Poets Series' through to his *Collected Poems* (1984) and beyond. He argues for a view of Ginsberg as a species of poet-taxonomist, a bard and teacher of 'the names' which lie within the making of America's modernity. R.J. Ellis, in turn, analyses Jack Kerouac through his classic Beat novel-diptych, *On The Road* (1957) and *Visions of Cody* (1972), two narrative versions of the West and the Kerouac/Cassady 'buddy' relationship as at once interconnected yet distinct.

In his account of Gregory Corso, Jim Philip suggests a poet whose whimsy or quizzicalness has often eclipsed the more consequential side of his work: the critic-witness to American economic and military oppression. Alistair Wisker argues for Lawrence Ferlinghetti as indeed both the 'poet-acrobat' of one of his own best-known (if untitled) poems and the veteran publisher-writer behind *City Lights*, but also a major American voice of place – in his case San Francisco and California at large.

Few figures can claim a more godfather role to the Beats than William Burroughs, Harvard-educated heir to an 'adding machine' fortune, junkie, Tangiers literary exile, the laconic vaudevillian of *The Naked Lunch*, in all an American Céline. At the heart of Williams Burroughs' satiric darkness has always been a concern with language's pre-emptive force, 'the word' in a corporatist world as itself a tactic of power-control and subordination. This is taken up by David Ingram in an account which explores Burroughs' counter-insurgent, often wickedly funny and disruptive, uses of language, not least in his debts to Alfred Korzybski and resort to techniques of cut-up and collage.

The essays which follow look to figures whose standing in the Beat pantheon has always been a touch oblique, whether as commentators, crucial mythic presences, or voices of Afro-America. Cynthia Hamilton re-evaluates the role of John Clellon Holmes, his considerable essay-work and fiction as themselves part of a new-born American Romanticism (linking in temper back to Melville and Whitman) which he identitied as the essential Beat signature. Clive Bush disinters, no inappropriate verb, Herbert Huncke and Neal Cassady, respectively Beat anarchist and hipster, figures as much of legend as life whose status and entrances and exits in the writing of others he annotates in detail.

My own essay addresses the African–American, the black, seam in American Beat writing, an analysis of the poetry and its sources and relationship to the Beat 'mainstream', of LeRoi Jones/Imamu Amiri Baraka, Ted Joans and Bob Kaufman. It thus argues for a multicultural perspective on the Beat gallery, Beatdom's black borrowings and yet at the same time anything but without its own originators.

Two further revisionary essays round out the collection, both of which re-excavate the gender dynamics of the Beat movement. Helen McNeil takes on the 'boy-gang' ethos, its implications both for the nature of male Beat writing and that of a generation of Beat-centred women from Diane Di Prima to Bonnie Bremser. Amy L. Friedman takes the latter issue still further, Di Prima and her successors as contributing to a timely, and needed, change in how the overall Beat canon is to be construed.

NOTES

1. John Clellon Homes, 'The Philosophy of The Beat Generation', *Esquire*, 1958. Republished in Seymour Krim (ed.), *The Beats* (Greenwich, Connecticut: Fawcett Publications, 1960) and John Clellon Holmes, *Passionate Opinions: The Cultural Essays* (Fayetteville, Arkansas: University of Arkansas Press, 1988).
2. Jack Kerouac, 'The Origins of The Beat Generation', *Playboy*, vol. 6., No. 6., pp.31–2, 42, 79. Reprinted in Thomas Parkinson (ed.), *A Casebook on The Beat Generation* (New York: Thomas Y. Crowell Company, 1961).
3. Gregory Corso, 'Variations on a Generation', *Gemini*, Vol. 2, No. 6. pp.47–51, Spring 1959. Reprinted in Parkinson, *A Casebook on The Beat Generation*.
4. Jack Kerouac, 'The Origins of The Beat Generation'.
5. 'America' was first published in Allen Ginsberg, *Howl and Other Poems*, Introduction by William Carlos Williams (San Francisco: City Lights Books, The Pocket Poets Series, Number Four, 1956).
6. Philip Rahv, 'The Cult of Experience in American Writing', reprinted in Philip Rahv (ed.), *Literature in America: An Anthology of Literary Criticism* (New York: Meridian Books, 1957).
7. 'The White Negro, Superficial Reflections on the Hipster', *Dissent*, Summer 1957, pp.276–93. Reprinted in Norman Mailer, *Advertisements For Myself* (New York: Putnam, 1959).
8. Kenneth Rexroth, 'Disengagement: The Art of the Beat Generation', *New World Writing No. 11* (New York: The New York American Library, 1957), pp.28–41.
9. Norman Podhoretz, 'The Know-Nothing Bohemians', *Partisan Review*, Vol. XXV, No. 2, Spring 1958, pp.305–11, 313–16, 318. Republished in Norman Podhoretz, *Doings and Undoings: The Fifties and After in American Writing* (New York: Farrar, Straus and Company, 1964).
10. Donald M. Allen, *The New American Poetry 1945–1960* (New York and London: Grove Press/Evergreen Books, 1960).
11. Henry Miller, Preface to *The Subterraneans* (New York: Avon Books, 1959), pp.5–7.

1

The Names:
Allen Ginsberg's Writings
John Muckle

> There are still other made-up countries
> Where we can hide forever,
> Wasted with eternal desire and sadness,
> Sucking the sherbets, crooning the tunes,
> naming the names.
> *John Ashbery, 'Hop O' My Thumb'*[1]

The inclusion of many names is perhaps one of the first things a new reader might notice in Allen Ginsberg's work. Whatever else he may or may not be, Ginsberg is a name-dropper on an epic scale. The proportion of familiar names to those vaguely recognised or unknown will of course vary between individuals. After noting their frequency and apparent range, such a reader might begin to count recurrences, devise categories based on the names, decide to investigate particular names further. On the other hand, he or she may tire quickly of all those unfamiliar or over-familiar names, apparently of some personal significance for the author, and lay the book aside.

Collected Poems (1984) includes an index of proper names with accompanying notes 'designed to make this large volume "user friendly"'. In 'Author's Preface, Reader's Manual' Ginsberg presents his life's work as a Poundian personal epic of consciousness, a 'life-long poem including history, wherein things are symbols of themselves'. Some names occur only once, some a couple of times close together; others recur time and time again. Ginsberg names friends and relatives, writers, politicians, musicians, various sorts of culturally-freighted famous personages, radical heroes, criminals, bums, and a panoply of deities drawn from Judaism, Islam, Buddhist and Hindu cosmogonies, Blake's prophetic books and ancient Greece.

The multiplication of names into symbol systems is part of what attracts Ginsberg to all these cosmogonies. In *Indian Journals* (1970), a volume that is one of his best, the process of mapping one on to another is clear:

> Krushchev's mouth in Kennedy's forehead ... Ganeshes for Peters, Buddhas for the Jacks, Kalis & Durgas for Bill and ilk – a huge cartoon religion with Disney gods with 3 heads & 6 arms killing buffalodemons.
>
> Imagine my father wandering around New Jersey in orange robes with big serious expression.
>
> Rishikesh – walking along path near house, three half naked men sitting with fixed eyes & beards crosslegged all afternoon in trance under tree – one with a pet cow with a monstrous deformed jaw his friend – & tin beg cups on the deerskin mat – fixed bloodshot staring open eyes on one, and Shiva Tridents stuck into the ground beside them.[2]

'Death to Van Gogh's Ear' (1957) is the poem in which he first assembles large numbers of names:

> Where was the House of Representatives when Crane read aloud
> from his prophetic books
> What was Wall Street scheming when Lindsay announced the doom
> of Money?

Allowing for some flexibility to include abstractions and names not strictly speaking those of persons, the poem's movement – its counterposition of martyrs with a series of abstracted or personalised villains, joky life-against-death, poetry against the machine politics (he makes Pound 'Secty Economics' in his cabinet of poets) – can be charted by reading its cast in order of appearance: Lorca, Whitman, Mayakovsky, Hart Crane, Platonism, Einstein, Bertrand Russell, immortal Chaplin, Genet, J. Edgar Hoover, Lao-Tze, the Sixth Patriarch, Russia, America, Hollywood, History, God, Man, Sacco and Vanzetti, Vachel Lindsay, Poe, Pound, Kra, Pukti, Alexander Blok, Artaud, Van Gogh's Ear, Theodore Roosevelt, Bickford's Employment Agency, Destiny, The Skeleton, Puerto Ricans, Elephants of mercy, Divinity, the Whore of Babylon, Capitols and Academies, Money, Eternity and Illusion.

Ginsberg's wholesale assembling of names and the properties he ascribes to them begins here as a protesting parody of and replacement for 'Hollywood whose movies stick in the throat of God'. His congeries of names – with relatively fixed characteristics, shared cultural meanings – owes a lot to the Hollywood star system. Stars recur in many disguises, speaking the same lines. Quite a number appear in the index. Garbo is there, Myrna Loy, Buck Rogers, Shirley Temple, cartoons and silent comedians. Chaplin is slightly ahead as both universal tramp and victim of McCarthyism. There are so many good losers among Ginsberg's names; it must be upsetting for a living person to find himself there.

The highest scorers are, perhaps predictably, Jack Kerouac (41), Peter Orlovsky (35), Buddha (31), Neal Cassady (27), Allen Ginsberg (24), Naomi Ginsberg (22), William Blake (20), Louis Ginsberg (16), Walt Whitman (16), William Burroughs (13) and Timothy Leary (12). Generally there is a correspondence between the importance of an individual to Ginsberg and the number of entries they receive, but not always. His relationship with William Carlos Williams (4) was crucial to his development as a poet, but he doesn't quite become a magic name, neither does Ezra Pound (6). Hart Crane (10), on the other hand, is invoked as symbolic personage many times.

Albert Einstein (10) recurs throughout in a variety of contexts, from his first appearance as symbol of science in 'POEM Rocket' (1957), and potential recipient of Ginsberg's 'flaming mss'. He is forever after a white-haired emblem of saintliness, genius and the culpability of science. The elements of this cultural myth of Einstein recur with differing emphases. Unlike Barthes he is not seeking to expose the myth, but to work with it. He talks to his Einstein, consults him in dreams and, in 'Plutonium Ode' (1977), invokes him as one of a pantheon who preside over the forces of creation and destruction, the release of energy at the beginning of the 'big bang' universe.

> Sabaot, Jehova, Astapheus Adonaeus, Elohim, Iao, Ialdabaoth, Aeon
> from Aeon born ignorant in an Abyss of Light,
> Sophia's reflections glittering thoughtful galaxies, whirlpools of star-
> spume silver thin as hairs of Einstein!

Legions of talismanic names appear less often. A small sampling of French writers reveals: Arthur Rimbaud (6), Jean Genet (3), Antonin Artaud (2), Max Jacob (2), Guillaume Apollinaire (2), Louis-Ferdinand Céline (1), Blaise Cendrars (1), André Breton (1), St John Perse (1), Raymond Radiguet (1) and Tristan Tzara (1); of comedians: Chaplin (3), Buster Keaton (3), W.C. Fields (2), Bob Hope (2), Laurel and Hardy (1), the Marx Brothers (1 each); of musicians: Bob Dylan (6), Thelonious Monk (1), Donovan (1), The Kinks (1), The Beatles (1 each), John Lennon (2), Frank Sinatra (4), Nancy Sinatra (1).

The villains of history score higher than its heroes; victims and martyrs feature prominently among the latter. Great world tyrants Adolf Hitler, Richard Nixon and Lyndon B. Johnson tie for first place with 13 entries apiece, while the authors of the military–industrial complex and postwar US foreign policy weigh in at Eisenhower (11), J. Edgar Hoover (8), Henry Kissinger (6) and John Foster Dulles (4), with uncharismatic Harry

Truman (2) bringing up the rear. John F. Kennedy (9), appears in a dual role as imperialist and assassinee, Lee Harvey Oswald and Jack Ruby repeat their roles as assassin and assassin's assassin three times. Martin Luther King (4), Abraham Lincoln (3), Malcolm X (2) and Robert Kennedy (2) complete a set of martyred leaders; Sirhan Sirhan claims his victim twice. Franklyn D. Roosevelt (6) and George Washington (3) appear together memorably in Ginsberg's vision of America as Kali Destroyer of Illusions, their severed heads each grasped in one pair of her hands; Ronald Reagan (3) appears as childhood matinee idol, the president only Birdbrain could have voted into office, concealer of atrocities; Jimmy Carter (1) as supplier of arms to El Salvador's military junta.

On the other side of the Cold War, Mao Tze Tung (7), and the (sometimes) sympathetic and colourful Fidel Castro (5) are ahead of Russian leaders Khrushchev (4) and Kosygin (2). Of the leaders of the Russian revolution, Lenin does not make it into Ginsberg's poems, Stalin (2) is paired with Hitler, Trotsky (2) appears with Zhdanov (1) as a creature of Naomi Ginsberg's Stalinist paranoia in 'Kaddish', 'mixing rat bacteria in the back of the store'. North Vietnamese leader Ho Chi Minh (3), with other world leaders, is wished Merry Christmas, believed to have enjoyed the support of 80 per cent of the Vietnamese people in 1954 by Eisenhower, imagined to be Chinese by ill-informed GIs. Finally, there is a late entrance by Margaret Thatcher (1), who 'scatters radioactive urine' over the green fields of England.

Domestic political martyrs include Ginsberg's favourites, the anarchists Sacco and Vanzetti (4) executed in Massachusetts in 1927, Julius and Ethel Rosenberg (4), executed for passing atomic secrets to the Russians, Soledad brother George Jackson (1), Black Panther Bobby Seale 'bound & gagged at Trial' and the Scottsboro boys (1), nine youths falsely accused of rape and sentenced to death in Alabama in 1931. Numerous trades union organisers, Jewish radicals, US communists and socialists of the 1920s and 1930s are also memorialised.

The names are invariably cited symbolically rather than with strictly historical intent. His Hitler/Stalin coupling refers not to the pact of 1940 but to their status as great world tyrants, to the point where the Frankfurt School in America met Truman and Dulles in the theory of totalitarianism.

Whenever Gertrude Stein (3) appears it is with the same reassuring air of wisdom and saintly tranquillity, except when we find 'the flayed skin of Gertrude Stein held down/fluttering over the gaping Yoni' of Kali Destroyer of Illusions. Ginsberg read her in the early 1950s. Her investigation of consciousness as eternal present, first with William James, has been related by Ginsberg to his attempts to document thought as it occurs, that is, in the order of its succession. Her lectures on narrative provide a distinction I have picked up in this essay. She speaks of poetry as naming, prose as telling how the names became the names. From an original unity of these functions in epic, poetry and narrative have developed a cleavage in which one names and the other tells. This, for Stein, is an impoverishment and a challenge to new ways of telling:

> In the American writing the words began to have inside themselves those same words that in the English were completely moving, they began to detach themselves from the solidity of anything, they began to excitedly feel themselves as if they were anywhere or anything ... words left alone more and more feel that they are moving and all of it is detached and is detaching anything from anything and in this detaching and in this moving it is being in its way creating its existing. This is then the real difference between English and American writing and this then can lead to anything.[3]

Walt Whitman was a lifelong amasser of vocabularies and taxonomies, a crank about names and the inexhaustible activity of naming:

> Names of home – the sacred names of mother and sister and wife – the sweet idyl of the names of children – the clustering associations of the names of the troop of amis! Names of bards, benefactors, martyrs, dear to the heart of the world – Names of the primeval supremes, of the founders of the antique Religions: Brama, Osiris, Zoroaster, Prometheus, Orpheus, Jove! The execrated names of tyrants and oppressors – names uttered with compressed lips – names of warriors and conquerors writing their fiery adventures on man's mind as the lightning writes on rocks! Names of the dead – names embalmed – tombs on a battlefield, o'ergrown with grasses and flowers![4]

Rambles Among Words, a book he collaborated on with William Swinton, goes on to explain the importance of names in the 'aesthetical realm'. Literary arts, particularly drama and the novel, 'require the creation of ideal Names. And often high and highest art is displayed in the working of the creative imagination on nominal emblems for these avatars of the mind.' America's need for new nomenclatures for its 'Geography, Inventions, Contributions Personalities' is invoked and writers are exhorted to 'quarry and build in the new architectures of humanity'.

'Eidolons' (1876) describes the processes of formation of such ideal names and their universal importance. The word had been used earlier in English by Scott, Carlyle and Poe. An eidolon can be a shape, an image in the mind, a spectre, an idea, a vision, or merely a fancy. It may also be a portrait, especially of a god, and hence a false idol.[5] Whitman's eidolons are both evanescent and eternal, 'Unfixed yet fixed', in a state of continual flux and reformulation: the names of natural and therefore of spiritual facts, but thereby leaving the physical universe giddyingly empty except for crumbling images:

> All space, all time,
> (The stars, the terrible perturbations of the suns,
> Swelling, collapsing, ending, serving their longer, shorter use,)
>   Fill'd with eidolons only.

Here Whitman seems to falter, to despair in the confidence of his naming. Inspirational eidolons are transformed into the myriad decaying shadows of shadows, philosophical doubt rhyming with the political despair in America expressed in 'Respondez!'

> Let all the men of These States stand aside for a few smouchers! let the few seize on
>   what they chose! let the rest gawk, giggle, starve, obey!
> Let shadows be furnished with genitals! let substances be deprived of
>   their genitals! ...
> Let books take the place of trees, animals, rivers, clouds!
> Let the daub'd portraits of heroes supersede heroes!

Robert Creeley finds Whitman's parallelisms of internal rhyme, recurrence, syntactical 'rhyming' to be also operative at the level of structures of thought and emotion. Comparison, association, opposition are part of an expanded definition of rhyme that governs the creation and structuring of Whitman's eidolons. He describes this as 'a process of seemingly endless gathering, moving in the energy of his own attention and impulse'.[6]

That, and the notion of a poem as 'agglomerative' and spherical rather than linear or cutting through language to 'a clear point' have both been related, by Ginsberg himself, to his use of Whitman's long line 'to build up big organic structures', to the former's prosody, but not, so far as I know, to the symbolic use of proper names in Ginsberg's poetry, and equally importantly to their smaller unit of construction. Ginsberg took up Whitman's challenge to manufacture new cultural symbols, to made eidolons:

> The present now and here,
> America's busy, teeming, intricate whirl,
> Of aggregate and segregate for only thence releasing,
>   Today's eidolons.

If the kind of poet Allen Ginsberg became is partly articulated against the kind of poet his father was, Louis Ginsberg's precedent as public figure, Paterson's most famous poet, whimsical journalist and genial wiseacre, must be important for the ease with which his son took on public life. But it is Pound who provides the true precedent. Ginsberg used him as a springboard, a series of warnings, a measure of greatness, a school, but also executed a series of reversals of Poundian practice. Having taken on all of Pound's roles vis à vis the other Beat writers, as agent, publicist, mediator, Ginsberg didn't claim to have invented anything. On the contrary, he claimed that his names had invented him. He provided himself with a context, in the way Pound was always telling you where he stole from, but didn't exactly assume proprietorship. Pound made infallible pronouncements, Ginsberg made a fool of himself in public. His whole poetic and public persona as a reasonable, self-deprecating individual is built out of and against Pound's cultural authoritarianism, the high modernists' projection of themselves as 'masters'.

At the same time as he became a parodic, self-ironising anti-Pound, Ginsberg was very attracted to the idea of cultural and spiritual masters. Such notions form part of his way of thinking with names, his creation of a pantheon of celebrity-eidolons. He has sought out many masters without, it seems, ever quite aspiring to be one himself. He operates an implicit critique of Pound as he reformulates and appropriates aspects of the poetic practice and project of the *Cantos*.

Ginsberg told the 82-year-old Pound that the *Cantos* did cohere as much as anything could, confronting him with a reading of the work in which its form was open-ended, personal, coherent as a record of his changing consciousness in time, Whitmanic. At this time Ginsberg was writing 'The Fall of America', beginning to see his own writing as a personal epic. Pound insisted that were 'all tags and patches',[7] but it must be admitted that whether the *Cantos* achieve 'major form' or not, they are an elaborate, evolving, consciously continuous work – as is Whitman's *Leaves of Grass* – in a way that *Collected Poems* isn't quite.

Ginsberg names names politically, exposes and elaborates conspiracies, his view of history centred on individuals, dependent on 'factive personalities'. These kinds of namings derive strongly from Pound, for whom names – and the research his reader must do to discover their significance – are part of the means by which that culture he wishes to preserve is to be reactivated in the present. Ginsberg's factive personalities aren't usually leaders, more often they are exemplary victims.

The Beats suck up influences, adapt certain writers and, through mutual interaction and one another's researches, arrive at their own synthesis of romantic and modernist ideas. The notion of 'Ordinary mind', or sometimes 'Original mind', is central to Ginsberg's poetics. The poem is a record or graph of the mind as it actually operates, of the movement of consciousness. 'First thought best thought', was Kerouac's slogan, because closer to perceptual and mental processes.

Many sources for this notion can be traced, including an interest in the perpetual present of consciousness that goes back to the beginnings of modernism. But transcriptions of 'ordinary mind' are also taken to reveal a transcendent realm, either religious or aesthetic: 'ordinary' shades into 'universal', through Emersonian manifestations in Whitman and his understanding of his 1948 vision of William Blake – that 'entire Universe was manifestation of One Mind'. He is also looking for a certain intimacy with the common, the average, the representative: 'ordinary mind' is a paradigmatic mind's flow of mental event. Here William Carlos Williams steps in.

'The Bricklayer's Lunch Hour' (1950) is transcribed from a notebook sketch, the first of the poems 'adapted from prose seeds', and possibly the best, before the liberating discoveries of Kerouac's sketching technique revealed their own problems and led to a period of attempting to imitate Williams. Louis Simpson is right to describe 'Paterson' (1949) with its Whitman line 'screaming and dancing against the orchestra in the destructive ballroom of the world' as 'the breakthrough, beginning and touchstone of his style,'[8] but it was to be years before he returned to that. 'A Supermarket in California' (1955) reads Whitman ironically, multiplicity in oneness (on the dollar bill, after all) turned to democratic consumerism in a supermarket's cornucopia of goods, but it's undeveloped, not made into anything except a humorous fantasy. Wincingly self-conscious glorying in bohemianism (charming in the 15-year-old Rimbaud on his way to Belgium) mars many early poems. 'In Back of the Real' (1954) is a railroad yard epiphany that first successfully articulates a 'Beat' point of view, bringing together Williams' crooked flower, 'like a used shaving brush/that's been lying under/the garage for a year' and a religious search for beauty in industrial debris, in the despised underside of America:

> Yellow, yellow flower, and
>   flower of industry,
> tough spiky ugly flower,
>   flower nonetheless,
> with the form of the great yellow
>   Rose in your brain!
> This is the flower of the World.

Ginsberg has spoken of the beginnings of 'ordinary mind' in his friendships with Kerouac and Neal Cassady, opening up to their own naïvety, to how one another 'really' thought beneath acquired literary or intellectual culture. Cassady's brilliant account of his mental processes and problems in writing is one of the high points of their correspondence. Montaigne-like, he insists on the paucity of his conceptions and his inability to carry them out. He offers us 'ordinary mind' failing but learning, and reveals a capacity to observe and chart its movements that belies his self-deprecation:

> After the first statement is out, and often before, I get hopelessly involved in words to contain the increasing number of ideas. As I progress this morass becomes larger and my head more and more deeply engulfed in recurrent themes which are infolded in sickening profusion, While on the paper. in attempting to snatch all I can before I forget, I am soon so over-extended – stretched grammatically and logically to the point where any semblance of clarity is lost – that I am forced to stop.[9]

At the time Ginsberg dismissed the taped conversations with Cassady in Kerouac's *Visions of Cody*, but later described this experiment 'as 'twere breakthru & historic first incidence of the later universal American style of anything we *do* is art ... The art lies in the consciousness of doing the thing, in the attention to the happening, in the sacramentalization of everyday reality.'

In this neat documentation of the self and its doings, Ginsberg becomes the clerk of his own inner life, archivist of his sensations; the unpublished taped journals of later years transcribed by research assistants, huge unread tracts of information gathered like the contents of the office wastebasket, sealed and vaulted as were Warhol's time capsules of ephemera and bric-à-brac, whose significance is as 'record of their time' but whose rationale – and actual reason – for being collected is proximity to the organising presence of the artist.

He himself began using tape recorders in the compositional process in 1965. Ginsberg is fascinated by intertextual transactions, by the processes of borrowing (without paying back), assimilation and reframing. After the fact of spontaneous composition he is a self-conscious writer and a punctilious acknowledger of debts:

> Jack always accused me of stealing from him, rereading 20 years later I see now how much was true. My Greyhound poem taken from his description of dock-loading President Adams for instance, the very syntax and phrasing is similar, 'cept his is half decade earlier: 'There's ammo in the hold and a special locker full of some priceless cargo bound for Penang, probably champagne ... Valentine's meat juice from Richmond ... – barrels for L.A.'

Later see 'whole families eating in Clifton's' similar to my Supermarket's 'whole families shopping at night.' His phrasing was archetypal for this moment of consciousness enlarging in wonderment to notice Americanist minute particulars aside from the centres of Attention-Power.[10]

He undermines the idea he ascribes to Kerouac, suggesting that theft might be more effective than simply 'doing anything', that what he learned from Kerouac was literary. From the re-creation of detail from the materials of memory and observation, Ginsberg develops an ability to memorialise the present, to define contemporaneity by naming contemporary objects and preoccupations, to combine these little nuggets of contemporary cultural signifiers, and make them sing and define their moment.

Inscribing thoughts in the order of their succession pays attention to the evanescence of the mind, but is also predicated on the idea of writing as ineradicable marks. If speech is the form of writing that cannot be erased, only added to, mind-notation makes the same rule for writing. An emphasis is placed upon writing as performance. The tumbling word orders this leads to – the writer does not know what's coming next – recall Romantic prose as much as Charlie Parker's solos. 'I struck it off at a blow,' was William Hazlitt's boast before Kerouac's. On the face of it, word-processors may seem well adapted to spontaneous bop prosody, but lack typing's irreversibility. Marks on a screen are always notional, provisional, subject to erasure.

Ginsberg's journals are the seedbed of his writing. Most of his poems are lifted from them. Just as the forward movement of the vortices he creates in 'The Fall of America' seems powered by physical movement through landscape and the succession of names and luminous details that offers, so in his travel journals – through South America, Europe, the Mediterranean, India, Africa, South East Asia – bombardment by that which demands to be notated (landscapes, people, domestic life, reading) makes for a writing that is unabashedly about the traveller's spiritual journey, taking place through the details he chooses, or which choose him. He doesn't so much reflect on the places he passes through as notate a movement through them, so that it is inner geographies that are described. His handling of memorialising images gives a very full sense of place, but little sense of a place's indifference to the traveller's itineraries. Ginsberg doesn't often seem overawed. On the contrary, the places he visits seem to gather around him. Faced by his directness and empathy, they offer themselves. He prepares himself by reading, but in many cases one feels that his relative ignorance about what he sees allows him to enter imaginatively its cultural spaces, to make them his own.

In the journals his characteristic lines fill up the page from margin to margin, but the line is whenever the mind breaks, and therefore can be one word or a long paragraph. His poems spill over into prose under the impact of powerful emotion. At its most intense, 'Kaddish' runs on too urgently for the hesitation of line breaks, telling overwhelms its means, although it may be that the true unit of meaning in Ginsberg is not the line at all but the phrase or sentence fragment – his larger formal structures are means to organise these. Whitman's long strophe is usually a speaking measure, a statement, as is the broken, triadic line of the later Williams; Ginsberg's long lines have so much more crammed into them, so many juxtapositions, changes of register and context, multiple linkages.

Ginsberg has said that he did not properly read Whitman until after the composition of 'Howl', and that imagist practices, Kerouac, the Bible, and Christopher Smart, were more immediate resources. Robert Creeley has spoken of coming to Whitman first through Hart Crane's encounter with him in Cape Hatteras, and this may also be true of Ginsberg. Crane's continent-spanning dips and pivots are from Whitman; Ginsberg is attracted by the way Crane's glittering archaisms are made to answer to modern America, his magniloquent lurches, his desperation, and shares his interest in surfaces:

> Stars prick the eyes with sharp ammoniac proverbs,
> New verities, new inklings in the velvet hummed
> Of dynamos, where hearing's leash is strummed ...
> Power's script, – wound, bobbin-bound, refined –
> Is stropped to the slap of belts on booming spools, spurred
> Into the bulging bouillon, harnessed jelly of the stars.[11]

The 'sharp ammoniac proverbs' of the stars, like 'the sky's acetylene', are contracted metaphorical yokings of the kind that Ginsberg developed through studying haiku and imagism. The long Whitman line, in his usage, holds within it Williams' techniques of presentation, the Poundian image, and a juxtaposition leaving out connectives that he learned from his reading of R.H. Blyth's four-volume study of haiku: 'Haiku = objective images written down outside mind the result is inevitable mind sensation of relations. Never try to write of relations themselves, just the images which are all that can be written down on the subject.'[12]

Such 'compressed haiku' are strung together into long lines by means of further gap-producing sentence fragments, dashes, elliptical word orders that Kerouac had mined out of Joyce and Céline. 'Hydrogen jukebox' is an example that Ginsberg has explained often. Pre-existent cultural associations of the simple but 'modern' nouns thus juxtaposed produce a more or less complex idea (about the relation of a newly realised potential for world destruction to the frenzy of postwar popular culture) in the reader's mind as he or she attempts to relate them.

Multiple layers of association are instantaneous only if you have the references and connotations at your mind's fingertips. Television has supplied such a competent audience for itself. TV's global audience presumably has a whole shared world now of the recorded century, that is, of its representations, at its fingertips in a way that few of Pound's readers can ever have possessed his kulchur of recovered fragments. There you are expected to investigate the materials, the contexts, for yourself, that is part of the purpose of the *Cantos* – the educational part. Ginsberg too has palpable designs, not exactly to persuade, but to initiate us into an implied literary culture, an attitude, a lifestyle and a way of looking at the world.

> ... when I read F.S. Fitzgerald I'm dealing with a writer I'm about equal to ... If I can't come to eventually write as good as he did I fear I'll honestly be pretty much of a failure, ego? no, truth. I realise he's not much and only extolled as American (at least a dozen, including your pal Jack K. are better) and I see him as a baby compared to Proust or Celino.[13]

The importance of Europe to the Beats couldn't be clearer than in this passage from Neal Cassady's letters to Ginsberg. Fifties' high cultural gloom about human possibility, Adorno's no poetry after Auschwitz slogan, God reported dead, 'tradition' (family, society, the state) bereft of moral authority, all were associated with a 'heavy humanist tradition'[14] that Americans wanted out of. 'Ordinary mind' was the American mind, theirs, uncluttered by angst, guilt, tragic historical experience. And yet the Beats are among the most 'European' of postwar American writers. Ginsberg's own 'heavy humanism' is from his parents' Russian Jewish heritage, his mother's communism, his Columbia teacher Lionel Trilling. He's always invoking tragic European or other historical or present experience. Rejecting the dullness of 'English' at Columbia, Ginsberg's first stop – via his friends Carl Solomon and Lucien Carr – was French existentialism, Rimbaud, Genet and Artaud. Having entered Columbia with the aim of 'helping the working class' he was soon provided with an alternative set of (bohemian) allegiances to criminals and the insane, and a fatal interest in the *acte gratuit*. Beat existentialism's common ground with Buddhism is that both offer spiritual discipline as a way out of 'le néant' or 'Void' – expanded consciousness, authentic being.

Ginsberg's interest in 'the rest of the world' is complex. Writing at a moment of supreme American cultural, economic and political power, he offers a trenchant critique of US imperialism while sharing in his country's cultural confidence. The Beats weren't shy about telling Europe the news; they came to instruct and to inherit. They brought their own versions of Europe, bartering a revised backwoods America and a clarion call to youth. The Beat version of French literature, for example, placed different emphases from the baccalaureat; Ginsberg's view of English romanticism was not often heard (at that time) on these shores.

While the abstract expressionists appropriated twentieth-century European painting and Frank O'Hara collected for the Met, the Beats made their own modest stab at inheriting Europe. John Ashbery was also living in Paris. Not, I imagine, a frequent visitor to the Beat Hotel, he discovered cut-ups at approximately the same time as Burroughs, publishing the results in *The Tennis Court Oath* (1962). What both groups of writers found there (Burroughs at several removes through Brion Gysin) was the heritage of French modernism. Ginsberg went to Paris to write 'On Apollinaire's Grave'; Kerouac, newly famous, paid his respects to Ferdinand Céline; Corso wrote intoxicatingly about the loud girls in the Sacré Coeur Cafe and had an affair with Peggy Guggenheim.[15]

William Burroughs lent *The Decline of the West* to all his friends. Oswald Spengler's view of the city is full of 'Beat' resonances. Modern cities are contrasted with those of antiquity as 'mere shells, fashioned not by blood but by utility, not by feeling but by the spirit of commercialism', in which, due to estrangement from 'organic' socially cohesive forces of community based in hearth, family and piety, and a 'vagrant existence from shelter to shelter', he prophesies the emergence of the city-dweller as a new kind of hunter or shepherd, an 'intellectual nomad': 'Each of these splendid mass cities harbours horrendous poverty, a brutalisation of all customs which even now, in the attics and garrets, the cellars and backyards, is breeding a new primitive man.'

Spengler's tone of portent and prophecy, his emphasis on the restless, rootless character of modern life, had varying impacts on the Beat writers. The vision of the city in 'Howl', both as a concatenation of the stories of its displaced jetsam, and the consuming industrial Moloch that has brought them together, is highly Spenglerian; as is their attempt to reclaim an unfallen, 'out there' America. Who, after all, fits the type of the 'new primitive man' better than Neal Cassady, their guide to 'out there': a one-man migrant workforce who turned his hand to many trades, who due to his pool hall and reformatory upbringing had several fathers, none of whom were about to provide a hearth, whose incurable restlessness was punctuated by so many attempts to provide himself with anchors and responsibilities. The difference is that, whereas the flotsam and jetsam of mass civilisation are contemptible to Spengler, they are Ginsberg's chosen people.

Theodor Adorno makes a similar inversion:

> The powerless, who at Spengler's command are to be thrown aside and annihilated by history, are the negative embodiment within the negativity of this culture of everything which promises, however feebly, to break the dictatorship of culture and put an end to the horror of pre-history. In their protest lies the only hope that fate and power will not have the last word.[16]

In Spengler's view of mass culture, democracy leads inevitably to decline:

> Through the newspapers, democracy has utterly excluded the book from the intellectual life of the people. The world of books, with its variety of standpoints which encouraged thought to select and criticise, is now truly possessed only by the few. The people read only one paper, 'their' paper, which thrusts its way into every house by the millions, drives books into oblivion through its format, and on the rare occasions when one book or another does appear, forestalls and nullifies its possible influence by 'reviewing' it in advance.

The freedom of the press, so beloved of 'weak minds', facilitates the rise of 'Caesars of world-journalism': 'Those who have learned to read succumb to their power, and the anticipated self-determination of late democracy turns into radical determination of the people by the powers behind the printed word.' Spengler's vision of a world in which the masses are dominated by media and in which the rise of industrialised leisure as 'the relief from highly intensive, practical, intellectual work through its opposite, consciously practised idiocy', must have seemed powerfully evocative of affluent postwar America and its emergent media culture, as it was for Adorno, for whom his view of history as 'blind closed, and fateful as any vegetable life' and his mystical faith in 'the unconscious archaic world of symbols whose expressive force intoxicate him' were less attractive.

However, Spengler's notion that a submerged, discredited 'culture', not high culture but a mystical 'being in form', can resist the decline into barbarism, is present in Ginsberg's naming of the names. He erects his own anti-tradition: a hidden wisdom literature of poetry and Eastern religious texts through which one might transcend contemporary mass civilisation and attain harmony with the forces of the cosmos: 'Recent history is the record of a vast conspiracy to impose one level of mechanical consciousness on mankind and exterminate all manifestations of that unique part of human sentience in all men, which the individual shares with his Creator.'[17]

'Only for a redeemed humanity is the past citable in all its moments,' writes Walter Benjamin,[18] envisaging some messianic day of reckoning. As a radical utopian, Ginsberg attempts, by naming names, to redeem the victims of history in the present, mingling radical *causes célèbres* like the Rosenbergs with memories of Sacco and Vanzetti, the Wobblies, the 'unknown' names of friends, stories encountered in newspapers. He names, as Benjamin says, 'without respect for division between major and minor events'. The persistence of his mother's socialism allows him to think of the bearers of these stories as a political force.

'The Names' (1958) is from the period of 'Death to Van Gogh's Ear' and 'America'. Unpublished before *Collected Poems*, this poem and its continuation 'Fragment: The Names II', 'falls into place, with motifs from Howl particularised'. 'Howl' had been a compendium of anonymous stories; now he names their owners:

> Time comes spirit weakens and goes blank apartments shuffled though
>   and forgotten
> The dead in their centotaphs locomotive highschools & african cities
>   small town motorcycle graves
> O America what saints given vision are shrouded in junk their elegy
>   a nameless hoodlum elegance leaning against death's military
>   garage

Death is military because the dead are an army, ranked, numbered. A military garage is a storehouse for the machineries of death, an infinitely capacious storehouse for the dead themselves. Particularised small-town hoodlums lean against garage doors in snapshots from their army days – elegantly death-defying but dead nonetheless.

> Hell the machine can't sentence anyone except itself, have I to do
>   that?
> It gives jail I give you poem, bars last twenty years rust in a hundred
>   my handwork remains when prisons fall because the hand is
>   compassion

The ranked names in Ginsberg's military garage are those of friends whose lives are 'shrouded in junk', in most cases dead, in others 'living dead'

(Huncke and Cassady come into this category), seemingly spent and wasted. The process of memorialising – and thus rescuing from oblivion – includes a capsule of their lives and encounters with the 'naming' authorities: prisons, armies, hospitals, morgues:

> Phil Black hung in Tombs, horsefaced junky, dreamy strange murderer,
>   forgotten pistol three buck holdup, stoolpigeon suicide I save him
>   from the grave ...
> Joan in dreams bent forward smiling asks news of the living as in life
> the same sad tolerance, no skullbone judge of drunks
> asking whereabouts sending regards from Mexican paradise garden
>   where life and death are one
> as if postcard from eternity sent with human hand, wish I could see
>   you now, it's happening as should
> whatever we really need, we ought get, don't blame yourself – a
>   photograph on reverse
> the rare tomb smile where trees grow crooked energy above grass

'Death's military garage' is one of Ginsberg's 'compressed haiku', an eidolon that yields a whole series of related ideas. 'Military' steps metonymically sideways from 'death' to a large and impersonal cause of death. 'Death' has been made abstract, personified by the possessive apostrophe, and defined. Death is military – it runs to precise but concealed timetables, its authority beyond appeal.

'Garage' is a further unexpected step. Garages are not particularly military in themselves. Death, and military death, are thus made familiar, part of the domestic scene. A military garage is a large garage, infinitely large. In each movement from word to word there's an agreeable swerve away from more habitual words that might have followed, a juxtaposition that leaves a gap for the reader's interpretive acts. A relation is made between abstractions and particular lives, again elevated (or degraded) into symbols, by the notion that the inhabitants of small-town motorcycle graves are or were 'saints given vision'.

The poem closes with a lament for Neal Cassady's 'lost bet racetrack oblivion' future death, and wishes for their reunion: 'O tenderness – to see you again – O tenderness – to recognize you in the middle of Time.'

Ginsberg's journal musings on 'my task as a politician' hardly suggest any great sophistication of programme, beyond a modest ambition to 'dynamite the emotional rockbed of inertia and spiritual deadness that hangs over the cities and makes everybody unconsciously afraid of the cops'.[19] He was the first to respond fully to the worlds opened up by

television. What we were watching in the 1950s and 1960s was the
emergence of a celebrity politics, of media dealing with social movements
or phenomena through preselected spokespeople, 'representatives',
that is, representations of forces that can thus be more easily defined
and controlled. Were Jerry Rubin and Abbie Hoffman guerrillas of the
superstructure or media pets? Likewise Leary and the rest. In their
globalism – in Ginsberg's earth-spanning, world-articulating juxtapositions – were they prophets of a new consciousness, pace McLuhan,
in which 'the electronic information environment allows for no fixed
positions or goals',[20] revolutionaries of airtime, or merely among its more
exotic fauna?

'America', 'Death to Van Gogh's Ear' and 'POEM Rocket' spoke an international language, addressed 'the world' from the belly of the beast in
a vocabulary television had begun to make familiar. They were also international in that the culture they enlisted against its versions of reality
– and asserted continuity with – included a pantheon of European
writers. During the period of these poems, Ginsberg had himself become
a Name and in the process helped develop and extend the range and
province of such compressed notation of cultural meanings by the
electronic information media. 'POEM Rocket' ('This is my rocket, my
personal rocket') has a quality of period opportunist topicality it shares
with sputnik lampshades, or many rockabilly songs of the time:

> Gonna buy me one of them rocket ships
> Something that'll take me there and back
> It ain't gonna be no fun being rich
> If it ain't Action-Packed.[21]

'Television was a Baby Crawling Towards that Death Chamber' (1961)
has at least a great title: an infant medium innocently led by curiosity
(an appropriate image for TV which gets its nose in everywhere) towards
the lurid, noisy and dangerous, a powerful baby god, not so much
manipulating as manipulated by forces it doesn't comprehend, possibly
Burroughs' Venusian arachnids.

> Octopus Death, with supernatural antennae spikes raying Awful
> waves at my consciousness, huge blind Ball invisible behind the
> rooms in the universe – a not-a-man – a no-one –
> Nobodaddy –
> Omnipotent Telepath more visionary that my own Prophetics &
> Memories – Reptile-sentient shimmer-fell-hole Here,
> Dense Soullessness wiser than Time, the Eater-Darkness hungry for
> All –

Later it is 'information' of one kind or another that is being conveyed. Poems become the instigators of campaigns. He is concerned, in the notes to his *Collected Poems*, to show that he was right about CIA involvement in the South East Asia drug trade and to excavate the political and historical contexts of his work in detail. A large part of Ginsberg's office's activity, small business headquarters, perhaps, has been gathering and disseminating information like a small independent campaigning newspaper, or one-man fifth international. A function of poetry is thus to bring together disparate experiences and relate them.

'Wichita Vortex Sutra' (1965) and the poems that make up 'The Fall of America', Ginsberg's attempt at 'a long poem of these States', combine media commentary, travel record, political meditation and self-document in a different way; the poet is a character glimpsed apparently making the poem (recording it on the portable Uher Bob Dylan had given him), moving through geographies and airtime, but invisibly present and ordering. In these poems the physical movement through landscape seems to provide the forward movement that sustains the vortex of notations:

Lightning's blue glare fills Oklahoma plains,
the train rolls east
          casting yellow shadow on grass
                              Twenty years ago
approaching Texas
          I saw
          sheet lightning
                                        cover Heaven's corners
          Feed Storage Elevators in gray rain mist,
                    checkerboard light over sky-roof
same electric lightning South
          follows this train
                    Apocalypse prophesied –
the Fall of America
                    signaled from Heaven

He achieves great flexibility and poise in this neo-Poundian measure; the craft, as in all his best work ('Howl', 'Kaddish', the poems from *Indian Journals*) brought into focus by the qualities, the demands of – and a sense of urgent responsibility to – the materials themselves.

There was some conscious intention to make a cultural breakthrough, to talk in public as we talked in private. How we behave in private is actually the ultimate politics. So the original literary inspiration was to behave in public as we do in private.[22]

Since the Beat programme was 'to behave in public as we do in private', private life too became strategic, part of various crusades, and thus involved him in myth-making, falsification, a further splitting or subdivision of the self. To be a smiling public man is to submit everything to the scrutiny of media-imposed agendas, even to 'history': to destructive pressures that a notion of 'private life' as protected, autonomous realm might have done something to dissipate. He's always opening the books (the Journals: the history of his transactions) on himself. As democratiser of bohemia and gay rôle model, he feels he has a great deal to answer for: 'How many people will go the wrong way, defy their parents and die in hovels alone, childless because they read, "I will be home in two months & look you in the eye"?'[23] – that is, his myth-making.

'Ego Confession' (1974) went in for a certain amount of self-dismantling, a certain amount of self-glorification:

Seaman knew ocean's surface a year
carpenter late learned bevel and mattock
son, conversed with elder Pound & treated his father gently
– All empty all for show, all for the sake of Poesy
to set surpassing example of sanity as measure for late generations
Exemplify muse power to the young avert future suicide
accepting his own lie and the gaps between lies with equal good humor
Solitary in worlds full of insects & singing birds all solitary
– who had no subject but himself in many disguises
some outside his own body including empty air-filled space forests
    & cities –
Even climbed mountains to create his mountain, with ice ax &
    crampons & ropes, over Glaciers –

The gaps between thoughts have become the gaps between lies. All is vanity – but not quite. An inextricable muddling of all aspects of Ginsberg's public, private and writing life make for a phenomenon of which writing is only apart, and in which the absolute value of writing as 'art' is called into question. Nevertheless, his political poems must surely be among the most widely read and effective, that is, politically influential in their own moment, in terms of their own intentions, in modern history. Politics is the core. For all that he turns upon himself in 'Ego Confession', his intentions are mocked as vanities but celebrated in their utopian ambition – 'and overthrew the CIA with a silent thought' – because politics – a paranoid world-embracing vision – is his mother's legacy:

> who died of the communist anticommunist psychosis ...
> complaining about wires of masscommunication in her head
> and phantom political voices in the air
> besmirching her girlish character ...
> (Witchita Vortex Sutra)

Ginsberg is interested both in naming and in telling. He names his names and there is always a kind of telling about the name. Frank O'Hara's names are those of whoever happened to be there, Jap, Vincent or Pierre Reverdy.[24] He refuses them any symbolic function – they are points between which the sliding T of the poems moves, defining and redefining itself. They may carry differing freights of association for different readers, a few like Ginsberg himself or Billie Holiday may be well known, but most are simply names to first-time readers of O'Hara and we are not really expected to investigate them as part of reading the poem. Ginsberg always tells us something about his names, even it is only of their place in his cultural and personal pantheon. In other words, he assigns them a symbolic function.

'Things are symbols of themselves,' the epigraph to his *Collected Poems*, is an ambiguous statement, reminiscent of Williams' no ideas but in things, similarly open to various interpretations. Is he saying there are no ideas, only things? That we must present ideas through things? On the one hand that word and object are identical, on the other that our words for things express ideas, that the general is to be sought in the particular? The last, as both Creeley and Ginsberg acknowledge, is the religious idea at the core of Williams' thinking, a belief in the value of common things and spiritual truth to be derived from involvement with them, 'the sacramentalisation of everyday reality'.

No ideas but in things contains all these contradictory notions: the word is both window and object, and through that tension is opened up the gap within the sign, between signifier and signified. It is there Williams is playing in 'Spring and All', territory explored by the Gertrude Stein of *Tender Buttons* (1913), where a vocabulary of everyday verbs and nouns is deployed both to denote 'Objects', 'Food' and so on and to reveal their status as linguistic counters. By playing in the gaps, Stein shows us both the apparent solidity and the elusiveness of the worlds of perception, time and objects in 'an arrangement in a system to pointing'. A rose is a rose is a rose is a linguistic paradox; the identity of sign and object is asserted, but 'rose' isn't a rose at all, it's a sign whose meaning changes – is qualified and attenuated – each time it is repeated.

'Things are symbols of themselves' tells us on the one hand that things are identical with and sufficient to themselves, on the other that they're already part of some transcendent order. Things, as they appear in poetry, are inevitably ideas, then, like Whitman's eidolons; merely to name is to participate in or construct a symbolic order.

The very afflatus of this epigraph, the index and highly informative notes (he nervously gives T.S. Eliot and Mary Shelley as precedent annotators), may suggest a failure of confidence on Ginsberg's part. Is his poetry simply a sprawling journalistic ad hoc account of 'our times' as they turn into airtime? Is there no overall spiritual narrative? Do the poems stand out of the contexts and order in which they were written, or are they to be read as a kind of intimate social history, for information in other words, which may include information about the limitations of their own strategies?

It is characteristic of Ginsberg to ask self-undermining questions, and this has made his poetry, quite apart from his role as publicist, more than rhetorical bardic posturings. 'Notations of ordinary mind', however romantically representative you take that mind to be, recording the gaps between thoughts, faltering, fumbling, associating, revealing the mind's less than unitary and Olympian status, even as a babbling oracle, runs against the implications of presenting yourself as a bard, a speaker of authoritative public truths. I sense that the bardic was deeply embarrassing to Ginsberg from the beginning, hence his constant milking of Whitmanic rhetorical grandness for its humour. Having written 'Howl', with its celebration of holy madness, he moves into a more intimate mode of address and territory, on to a sorrowful consideration of real madness and its effects in 'Kaddish'.

Such is the undecidable status of Ginsberg's names, personal, and 'appearing as themselves', also a dramatis personae. It all turns on whether his personal cultural matrix is valid or not beyond its significance in the growth of his own mind. Enough people have thought so to follow his paths, investigate his names, ingest his tradition. Which can also be enthusiastically added to: as I write Marianne Faithfull has been inducted into the Jack Kerouac School of Disembodied Poetics. The 'canon' becomes a kind of alternative Country Music Hall of Fame (no disrespect to either institution), but for his own part Ginsberg seems rather to embarrass himself. In his efforts to overcome this he embarrasses us. There is a cycle of overstatement, embarrassment, retreat, of cutting a pathetic 'all too human' figure with his reader, reconsideration, and an impatient lurch back to bardic rhetoric or personal revelation.

These movements, cycles or alternations, can also be found in his swing back and forth between religion and politics. It is not that religion, his much discussed Blake-vision (which now seems to embarrass him) or his Buddhism signify, as some commentators have said, a retreat from politics, rather it provides means of renewing his politics, of setting a wider framework for his activities. His vision of Blake in Harlem, for example, may have laid an intolerable burden on him, but it also provided him with permission: evidence that he was a visionary, a position from which to speak his political critique of America.

'The Change' (1963) was written on a train in Japan. Ginsberg describes the poem as 'prophetic of a more literal change later on' in respect to his 1948 vision of Blake in Harlem, 'Because, finally the memory of the Blake vision left such a strong impression of universal consciousness that it didn't seem right to abandon it. In fact, my first thought when it happened to me was "I must never forget this".'[25] The preoccupation with the significance of this experience, and attempts to replicate it, had taken him over and led to a neglect of what he felt were his responsibilities to 'awareness of present time'. This led to a renunciation of visions, of the prophetic, shamanic role they implied for the poet, a return to the body, and acceptance of the Buddhist doctrine of Anatma – no permanent selfhood:

> I am false Name the prey
> of Yamantaka Devourer of
> Strange dreams, the prey of
> radiation & Police Hells of Law
>
> I am that I am I am the
> man & the Adam of hair in
> my loins This is my spirit and
> physical shape I inhabit
> this Universe Oh weeping
> against what is my
> own nature for now

His *Indian Journals* and the poems he wrote there in the early 1960s, returning to his Williams mode of 'Empty Mirrors', found him exploring the actuality of India, an experience to overpower the dangers of self-congratulatoriness and a sense of unreality that is bound to attend a newly famous man:

Old man,
        the dozen green
bits of pepper in a bowl
on marble table top,
            all the details
I mean all the yellow rice and mutton
in my Mohammedan hotel are yours
        in Calcutta –
I love you,
        with interruptions....[26]

India was a way out of a constricting role as beatnik humorist, a way to shake cultural certainties, deepen his politics and those of his audience. A Buddhist sense of the forms of authority being worldly impostures provided a transcendent rationale for his mid-1960s politics. He moves between religion and politics, incorporating and reformulating various elements of a previous stance. 'Plutonium Ode' (1977) amasses a legion of wrathful deities, widespread borrowings from apocalyptic literature – a wholesale naming of names – to do battle with the American nuclear industry, a means of comprehending the magnitude of plutonium's destructive potential, and of wryly suggesting the scale of the powers that would be necessary to stop it.

The Beat stance is built out of a number of negations of official options, aesthetic and social, yet the Beat writers (particularly Ginsberg) mirror the academy in their archivism. He always kept lines of communication open to the academy, sought approval in a sense, wanted to take over, recognised its importance – as access to young minds, audiences. He concerned himself with making alternative 'traditions', a faculty, living and dead, for the academy of the future, and finally incarnated that in a school of his own. His influence on subsequent American poetry is vast, but his celebrity and the singling out that this entails muddies the picture: it's impossible to say what is direct and what arises from an independent shared poetics or other connections. The most famous poet is the one you first hear of, initially over-praised, denigrated by initiates.

A constant theme in the early biography is of being invaded, taken over, robbed of identity, displaced by others; a process he is seemingly powerless to stop. Huncke, the Times Square junkie Burroughs had introduced him to, whom New York cops had considered too much of 'a creep' to hang out with the other lowlife, moves in, steals from him, takes over his apartment; other friends use it as a store for stolen goods.

In many relationships there seems to have been an inability, or unwill-ingness, to set boundaries between self and other, and a consequent tendency apparently to welcome imposition, abuse, exploitation.

But it is this hospitality to others, a seeking of himself in them, that made Ginsberg such a powerful catalyst, available to Burroughs, Kerouac, Cassady and others as sounding-board and scribe. He has been a meeting place for other consciousnesses, for whole constellations of contemporary concerns and restlessly tried-on identities, religions, geographies. That is how he was able to being news of elsewhere:

Ayers Rock/Uluru Song

When the red pond fills fish appear.
When the red pond dries fish disappear.
Everything built on the desert crumbles to dust.
Electric cable transmission wires swept down.
The lizard people came out of the rock.
The red Kangaroo people forgot their own song.
Only a man with four sticks can cross the Simpson Desert.
One rain turns red dust green with leaves.
One raindrop begins the universe.
When the raindrop dries, worlds come to their end.
                                         Central Australia, 23 March 1972

Ginsberg has claimed the Beats (though not necessarily himself) as precursors of practically any late twentieth-century aesthetic or social movement you care to name, but I sense a defensiveness in some of these statements, as though he has been, or expects to be, passed over.

His notion of poetic line as breath, for example, in common with that of Olson, annexing Williams' notions of speech-rhythm, is full-bloodedly physiological, and as such vaguely embarrassing to postmodern critics. Writing (and thought) are assimilated to speech, apparently; recent criticism is more comfortable with the visual, with the page, with syntactic disruption.[27] But if he is recording the jumps, the gaps in thought, he thereby reveals the interstices of subjectivity. He allows language to recombine, to play out its own structures on the page. Kerouac taught him how to 'let the mind find the language', he tells us, a process that is not 'automatic writing' but 'a highly conscious attention to the shapes in which language appears in the mind'.[28] He goes on to say that a sense of rhythm or virtually wordless verbal structure – a grammar of the poem, if you like – is often there before the words, which are then 'filled in by process of association'.

An ad hoc vocabulary from literature, the world's religions, newsprint, television advertising, American vernacular, word orders that impede immediate comprehension, polyvalent syntax, articleless juxtaposi-tions disrupting the rolling forward of movement of his long line, all deployed as contemporary cultural commentary – such ideas are a common legacy of current poetries that take off from the 1950s, however remote they may appear from Ginsberg.

Not only did he make moves that opened up new audiences, he seized the opportunity to make a poetry of public address, became 'paterfamilias' and laureate to the last youth movement to be based on reading. His input into the political manifestations of the 1960s was both internationalist and communitarian.[29] Electing to speak in a public arena in a public voice, he began to include within his work the possibility of a number of responses to it, including the hostile ones that its author is either a person who has failed to develop a mature attitude to the world and its problems, or is simply a buffoon. This is what makes for his wild contortions and instabilities of tone. Diaristic notation, mock-prophecy, lyric, bathos – all are constantly in play. In 'Capitol Air' (1980) and more recent poems he mocks his own earnest liberalism and agenda-based politics. 'Cosmopolitan Greetings' (1994) returns to one of Ginsberg's earliest successful modes, the self-mocking protest poem, and hopes his asshole will hold out.

Problems arise in all attempts to reread recent literary history for validation, inevitable though that process may be. For much as you wish to provide yourself with a historical precedent, there are usually good reasons to distort or even begrudge your benefactor from the past. Ginsberg's breath poetics have recently been praised for having 'oddly anticipated the recent French feminist idea of "writing the body"'.[30]

In the end it's a matter of making your own version, as I have done. Ginsberg, after all, made up his own ad hoc versions of literary history and of the second half of the twentieth century, in order to reactivate silenced voices, to disseminate hidden strains in writing. His influence extends to all those who begin by investigating his names, as well as to many who have never heard of him, company too numerous even for death's military garage. This may be a paradox of his work, since he is at his best, for this reader, not when conjuring with his names, but when he has something in front of him.

New York poet Clark Coolidge has a long-standing interest in lists and names, evidenced in his long poem 'In Virginia' (1975), excavated from surveys of caves in that state. His recent version of 'The Names'

(1994) continues that and also parodies the reminiscence in Ginsberg's poem:

> Marble Dando is not the name of anything
>
> Flash Coolihan, the Hamadryad Bactrician
> or kneedeep bouncer from Limerick
> Closed
>
> Insouciance of the Steed, that's a name
>
> Billy Neuter was a hod carrier, no, a nose thief, no,
> a rod of justice, no, bartender in a wheat row hallway, no,
> the embolism at the end of your cow, no, a veer,
> no, there is no resemblance to this name
>
> We sit in a transparent green room and view
> Heady Carrier
> there is nothing on the flow but a new dog
> and nothing further to say but amplitude[31]

These invented proper names return naming to the province of telling. Clark Coolidge's poem is an 11-page improvisation, an exercise in an expanded sense of rhyming, pure invention, cultural-linguistic play with proper names. His poem seems to complete a circle in this essay, arriving at a point where the historical cleavage between naming and telling that Stein speaks of has been overcome: a notionally endless flow of epic naming and telling, where naming the names and telling how they became the names are one activity.

NOTES

I wish to thank Yiannis Patsakas for his conversation during the writing of this essay.

Quotations are mostly taken from:
Collected Poems 1947–1980 (London and New York: Viking, 1984) = CP
Indian Journals (San Francisco: City Lights, 1970) = IJ
Journals Early Fifties Early Sixties (New York: Grove Press, 1977) = JEFES
As Ever: The Collected Correspondence of Allen Ginsberg and Neal Cassady (Creative Arts, 1976) = AE
Barry Miles, *Ginsberg: A Biography* (London and New York: Viking, 1989) = Miles

1. John Ashbery, *Selected Poems* (London: Paladin, 1987) p.189.
2. IJ, p.62.
3. Gertrude Stein, *Narration* (Chicago: University of Chicago Press, 1935) p.10.
4. *The Harvard Collected Works of Walt Whitman*, Vol. 5, p.1649.
5. Liddel and Scott's *Greek Lexicon* (1892).
6. Robert Creeley, Introduction to *Poet to Poet: Whitman* (London: Penguin, 1971).
7. For a full account of their conversations, see Miles, pp.400–6.
8. Louis Simpson, *Studies of Dylan Thomas, Allen Ginsberg, Sylvia Plath and Robert Lowell* (London: Macmillan, 1978), p.67.
9. AE, p.111.
10. Allen Ginsberg, *The Visions of the Great Rememberer* (Northampton, Massachusetts: Mulch Press, 1974).
11. Hart Crane, *The Bridge* (New York: Liveright, 1930), p.41.
12. JEFES, p.95.
13. AE, p.113.
14. Robert Creeley interviewed in Ekbert Fass (ed.), *Towards a New American Poetics* (Santa Barbara, California: Black Sparrow, 1978), p.172.
15. Miles, pp.231–47.
16. Theodor Adorno, 'Spengler After the Decline', in *Prisms* (London: Neville Spearman, 1967), p.72. All quotations from Spengler are taken from Adorno's essay.
17. Allen Ginsberg, *Village Voice*, 25 August 1959; quoted in George Bowering, 'How I Hear "Howl" in *On the Poetry of Allen Ginsberg* (Ann Arbor: University of Michigan Press, 1984).
18. Walter Benjamin, 'Theses on the Philosophy of History', in *Illuminations* (London: Fontana, 1976).
19. 23 March 1961, in JEFES, p.192.
20. Marshall McLuhan, *The Medium is the Massage* (London: Penguin, 1966).
21. 'Action Packed' by Ronnie Dee.
22. Miles, p.531.
23. Ibid., p.511.
24. Frank O'Hara, *Selected Poems* (New York: Knopf, 1974).
25. Fass, (ed.), *Towards a New American Poetics*, pp.225–8.
26. 'To W.C.W.' in IJ, p.60.
27. See Marjorie Perloff in Robert Frank and Henry Sayre (eds), *The Line in Postmodern Poetry* (Urbana: University of Illinois, 1988).
28. Fass, (ed.), *Towards a New American Poetics*, p.257.
29. See Jane Kramer, *Paterfamilias* (London: Gollancz, 1970) and Norman Mailer, *The Armies of the Night* (London: Penguin, 1967) for full accounts.
30. Sandra M. Gilbert, 'Glass Joints', in Frank and Sayre (eds), *The Line*, p.43.
31. Clark Coolidge, 'The Names' (1994), unpublished MS; to appear in *Active in Airtime* No. 5.

2

'I am only a jolly storyteller': Jack Kerouac's *On The Road* and *Visions of Cody*

R.J. Ellis

How distinct, how related, are Kerouac's two landmark novels, *On The Road* and *Visions of Cody*? Are they, as critics like Timothy Hunt suggest, best regarded as versions of the same evolving narrative or should they be read as each self-standing, distinct if comparable accounts of an emblematic male friendship in immediate postwar America?[1] My own preference is to regard them as the latter, the one out of a modernistic-inspired revision of picaresque and *bildungsroman* traditions (replete with accompanying quest-motif) and the other out of a more concertedly modernist lineage (its debts, among others, being to Joyce and Faulkner).[2] If, too, *On The Road* revises the picaresque to its own ends, so, in turn, it forecasts something of the more overtly experimental nature of *Visions of Cody*.

On The Road deviates from the traditional *Bildungsroman* in one key way: it subjects it to a framing – a meta-narrational – irony. For Kerouac is concerned to expose the process whereby the myth of the Western Frontier has become essentially bankrupted and ideologically deformed. It is, too, an exposé whose urgency derives from an especially keen, inward sense of the 1940s, when the novel is set and when Kerouac commenced working on it. Early in the book we are told: 'In the month of July 1947, having saved fifty dollars from old veteran benefits, I was ready to go to the West Coast.'[3] Sal Paradise has already mentioned a 'miserably weary split up' with his wife, and a (partly resulting) 'serious illness'. The text makes available here a symbolic reading that invests Sal and his quest with mythic (national) significance: a coherent rereading of this pattern of ejection from domestic stability into a period of illness could result from flatly observing that the US had emerged from a long period it represented as one of isolation within domestic concerns into reluctantly overt global engagement via the Second World War. Armed with his $50 worth of veteran's checks, Sal adventures into America's interior. The resulting narrative constitutes a reassessment of America's national myths in the resulting postwar climate.

The quest motif for a 'pearl' is clearly announced in the opening chapter, as is the fact that Sal's initially naïve search will involve a process of learning which comically recasts one central American myth pattern: the West as frontier territory, beyond societal controls, where an American identity can be forged. Eleven times in nine pages we hear of this 'so-longed-for' West. All this is conventional enough: numerous American narratives incorporate into their picaresque form a *Bildungsroman* motif in which a naïve hero locates his 'pearl' in the West.[4] A relevant continuity here is with popular literature, particularly Western cowboy novels and films, exploring the 'Frontier' as a fictive space, a territory of (often anxious) freedom and possibility.[5] Indeed, *On The Road* adopts another characteristic of cowboy narrative, namely the 'Buddy' tradition, where the raw newcomer is initiated by his more experienced friend (in this novel, Dean, a Gene Autry lookalike) into the arts of survival. The myth pattern, then, incorporates male initiation; *On The Road*'s narrative, however, re-represents this pattern through ironic parody.

Sal's attempt to act out this central US Western myth-pattern in 1947, as a returned GI, just following a period when America's global military interventions created a need for national redefinition, generates significant dissonances. That the 'West' is being contemporaneously redefined as set against the 'Communist East' is one sign of this process. The resulting ironies continually cut against unproblematic acceptance of Sal's story. Obviously his naïvety itself highlights one basic situational irony: that to regard to West as an arena of (self) discovery is circumscribed by the fact that the Frontier, according to Frederick Jackson Turner, has been closed for over half a century.[6] This becomes comic in Kerouac's revisions: Sal's experienced buddy is a twentieth-century cowboy – a car thief rather than a horse thief, his job in New York that of a 'parking-lot attendant'. Sal's narrative is thus repeatedly marked by ambivalence concerning Dean – though largely retrospectively. Once again, this is established in the opening paragraph. Dean may be 'a side-burned hero of the snowy West', but he is also 'conning me and I knew it'. It is impossible finally for Sal to 'cast' Dean unambiguously into the stereo-typical role of the initiated cowboy buddy. His attempt to resolve the problem is fraught with tensions: '… his "criminality" was not something that sulked and sneered; it was a wild yea-saying overburst of American joy; it was Western, the west wind, an ode from the Plains …'. Such hyperbole ironises its own attempts to re-integrate Dean into a conventional heroic representation – the good bad (cow)boy who 'only stole cars for joy rides'.

Crucially, this ambivalence is accompanied by doubts about the promise of the West saturating the novel's early narrative. The West recurrently poses serious threats to Sal's romantic effusiveness:

'Hell's bells, it's Wild West Week,' said Slim. Big crowds of businessmen, fat businessmen in boots and ten-gallon hats, with their hefty wives in cowgirl attire bustled and whooped on the wooden sidewalks of old Cheyenne ... Blank guns went off ... I felt it was ridiculous: in my first shot at the West I was seeing to what absurd devices it had fallen ... (p.29)

While Sal retains shreds of his dream, believing these 'absurd devices' enabled the West 'to keep its proud tradition', Jack Kerouac's satire has become unrelenting. Confronted with 'long flat wastelands of sand and sagebrush', Sal is alarmed: 'What the hell is that?' He needs the reassuring signifier 'the rangeland' to be supplied to secure the necessary conceptual relationship and recover his balance.

These points should not need labouring, but that this interplay is, at least early on, represented comically still needs emphasis. Orientational confusion provides another source of this: the rose dropped into the Hudson by Sal would float east, and the blonde-haired girl Sal meets in Cheyenne turns eastward, too – in a flowerless prairie:

'... listen, we'll take a nice walk in the prairie flowers.'
'There ain't no flowers there,' she said ... . '... I want to go to New York. I'm sick and tired of this. Ain't no place to go but Cheyenne, and ain't nothin in Cheyenne.'
'Ain't nothin in New York.'
'Hell there ain't' she said ... .(p.31)

Things are getting confusing: romantic opportunity flows eastwards, and this comic inversion underscores the irony that the Western territories are not, in the late 1940s, a social wilderness, but like Denver, increasingly urbanised communities separated by space.[7] Sal's comic series of symbolic failures to rendezvous with friends there are thus 'missed connections' in 'a war with social overtones', satirically exposing class divisions that really exist, contradicting the myth-representations of an agrarian-rooted, egalitarian, democratic individualism. But Sal is a comically slow learner, destined in San Francisco to become a species of cop. Perforce, Sal finally resorts to a crucial, plainly ironic, reorientation: New York becomes for him, as for blonde-haired prairie women, 'brown and holy'. He faces 'East' and determines 'to make my trip a circular one ...'. (pp.66–7)

This step crystallises the book's overarching structural pattern: Parts Two and Three reproduce Part One's pattern of departure from and return to New York, as do Parts Four and Five when taken together. Such a repeated pattern can be regarded as an element of the narrative's engagement with myth. The function of this repetition is plainly 'to render the structure of the myth apparent'.[8] However, there are successive revisionary inflections to these repetitive circular returns to New York. The circlings steadily become more pre-emptively treated. Parts One, Two and Three all describe successive round trips, but Part One is by far the longest. Parts Two and Three are each only half as long. Parts Four and Five, which, taken together, make up a fourth round trip, are very much shorter still.

The way in which the descriptions of Sal's trips grow progressively more cursory provides structural reinforcement for a growing feeling of a narrative vortex. The increasing desperation and loss of energy which comes to characterise Sal's quest is replicated by the narrative's increasing rapidity. Early in the second journey around America Sal may still be able to preserve some faith in his quest: '... I suddenly saw the whole country like an oyster for us to open; and the pearl was there, the pearl was there' (p.114). But for the reader this reassertion of faith in a pearl is disturbing. The final repetition of its location lends a note of querulousness, and the greater specificity given to the metaphor shakes one's faith: prising open an oyster kills it. The image is tainted with rapacity. Sal's initial point of departure is Paterson, where past history manifests such rapacity:

> In February 1857, David Hower, a poor shoemaker ... collected a lot of mussels from Notch Brook near the City of Paterson. He found in eating them many hard substances. At first he threw them away but at last submitted some of them to a jeweler who gave him twenty-five to thirty dollars for the lot. Later he found others. One pearl of fine lustre was sold to Tiffany for $900 ... .
>
> News of the sale created such excitement that search for the pearls started throughout the country. ... A large round pearl, weighing 400 grains which would have been the finest pearl of modern times, was ruined by boiling open the shell.[9]

Part Two of *On The Road* drives home this sense that a search for pearls throughout the country is ruinous. On Sal's second transcontinental crossing the route is different, but the destination, San Francisco, is unchanged and the disenchantment on arrival more acute: 'I was out of my mind with hunger and bitterness ... I walked around picking butts from the street.' (pp.142–3) This is an exact reminder of Sal back in the East, standing in a 'subway door', trying to 'get enough nerve' to pick up a 'beautiful long butt' on Times Square (p.90). Sal's hope then, in

Part One, that the East would prove to be 'brown and holy' inevitably dissolved in 'the absolute madness and fantastic hoorair of New York with its millions and millions hustling forever for a buck among themselves – grabbing, taking, giving, sighing, dying, just so they could be buried in those awful cemetery cities beyond Long Island ...' (pp.89–90). For Sal, New York instead becomes 'the place where paper America is born' – 'paper America' stretches from Coast to Coast. As Sal had warned us, the East only seemed holy to him when first on the West Coast: 'that's what I thought *then*' (my emphasis).

A symbolic wilderness thus pervades both poles of the East–West opposition: Sal's encounter in Part One with the 'Ghost of the Susquehanna', the old man driven out of his mind by his hoboing, dramatises this: 'I thought all the wilderness of America was in the West till the Ghost of the Susquehanna showed me ... a wilderness in the East.' (p.88) On one level this is literally true of the East's backroads, but Sal's simultaneous mention of Franklin, Washington and Boone, and the high hopes for America enshrined in the legends attached to their names, gives this Wilderness symbolic and ironic resonance. The old binary division of America into East and West simply won't hold good: the Ghost, heading off the wrong way, has now literally lost his sense of direction.

The verdict in the final paragraph of Part Two thus provides a deadening climax: 'What I accomplished by coming to San Francisco I don't know.' It dramatises Part Two's overt questions about direction. Part One had obliquely introduced this motif, when, with comic irony, the question is raised by a carnival operator:

> A tall lanky fellow ... came over to us ... 'You boys going to get somewhere, or just going?' We didn't understand his question, and it was a damned good question.
> ... I said, 'I don't know, I'm going as fast as I can and I don't think I have time.' (p.20)

Once again, the phrasing is crucial: the question was 'damned good' because it queries whether Sal's journey possesses any goal. Sal's answer conspicuously fails to name any destination. This silence is exposed more fully in Part Two:

> Finally [Carlo] ... said, 'I have an announcement to make.'
> 'Yes? yes?'
> 'What is the meaning of this voyage ... I mean, man, whither goest thou? Whither goest thou, America, in thy shiny car in the night?' (p.99)

Again, no answer is forthcoming: '"Whither goest thou?" echoed Dean with his mouth open. We sat and didn't know what to say; there was nothing to talk about anymore. The only thing to do was go.' The exchange confirms that Sal's crisis about East–West orientations also confronts the cultural myth. Within twenty pages, this question of purpose is raised again, this time by Old Bull Lee:

> 'Now, Dean, I want you to sit quiet a minute and tell me what you're doing crossing the country like this.'
> Dean could only blush and say, 'Ah well, you know how it is.'
> 'Sal, what are you going to the Coast for?'
> 'Only for a few days ...' (p.121)

Kerouac deliberately marks this comic interrogation, even to the extent of making Lee repeat it six pages later, but still Sal cannot properly reply.

This crisis of direction crystallises in Part Three. Firstly, the trip now consists only of revisits, except, significantly, for the automobile town of Detroit: geographic repetitiveness predominates. Secondly, the bulk of the descriptive detail is given over for the first time to an Eastward journey. The narrative deliberately marks this key inversion:

> I saw flashing by outside several scenes that I remembered from 1947 .... All that old road of the past unreeling dizzily as if the cup of life had been overturned and everything gone mad. My eyes ached in nightmare day. (p.193)

This reverse movement conveys a sense of threat and nausea:

> Great horrors that we were going to crash ... took hold of me ... now I could feel the road some twenty inches beneath me, unfurling and flying and hissing at incredible speeds across the groaning continent. (p.193)

Disillusionment now definitively dominates. Sal realises that he is 'beginning to cross and recross towns in America as though I were a *traveling salesman*' (my emphasis). The residue of naïve enthusiasm is, in terms of the myth, now incongruously mis-oriented: 'We were hot; we were going *east*; we were excited' (p.171; my emphasis). To underline this inversion further, the specified destination – Italy – lies (necessarily) outside of the United States. Appropriately, given the dominant tone of sterile exhaustion in this section, Italy is never reached; the final words of Part Three are 'So we didn't go to Italy.' But the intention of effecting a break-out from this East–West circling is immediately enacted in Part Four. The Mexican border becomes (conventionally) the selected exit point, and the narrative defines the incumbent geographical reorientation: 'I couldn't imagine this trip. It was the most fabulous of all. It was no longer east–west, but magic south.'

The ironies are comically inescapable. Part Three described an inverted West–East trip, and Part Four's new direction offers no resolutions. 'Paper America' still accompanies them. Mexico may seem, on arrival, 'the magic land', but only because 'our wonderful ... money went so far'; 'the whole of America' cannot be put 'behind' these 'moneybags Americans' (pp.225, 230). Predictably, Mexico terminates in dysentery, Dean's desertion, and a drained return North to New York before the final split-up. The pattern is now completed: Part One – Westwards; Part Two – Westwards; Part Three – Eastwards; Part Four – Southwards; Part Five – (implicitly) Northwards. The initial repetition of Westward movement provides initial irony; the latter half of the novel repeatedly dislocates the conventional geographic orientation of the Western myth. The only pattern constantly sustained is that of deflated returns to the starting point, in what are, in terms of narrative detail, increasingly rapid cycles. And this vortex-movement, I would argue, creates a reorientation inwards, into an inner space in which a second narrative trajectory unfolds – that of Dean Moriarty.

II

Kerouac's assertion that *On The Road* is 'a horizontal account of travels on the road' is fulfilled by the end of the second section.[10] After this, the increasing loss of orientational clarity within the American myth of the Western frontier forces the characters inwards, during the third section's inverted West–East journey. This sickening inversion structurally marks the breakdown in the capacity of the myth coherently to represent America's social development: by now the repeated journeys cumulatively reveals the myth to be not timeless, but part of a process of history. As Claude Levi-Strauss has argued, for advanced capitalist societies modern myth (unlike primitive myth) functions 'in history'.[11] This distinction is for me crucial. Levi-Strauss claims that myth seeks 'to provide a logical model capable of overcoming a contradiction ... [which is] impossible ... if ... the contradiction is real'.[12] Since America's 'modern myth' of the West is located in history and so cannot be timeless, it does impossibly seek to overcome a real contradiction within its culture. The tension between the modern Western myth's attempt to secure asocial timelessness and its presence within history is therefore a symptom of what Roland Barthes describes as modern myth's 'ideological' function.[13]

Sal's travels ironically expose this myth's conventional representation of immediately available freedom in the frontier West. But, I wish to argue, this exposé's real penetration into the myth's ideological formation occurs when the novel's vortex bores progressively inwards, into the myth-narrative, and lays bare the existence of what Barthes describes as a second-order sign-system, extant within the first-order system – embedded within Sal's comically purblind 'Western' story. This represents, in effect, an extension of Levi-Strauss's point that myths function as narratives dialectically – in a constantly revisionary process that in this case leads Sal to embrace Dean as his myth-hero, his 'insider'.[14] The West's ability to retain mythic meaning for Sal beyond its demonstrable coherence is an ironic indication of its second-order, meta-linguistic (and so unvoiced) ability to allude 'imperatively' to the illusion of timelessness.[15] Barthes describes this as 'The privation of History': history 'evaporates'.[16] The modern myth can therefore function ideologically as the road 'unwind[s] *into* Sal Paradise' (my emphasis).

This inward exploration functions simultaneously as a continuing narrative search for release and a meta-narrational exploration of what Barthes describes as the 'turnstile' of modern myth, winding together the myth's first-order sign system (the story) and its second-order system – its ideology.[17] Sal seeks to act out the first order story. For the reader, it is ironically *unwound*, through the comic portrait of Sal's attempts to preserve its romantic efficacy. This process increasingly centres on Sal's representation of Dean as heroic, and finds its focus in Sal's construction of Dean as developing. This is hinted at in the very first chapter, when we are told that Dean in 1947 was 'not the way he is today'. Significantly, however, this does not begin to emerge as a central theme until Sal's disillusionment with the naïve version of the myth in Part One endangers its explanatory adequacy. Only four pages into Part Two, however, the new, Dean-oriented dimension starts to unfold, when we are told that 'The madness of Dean had bloomed into a weird flower.' As Sal puts it, '"My God, he's changed"' (pp.94–5). This change is soon clarified, when Sal asserts 'I had never dreamed that Dean would become a mystic' and claims that this represents a first phase, 'the first days of his mysticism prior to the strange, ragged, W.C. Fields saintliness of his latter days'. Crucially, his later saintliness occurs in Part Three, on the inverted journey, when 'That [broken] thumb became the symbol of Dean's final development.' Thus Dean's evolution in Sal's story is both necessarily contradictory and *inward*, a spiritual ascent converting him into, progressively, a mystic, a saint, then an 'Angel', and finally 'God'. In order to sustain the myth-narrative's coherence Dean grows ever more immaterial. And on each of the occasions that this inward growth is apparent to Sal, it is welded to Dean's pronouncements on time.

Deprived of any coherent spatial representation for the myth, now overtly constrained by history, Sal is drawn to Dean's intuitive, mystical, second-order exploration: as Dean explains it, just after Sal first realises he has 'changed', '"now is the time and we all know time."' Dean's explications of this knowledge remain necessarily gnomic, but as he develops, the notion is gradually elaborated upon. Thus, when Sal realises Dean has become a mystic, this occurs just after Dean's explanation: '"Everything is fine, God exists, we know time. ... You can't make it with geometry and geometrical systems of thinking. It's all this!" He wrapped his finger in his fist; the car hugged the line straight and true.' It is significant that Dean's attempts at explication recurrently occur either in moving cars or when listening to jazz improvisations. Thus the solo by Rollo Greb inspires Dean to exclaim:

> 'That Rollo Greb is the greatest ... . He's never hung-up, he goes every direction, he lets it all out, he knows time ... . You see, if you go like him all the time you'll finally get it.'
> 'Get what?'
> 'IT! IT! I'll tell you – now no time, we have no time now.' (p.106)

To 'tell' is to revert to syntagmatic presentation, but since the linear (geographical) syntax of the myth has broken down, narrative (linearity) threatens the coherence of Dean's experience.

The key exposition comes in Part Three, in a car speeding East. Once more it is stimulated by jazz improvisation, which Sal realised, the night before, marks the attainment of 'it'. Dean now explains:

> 'Now, man, that alto man last night had IT – he held it once he found it; I've never seen a guy who could hold it so long.' I wanted to know what 'IT' meant. 'Ah well' – Dean laughed – 'now you're asking me impon-de-rables – ahem! Here's a guy and everybody's there, right? Up to him to put down what's on everybody's mind. He starts the first chorus, then lines up his ideas ... . All of a sudden somewhere in the middle of a chorus he *gets* it – everybody looks up and knows; they listen; he picks it up and carries. Time stops. ... everybody knows it's not the tune that counts but IT – ' Dean could go no further; he was sweating telling about it. (p.170)

'"Time stops"': the search for freedom and spontaneity is paradigmatically occluded from the trap of history threatening the myth of the West. The fusion of experiences, emotions and confessions within 'it' constitutes in that instant spontaneous release. The meta-narrational irony is that plainly this experience is illusory – only momentary and context-bound, it makes no sense, nor can it, in the passage of time, in history. Sal's story unwinds its momentariness. Just to speak of 'it' acculturates it, gives it 'time'. The pursuing 'shrouded traveler', besides representing death when Sal 'look[s] back on it',[18] also signifies the decay

of the moment and imminent re-entry into history. Dean's experiences of momentary occlusions inwardly illuminate the duplicit
revolutions of the myth-turnstile of Western release and its ahistorical
East–West linear axis illusorily depriving time of history. 'It' actually
threatens this second-order ideology – from *within* its apparent recon-
firmation, because 'knowing time' is an active penetration of the story
of America, not a passive retelling. Sal senses this threat to his story and
draws back: his 'vision of Dean' sees him as descending 'like wrath to
the West' – 'like wrath' because the futility of the quest-process leads
to angry exposure of the actual class-bound materialist West. Thus the
climactic paragraph describing Dean's and Sal's attainment of 'IT'
concludes with the ironic, distancing statement: 'We were hot; we were
going east; we were excited.' The reflective narrator undermines Dean's
experiential release by inserting the implication that the direction is
wrong. The tensions extant between myth and history exposed by this
allusion to mis-orientation are part and parcel of the ambivalent pattern
of attraction–repulsion that Sal feels towards Dean, a product of Sal's
own ambivalence concerning unconditional immersion in the moment.
Gripped by the story of the West, Sal cannot enter this experience of
immediacy. Dean is both celebrated and ironically 'framed' by Sal – to
risk a pun. Sal's story finally forces Dean back into the Western myth.

The novel's structure carefully preserves its early distance from Sal,
to prepare us for the inadequacy of his response. His naïvety recedes,
but his commitment is constrained: the episode with the Mexican
Terry and her son Johnny is thus carefully positioned. In a sense it is a
return to the land, set in the West, but now as a hired hand – picking
cotton. Ironies here are replete: Sal is less adept than either Terry or
Johnny. Sal later may 'wish ... I were a Negro ... a Denver Mexican, or
even a poor overworked Jap, anything but what I was so drearily, a "white
man" disillusioned', but this is immediately undercut by a reminder of
Terry: 'All my life I'd had white ambitions; that was why I'd abandoned
a good woman like Terry ...'. In the end, Sal can always fall back on
some 'rich girl [he] knew', who in the morning can pull 'a hundred-
dollar bill out of her silk stocking ... . So all my problems were solved.'
This reminder of social location combines with his awareness of the
destructive egotism inherent in Dean's search to hold him back from
full commitment to what he recognises as 'the root, the soul' of 'BEAT'.
His dilemma emerges as Dean, the 'Holy GOOF', is attacked by Galatea:

'You have absolutely no regard for anybody but your self and your damned
kicks. All you think about is what's hanging between your legs and how much
money or fun you can get out of people and then you just throw them aside.'
(p.160)

Sal speaks here of Dean's 'enormous series of sins' making him 'the Saint of the lot'. But Dean's canonisation by Sal is not religious, it is ideological, and his crucifixion stems from the historical imperatives forcing the Western myth of release inwards. Dean, the sinful saint, thus replicates the revolutions of Barthes' turnstile of myth, simultaneously concealing and revealing its workings though his inward incarnation of the myth of 'release'. He is both its victim and an instrument of its ideology: a meritorious and meretricious exemplar.

This ensures Dean cannot be regarded as purely innocent. As Galatea notes, he is a sexist, and, as she forecasts, he eventually deserts Sal, in Mexico. But, as the symbolic inward cup-bearer of the displaced timeless myth, Dean is also in a sense carrying the sins of them all: 'his bony mad face covered with sweat and throbbing veins, saying "Yes, yes, yes," as though tremendous revelations were pouring into him all the time now, and I'm convinced they were'. Dean's momentous search for autonomous release from the bonds of society is contradicted by the historical realities of modern America, so that we view this 'Western kinsman of the sun' as an ironic hero, pursued by his own mortality, spinning on the axis of an unresolvable contradiction (space become speed) that exposes the ideological co-ordinates of the unrealisable myth. Dean's egotistical urge towards freedom is ironically constrained by history. Sal's failure to grapple with these paradoxes is marked by his 'wash[ing his] hands of the whole matter'. He never fully confronts the ironies that gather around his election of Dean as the heroic 'shrouded traveler'.

Instead, Sal's focus falls upon the continuing desire for release, which gives his narrative a constraining generic identity – the social dimension of his discourse. As Barthes expresses it in *Writing Degree Zero*: 'It is under the pressure of History and Tradition that the possible modes of writing for a given writer [here, in fact, Sal as storyteller] are established.'[19] The text's ironic revelations of these pressures of history indicate Sal's socio-historical location: a doubt-ridden postwar celebrant of the timeless West.[20] The reader is thus directed to a recognition that 'when History is denied ... it is most unmistakably at work'.[21] Dean's megalomaniacal search for an alternative space–time continuum thereby reveals the mendacity of modern myth: he is indeed a 'mad Ahab at the wheel'. The myth of the West subsists in a duplicit collapsing of its gesture towards an obsolete timeless 'covered wagon' essence into its modern, ideology-suffused 'Coca-Cola' present in an inextricable second-order fusion: 'I was more interested in some old rotting covered wagons and pool tables sitting in the Nevada desert near a Coca-Cola stand.' The terrain is saturated with the commodity code.[22] That Dean's signifier of movement, his hitchhiker's thumb, is broken in the latter third of the book is plainly symbolic. As Gary Snyder put it (speaking of Neal Cassady):

> [He] was like so many Americans who had inherited the taste for the limitless … [but] when the sheer physical space disappears you go crazy. Which is like the story of America … Initially you are moving very slowly in a totally wide area … . What you end up doing is going very fast in a densely populated area. Space becomes translated into speed … the energy of the archetypal West, the energy of the frontier … the cowboy crashing.[23]

The vortex draws Dean inside – his travels are no longer simply physical – into self-centred and inherently contradictory confrontations with this crash. But release from the continuing hold of the modern myth can only now adhere in such obsessive confrontation, not by washing one's hands of any engagement with the paradoxes – as Sal does in his final response when leaving Dean and sweeping off in 'the back of [a] cadillac'.

In this closure, *On The Road*'s picaresque/*Bildungsroman* structure decisively bifurcates. Sal's *bildungsroman* concludes with a step back into society – the *Bildungsroman*'s classic generic pattern: '… the *Bildungsroman* … ends with a self-imposed limitation; although the hero gives up the problematic search, he does not accept the world of convention or abandon the implicit scale of values …'.[24] Sal's final, internal adherence to the implicit scale of American values enshrined in the Western myth is textually marked by his final thoughts of Dean, now nostalgically sentimentalised, and tellingly accompanied by a proto-Disneyland representation of God as 'Pooh Bear'. but Dean is left on the roadside, rounding the corner, still seeking to resolve his inward conflict between history and the myth of release, still churning within the turnstile of modernity. To a significant degree, Dean's mysticism has brought him into congruence with the characteristics of Georg Lukács' 'abstract idealist', his soul 'narrowed' because: 'the complete absence of an inwardly experienced problematic transforms such a Soul into pure activity … . He has to be an adventurer' and displays a 'grotesque failure to meet' with the world. Significantly, Lukács relates this 'abstract idealist' to the picaresque hero.[25]

Sal's contrasting unpicaresque final retreat marks also his failure to attain the role of 'mythologist', as Barthes terms it.[26] I thus read the incident in the Detroit cinema as a key to the book's symbolic explorations:

> The people who were in that all-night movie were the end … . If you sifted all Detroit … the beaten solid core of dregs couldn't be better gathered. The picture was Singing Cowboy Eddie Dean and his gallant white horse Bloop, that was number one; number two … was George Raft, Sidney Greenstreet

and Peter Lorre in a picture about Istanbul. We saw both of these things six times each during the night. We saw them waking, we heard them sleeping, we sensed them dreaming, we were permeated completely with the strange Gray Myth of the West and the weird dark Myth of the East when morning came. All my actions since then have been dictated automatically to my sub-conscious by this horrible osmotic experience. (p.201)

In this depiction of the interpellative power of a modern myth's ideo-logical complicity the novel offers a meta-narrational recognition of the saturated status of culture and society under the myth-code of Western freedom – to which the individual is subjected, and upon which such a subject can obtain no perspective, since to seek release is merely to rehearse the terms of the myth.[27] Sal's failure is already coded by his *Bildungsroman*'s 'osmotic' generic structure, which dictates a return to a culture within which his desire for freedom is given endless, timeless, discursive replication.[28]

Our ironic distance from Sal's perspective on Dean promotes this recog-nition. Sal is swept up into a commodified subject-position and ultimately becomes part of 'rubbish America'. Symptomatically, for this is part of the myth, it is his buddy Dean who watches over him and only he can rescue him:

> I was sleeping with my head on the wooden arm of a seat as six attendants converged with their night's total of swept-up rubbish and created a huge dusty pile that reached to my nose as I snored head down – till they almost swept me away too … . Had they taken me with it, Dean … would have had to roam the entire United States and look in every garbage pail from coast to coast before he found me embryonically convoluted among the rubbishes of my life, his life and the life of everybody concerned. (p.202)

For Sal, Dean, in 'pure activity', lays his tortured soul to 'rest'. But this remains a mythic projection of hoped-for rescue. The ironic critique of Sal's perspective establishes what Linda Hutcheon describes as a 'paradoxical' detoxification. Sal's 'inevitable ideological grounding' is shared by Dean, but Dean's continuing inward struggles offer a potential (and only a potential) 'site of denaturalising critique'.[29]

What remains crucial is the response offered to Dean's intervention and Sal's response is a generic retreat: 'What would I have said to him from my rubbish womb? "Don't both me, man, I'm happy where I am."'. The implicit question here is whether conventional media representa-tions are to be the controllers of the turnstile of meanings contained in modern myth, or whether a relative autonomy is possible in mediating between the conflicting demands of freedom, history and ideology: 'This is *the story of America*. Everybody's doing what they're supposed to do' (my emphasis). Sal, ironically, when he utters these words, is a security guard with Remi Boncoeur, his companion once again in the chauffeur-driven Cadillac in the closing accommodation of his *Bildungsroman*. We read Sal's words with meta-narrational irony: he is indeed here – and always – doing as he is 'supposed to'. The unanswered questions are ones concerning release from the commodified subject-position which Sal finally embraces, abandoning resistance.

III

Visions of Cody in part seeks to address these unanswered questions more concertedly. They remained unanswered precisely because *On The Road* established a narrative position for Sal which excluded penetrative understanding of the continuing inward spirals of Dean. Crucially, *Visions of Cody* establishes a different, and contrasting, location for its narrator, Jack Duluoz. Where Sal Paradise had commenced as naïve and ended up as a *Bildungsroman*'s hero, accepting a self-imposed limitation, Jack Duluoz offers a narrative with no sense of such linear progression. In a sense *Visions* tells no story, and so avoids retelling the myth-stories of America.

This lack of linearity provides me with an excuse for jumping to the final third of *Visions of Cody*, where in the section 'Joan Rawshanks in the Fog' a description occurs of the making of a movie in the streets of San Francisco that the narrator chances upon.[30] This section I regard as very carefully positioned, just preceding as it does the representations of Duluoz's visions of Cody, the continuing 'imitations' of the tape scripts and the rehashing of the road adventures that conclude the book (pp.374–98). In these pages Duluoz is quite differently placed from Sal Paradise in the Detroit cinema. He is now not a consumer of the movie product but an observer of a movie's production: now not subject to its interpellations but witness to its 'strategies', not gazing but watching. Considerable stress is placed on this process of construction and its artificiality: constant retakes lead up to the final 'TAKE'. This experience is explicitly contrasted to Duluoz's (radically different) imagining of the making of Hopalong Cassidy films, making the comparison to *On The Road* all the more germane:

> ... on the road itself Hopalong Cassidy, in his white hat and on his famed pony, loping along intently ... grave, bemused in the night, thinking thoughts ... all pure California night scenery and landscape... (p.285)

Even in this there is a note of discord: the posse Duluoz pictures in pursuit is actually composed of 'rustlers posing', just as the Joan

Rawshanks 'TAKE' is a vast mechanism of deceitful effects, down to the contrived tears in her eyes. This is 'the general materialism of Hollywood', we are told, a piece of instruction that helps us understand the symbolism involved in the depiction of the crowd of onlookers being herded around by the movie-makers (as media 'ranchers'): 'surrounded ... looped in ... cooped up', denied access to their homes. This callousness is matched by the 'cruel' act of the director, when he pulls Joan's head down in a 'scarf noose' as he makes a point to her about the required performance. Symptomatically, concerted resistance to such crowd herding derives only from the middle classes, 'businessmen who lived in this charming district' or the suggestions of the police.

This exposé of the film production process is a climactic representation of the relationship of imagination and dream to the movies in *Visions of Cody*. The opening sections predominantly consist of a carefully structured collage of facets of America, particularly urban America, within which references to the movie industry, especially B-movie houses, are recurrently embedded. On the book's second page, in the second of the opening short sections, 'THE CAPRICIO B-MOVIE' house is described, its illuminated sign misspelt 'by crazy dumb kids who earn eighteen dollars a week', offering 'terrible B-movies' just across the street from 'a hotdog-Coke-magazine establishment with a big scarred Coca-Cola sign'. This, we are told, is 'the bottom of the world'. In this environment, the evolving representation of America leads to its definition, in a long anaphoric depiction, as 'a lonely crockashit'. The collage of depictions that surround this definition are an attempt to describe rather than to tell: to resist any reformulation of 'the story of America' – as told by the film 'productions' of Joan Crawford and Hopalong Cassidy in Hollywood B-movies.

In fact, the very long third section, consisting of transcripts of tapes, which follows these opening collages, is concerned with a resulting aesthetic problem: the way in which experience, in being verbalised, becomes a narrative, becomes linearised, as talking becomes telling, and, more fundamentally, how in successive retellings, experience becomes more and more of a story. At one key point in these tape discussions, this issue becomes a central concern of Jack Duluoz and Cody Pomeray. What has to be sought, but which cannot be retained, is the 'spontaneous':

... what it actually was, was a recalling right now on my part ... all I did now was re – go back to that memory and bring up a little rehash ... a little structure line, a little skeletonised thing of the – what I thought earlier, and that's what one does you know, you know when you go back and remember about a thing that you clearly thought out and went around before, you know what I'm sayin', the second or third or fourth time you tell about it or say anything like that why it comes out different ... the effort to go back and remember in detail all those things that I've thought about earlier, is such a task, and unworthy ... (p.145)

What prompts this statement of Cody's is his reading of Duluoz's transcript of the previous night's tape, which has become, in this very transcription process, a telling – posing for Duluoz, as he admits, problems of punctuation. Cody now goes on to explain how, even in the initial talking, syntax is a dilemma:

Used to not feel couple of year ago hardly worth it to complete a sentence and then it got so try as I might I couldn't and it developed into something that way, see, so now in place of that I just complete the thought whatever ... like I see it complete whatever thought comes, see, instead of trying to make myself hurry back to where I should be here ... (p.145)

The risk is that if syntax and/or retelling dominate, then all that results is 'meaningless talk' a 'mo-difi-cation' of the event or experience, the 'first happening'. The book is here explicitly probing at some of the paradoxes that had remained meta-narrational in *On The Road*.

In *On The Road*, we have seen how these meta-narrational paradoxes are signposted by Dean's inability to find social accommodation (beyond reform school/prison), creating deep inward fissures summoning us to a deconstruction of the Frontier's loss of geographical specificity and its story's assumption of a new, historically-constrained ideological function. Dean's rejection of limitations and his search for endlessness penetrates both the Western myth of release's ahistoricity and its generation of a simulated reality and excludes him from closure. But this is constrained within Sal's narrative, an ultimately syntactical account paradoxically containing and disabling such protest, driving it off in the back of a Cadillac, capturing it as just another American story. Sal's containment of Dean's idealism in a *Bildungsroman* structure marks his ideological appropriation by the modern Western myth. Our ironic understanding of Sal's limitations and Dean's contradictions, however, give us as readers the meta-textual potential to become mythologists on our own account, not outside of but exploring warily from within the insoluble paradoxes, enacted in the unresolved double-ending offered by this picaresque/*Bildungsroman*. The abstract idealist's adherence to pure activity is not compatible with the *Bildungsroman* hero's insistence on arrival. This incompatibility creates a potentially subversive interrogation of the contradictions imperfectly contained within the available myth-representations of the West in postwar America. But it remains meta-narrational: 'The contradictions ... are positioned within the system and yet work to allow its premises to be seen as fictions [and] ... as ideological structures.'[31] So *On The Road*'s first-person narrative remains 'within the system', telling 'the *story* of America' (my emphasis).

In contrast, in *Visions of Cody* the level of analysis that exists outside of Sal's narrative in *On The Road* becomes a central structuring element. Specifically, the determination to avoid linearity – of syntax, of 'structure-line', of 'mo-difi-cation', debated by Cody and Jack – permeates the book as a whole, in terms of both structure and content. The determination is to avoid 'making the mistake of following a bum story line *already written*', (my emphasis) – already written, that is, as an ideological narrative. What has to be resisted is a reductive reproduction of *Visions* as 'our B-movie again'. What has to happen is a break-out from the dream movie-house where the collective story of America is told:

> 'This movie house of mine in the dream has got a golden light to it though it is deeply shaded brown, or misty gray too inside, with thousands not hundreds but all squeezed together children in there diggin the perfect cowboy B-movie which is not shown in Technicolor but dream golden...' (p.251)

The recognised risk is that these cinema showings function as instructions in the American Western myth, now a bankrupt offer of escapism, and, furthermore, contributing to the cultural atmosphere of mid-twentieth-century America: 'All my B-movies, all our B-movies, taught us what we know now about paranoia and crazy suspicion.' It is perhaps worth mentioning here that *Visions of Cody* was worked upon by Kerouac most concertedly in the early 1950s – chiefly in 1951.[32] McCarthy made his allegation about his list of names on 9 February 1950. Kerouac is here interrogating the permeation of the modern myth of (Frontier) release in postwar America. His recognition of its ideological inexhaustibility serves as a warning of its corrupt domestic employment, specifically during the Cold War. As Cody explains to Jack: 'I think your mind is too much on the writing so that you don't have time to really sit down and go into whatever it is that's flailing you, all these people flailing you.'

IV

I am not simply claiming that Kerouac, in these two novels' differing interrogations about the hegemonic potential of discourse, should be read as a species of postmodernist. I am, of course, claiming that his writing is modernist, by virtue of his formal and thematic concern with the problematic roles of time and history upon the shaping of human institutions in process.[33] But I'm also claiming that Jack Kerouac recognises that even a satiric appreciation of how time and history are recurrently prefigured by a culture's conventional, mythic representation of the identity of self and social institutions is itself, ironically, in danger of being constrained by such representations, as talking becomes telling. And I am further claiming that this recognition obtains within a specific historical conjunction – the immediate postwar period in which the hegemonic myth-representation of the self in America has become mendacious – in a society breaking out into a period of anxious redefinition in which the issues represented in the texts, issues of class identity, gender identity and (even) race identity, are drawn into problematic and contradictory confrontations with 'the story of America'.

My point here is rather that, crucially, this recognition becomes, in *Visions*, more comprehensive and foregrounded. We are told (quite literally as a point of departure) that we have to realise that 'Not even success in America … matters.' The stimulus for this instruction is an encounter with 'a very successful young American … executive' who is 'just … bored … nothing to do in his soul but flounce around and yawn and wait, always wait, wait; the dullness of the heart gone dead'. What *Visions* concertedly does in this domain is bring the issue of class into sharper focus than in *On The Road*. Ironically, this is achieved by abandoning the device of drifting the narrator's class location off towards the middle class, as set against his working class subject (the Sal–Dean dichotomy), and instead locating Duluoz and Cody in the same working class. Thus the opening two sections of *Visions*, with their collage of urban America, constantly interweave basic life-ingredients (food, defecation, sex, masturbation, work) recorded as sights, sounds and smells (strongly olfactory in presentation, in fact). The viewpoint is established as from 'the bottom of the world', which can establish a perspective from which 'Everything belongs to me because I am poor' (p.33). Plainly, the risk here is of sentimentalisation – whether of 'little raggedy Codys' (p.5), or of Denver working-class and coloured suburbs. The point exactly is that this risk is resisted: thus we are told that 'little raggedy Codys dream, as rich men plan', and that these Codys' dreams are populated by B-movie images which can take over lives to become 'all the movies we've even been in', in which the images are real – little raggedy Codys casting themselves as Hopalong Cassidys, or, more pertinently, the Three Stooges:

Supposing the Three Stooges were real? (and so I saw them spring into being at the side of Cody in the street right there …) … goofing on the screen and in the streets that are the same streets as outside the theater only they are photographed in Hollywood by serious crews like Joan Rawshanks in the fog, and the Three Stooges were bopping one another … until, as Cody says, they've been at it for so many years in a thousand climactic efforts superclimbing and worked out every refinement of bopping one another so much that now, in the end, if it isn't already over, in the baroque period of the Three Stooges they are finally bopping mechanically and sometimes so hard its impossible to bear (wince), but by now they've learned not only how to master the style of the blows but the symbol and acceptance of also, as though inured in their souls and of course long ago in their bodies, to buffetings and crashings in the rixy gloom of Thirty movies and B short subjects (the kind made me yawn at 10 A.M. in my hooky movie of high school days, intent I was on saving my energy for serious-jawed features which in my time was the cleft jaw of Cary Grant), the Stooges don't feel the blows any more, Moe is iron, Curley's dead, Larry's gone, off the rocker … (pp.304–5)

In this complex passage the constant slide between movie screen and 'real' street, which is not systematically marked syntactically, metonymically rehearses the process of internalised control – an ideological 'flailing', indeed: the American working class beating itself into submission with movie images in a rhetorical structure that seems to me akin to that of an aporia – a movement of doubt/complexity within which the 'otherness' of meaning, its construction and deferment, can be revealed self-reflexively.[34] Cody, importantly, offers a 'savage mimicry' of this.

I do not think it is accidental that this passage is closely followed by the words '"Obviously an image which is immediately and unintentionally ridiculous is merely a fancy." – T.S. Eliot, *Selected Essays, 1917–1932*, Harcourt, Brace and Company.' In discovering an intention in the principled spontaneity of structure of *Visions*, inevitably the reader is being left to fill in the gaps. To do otherwise would be to re-establish linear narrative controls: to re-mythologise release.

It is thus worth noting that Kerouac proposes that the unmarked section which offers these 'Visions of Cody' could quite literally have been the point of departure, the actual start of the book. The section is even proposed as a 'preamble' to the 'VISIONS OF CODY' and it is here that, 'in the Summer of 1949', Duluoz starts on his journey 'out West to find' Cody. The actual start of the book is the interior of 'AN OLD DINER' which introduces the food motif so central to its opening sections. One obviously can attempt to systematise this organisation by describing it as a prolapsed structure, within which details of Cody's past are held back, a potential opening paragraph is withheld, and where the road adventures do not get started until still later in the novel: 'IT BEGAN IN DENVER'.[35] More to the point would be to regard this structure as constituting overall a spontaneously unstructured biography, or rather 'lifewriting', of the fictional Cody Pomeray – a working-class American brought up during the Depression and struggling to come to terms with postwar America at mid-century.

I am here diverging from the view of *Visions of Cody* that regards it as the version of the evolving *On The Road* saga that introduces Kerouac's spontaneous prose experimentation. For *On The Road* itself offers modulations between a colloquial American style, laced with hip slang, and passages where hip talk predominates – when time is known and 'it' attained: in jazz solo descriptions, conversations (talking) and in momentary descriptive passages. Warren Tallman, in his essay 'Kerouac's Sound', has best defined the qualities of hip talk which make this careful deployment stylistically significant:

> Hip talk ... is in fact ... a language art in which spontaneity is everything. The words are compact, mostly monosyllabic, athletic ... sensitive to the nuances and possibilities ... of [the] always threatened moment ... .[36]

These moments in *On The Road* when hip talk takes over within Kerouac's style spring from what he himself, in his essay 'Essentials of Spontaneous Prose', labels as his 'jewel centers':

> CENTER OF INTEREST Begin not from preconceived idea of what to say about image but from jewel center of interest in subject of image at moment of writing, and write outwards swimming in sea of language to peripheral release and exhaustion.[37]

LeRoi Jones rechristens these 'jewel centers' Kerouac's 'trigger inferences ... usually very easy to recognise [as] the key-image ... acts as a trigger.'[38] These sequences of 'spontaneous prose' are, I would claim, carefully positioned in *On The Road* to notate the knowing of time, the attainment of 'it'. Thus the depiction of Dean's 'work ... in parking lots' uses this phrase as the trigger-inference:

> " ... he only worked like a dog in parking lots. The most fantastic parking-lot attendant in the world, he can back a car forty miles an hour into a tight squeeze and stop at the wall, jump out, race among fenders, leap into another car, circle it fifty miles an hour in a narrow space, back swiftly into a tight spot, *hump*, snap the car with the emergency so you see it bounce as he flies out; then clear to the ticket shack, sprinting like a track star, hand a ticket, leap into a newly arrived car before the owner's half out, leap literally under him as he steps out, start the car with the door flapping, and roar off to the next available spot, arc, pop in, brake, out, run; working like that without pause eight hours a night, evening rush hours and after-theater rush hours, in greasy wino pants with a frayed fur-lined jacket and beat shoes that flap. (pp.9–10)

The flood of recollection of Dean knowing time as a parking-lot attendant is released by the trigger-inference: Dean's moment is momentarily held in the prose, just as in the justifiably famous descriptions of jazz solos.[39] But such moments are also framed – by Sal's romantic effusions and an undercutting of these by a more prosaic, restrained, reflective, style (drawing on Burroughs' factualist adaptations of Kerouac's own earlier style).[40] Thus, the suspension of narrative constraint in spontaneity is constantly framed in *On The Road* by a drive towards analytical mastery: to try to understand and contain Dean.

In *Visions of Cody*, Duluoz does not provide any organisational framing. Instead he offers a prose-style founded on free association and an accompanying syntactical uncertainty which constantly replicate Dean's arguments concerning telling and retelling: the way in which, in Derrida's terms, 'language ... is born ... from falling short of itself'.[41] Importantly, Dean mistrusts speech almost as much as its subsequent narrative organisation; he values incompleteness, the refusal of analytic mastery. This valuation is reproduced in the text by a steady desertion of modulations of narrative voice in favour of a gathering accent on drift, which interacts with increasing drift in the narrative voice: first person modulated by audio tape-scripts, imitations of these, even third person narration. Thus any narrative sense of a monolithic depiction of a defined self is eroded. This reinforces the refusal of narrative linearity and creates a fictional biography existing only when taken holistically. The story of America is not told, but broken up, and radical interrogation results, exposing a national crisis of legitimation that had helped foster the Cold War-invested confusions of mid-century America.[42] This is to become the story of postwar America, told not as a dream but, precisely, as a vision – a vision of Cody (Duluoz's vision of Cody and Cody's vision) that is 1950s America's *pharmakon*: its poison and cure.

NOTES

1. Tim Hunt, *Kerouac's Crooked Road* (Handen, Conn.: Archon Books, 1981). I do not intend to undertake a preliminary survey of recent Kerouac criticism. See Warren French, *Jack Kerouac* (Boston: G.K. Hall, 1986), pp.136–43 for a sound annotated and fairly recent survey. French's study, Hunt's, and Regina Weinreich's *The Spontaneous Poetics of Jack Kerouac* (Carbondale: Southern Illinois University Press) are books I would nominate as of particular interest. The title quote to my article is taken from Jack Kerouac's 1957 'Biographical Resume', written for Donald Allen, and quoted in French, p.54. It is meant ironically.

2. These debts have been pretty well established: particularly by French, Hunt and Weinreich. See also: Morris Dickstein, *Gates of Eden: American Culture in the 1960s* (New York: Basic Books, 1977); John Tytell, *Naked Angels: The Lives and Literature of the Beat Generation* (New York: McGraw Hill, 1976); and Tom Clark, *Jack Kerouac* (San Diego: Harcourt Brace Jovanovich, 1984).

3. Jack Kerouac, *On The Road* (New York: Viking Press, 1957), p.11. Future page references to this novel will appear in the text.

4. This continuity has been touched on by previous critics. Two (unsatisfactory) examples would be: Melvin W. Askew, 'Quests, Cars and Kerouac', *University of Kansas City Review*, Vol. 28, No. 3 (Spring, 1962), pp.231–40; Kingsley Widmer, 'The American Road', *Univ. of Kansas City Review*, Vol. 26, No. 4 (Summer 1960), pp.309–17. Both of these, for example, do not confront the inflection the phrase 'on the road' carries of 'having no fixed abode'. Interestingly, given Kerouac's origins, the French title, in this respect, could have become not *Sur la route*, but 'Sans domicile fixe'. Incidentally, the German title, *Unterwegs*, translates back best as 'On the Way', or 'Moving'.

5. See Harry Russell Heubel, *Jack Kerouac* (Boise: Boise State University Press, 1979): 'Kerouac's dependence upon popular novels, radio programs and the movies is impossible to overestimate' (p.27); the Western film's uncertainties are explored in, e.g., John Cawelti, *The Six Gun Mystique* (Bowling Green: Bowling Green Popular Press, 1973).

6. Frederick Jackson Turner, 'The Significance of the Frontier in American History', 1893, rpt. in F.J. Turner, *Frontier and Section*, ed. R.A. Billington (Englewood Cliffs: Prentice Hall, 1961), p.37.

7. See Gerald D. Nash, *The American West in the Twentieth Century: A Short History of an Urban Oasis* (Englewood Cliff: Prentice Hall, 1973).

8. Claude Levi-Strauss, *Structural Anthropology*, 1958, rpt., trans. C. Jacobsen (London: Allen Lane, 1968), p.229.

9. William Carlos Williams, *Paterson: Book I* (1946), rpt. in *Paterson: Books I–V* (New York: New Directions, 1964), p.17.

10. Jack Kerouac, 'Introductory Note' to *Excerpts from Visions of Cody* (New York: New Directions, 1960), p.5.

11. See, in particular, Claude Levi-Strauss, 'Response à quelques questions', *Esprit*, Novembre 1962, pp.596–627. For a useful summary of his distinction, see Edmund Leach, *Levi-Strauss* (London: Collins, 1970), pp.16–17.

12. Levi-Strauss, *Structural Anthropology*, p.229.

13. See Roland Barthes' seminal essay, 'Myth Today' in *Mythologies* (London: Jonathan Cape, 1972), pp.109–53.

14. Levi-Strauss, *Structural Anthropology*, pp.220ff.

15. Barthes, *Mythologies*, p.124.

16. Ibid., pp.151, 110.

17. Ibid., p.118.

18. See Robert Hipkiss, *Jack Kerouac: Prophet of the New Romanticism* (Lawrence: The Regent's Press, 1976).

19. Roland Barthes, *Writing Degree Zero* (1953), rpt., trans. A. Lavers and C. Smith (London: Jonathan Cape, 1967), p.2. Interestingly, Kerouac's location of

these dilemmas as those of a *narrator* echo some common criticisms of the later Barthes. Christopher Norris usefully and briefly reviews this debate, in his *Deconstruction: Theory and Practice* (London: Methuen, 1982), pp.8ff and passim.

20. To raise the question of the clarity of Kerouac's realisation of this constraint with reference to his own immediate situation as a writer is here germane; this idea will be be pursued later, when I suggest that possibly *Visions of Cody* represents an attempt by Kerouac to elude the fate of becoming 'a prisoner to his own formal myths'. (Barthes, *Writing Degree Zero*, p.84.)

21. Barthes, *Writing Degree Zero*, p.8.

22. See Jean Baudrillard, *Selected Writings*, trans. Mark Poster (Cambridge: Polity Press, 1988), pp.57 ff., and passim.

23. Gary Snyder, 1969, quoted in Ann Charters, *Kerouac: A Biography* (San Francisco: Straight Arrow Books, 1973), p.287.

24. Lucien Goldmann, *Towards a Sociology of the Novel*, trans. A. Sheridan (Salisbury: Tavistock Publications, 1975), p.3. Goldmann is drawing upon George Lukács' taxonomy in his *The Theory of the Novel*, trans. A. Bostock (London: Merlin Press, 1971).

25. Lukács' *Theory of the Novel*, pp.98–9.

26. Barthes, *Mythologies*, p.124.

27. Jean Baudrillard, *Selected Writings*, pp.166ff.

28. See Andrew Ross, *Universal Abandon? The Politics of Postmodernism* (New York: Columbia University Press, 1988) for another mode of discussing the ideological grip upon discourse of the myth of immediate release.

29. Linda Hutcheon, *The Politics of Postmodernism* (London: Routledge, 1989), pp.11, 3.

30. Jack Kerouac, *Visions of Cody* (London: Andre Deutsch, 1973), pp.275–90 and ff. Future page references appear in the text. It is perhaps worth noting here, just as a reminder of the dangers of reading off Kerouac's fiction against his biography, that insofar as this incident can be traced back to Kerouac's life, it relates to an incident on a Hollywood film lot. The incident in the book occurs on the actual streets of San Francisco – a critical relocation, in terms of my argument. See French, *Jack Kerouac*.

31. Linda Hutcheon, *A Poetics of Postmodernism* (London: Routledge, 1988), p.13.

32. See Timothy Hunt's account of the evolution of *On The Road* and *Visions of Cody* in his *Kerouac's Crooked Road*, pp.85 ff. I certainly agree with him that *Visions* offers not 'a ... survey of travelling [but] ... a project that consciously and unconsciously evoked Cassady in his many dimensions' (p.120). What I want to emphasise here is how the narrative transition that occurs between *On The Road* and *Visions* leads to a fundamentally more forthright and sustained exposition of the enmeshing dangers of the web of American myth discourse.

33. One way of dramatising this affiliation is to offer this extract from Rainer Maria Rilke's *Duino Elegies* as a possible epigraph for *On The Road*:

Jede dumpfe Umkehr der Welt hat solche Enterbte,
denen das Frühere nicht und noch nicht das Nächste gehört.

– Rainer Maria Rilke, *Duino Elegies*, trans. J.B. Leishman and Stephen Spender, Third Edition (London: The Hogarth Press, 1948). Their translation:

> Each torpid turn of the world has such disinherited children,
> to whom no longer what's been, and not yet what's coming, belongs.

34. The reference to Derrida here is deliberate: see his *Writing and Difference* (1967) trans. A. Bass (London: Routledge, 1978).
35. See, for three systematising attempts, Hunt, French and Weinreich.
36. Warren Tallman, 'Kerouac's Sound', *Evergreen Review*, Vol. 4, No. 11 (Jan.–Feb. 1960), p.156.
37. Jack Kerouac, 'Essentials of Spontaneous Prose', *Evergreen Review*, Vol. 2, No. 5 (Summer 1958), p.73.
38. LeRoi Jones, 'Letter to the Editors', *Evergreen Review* Vol. 2, No. 8 (Spring 1959), pp.254–5.
39. It is true that Kerouac formulated this theories of sketching – the prototype version of spontaneous prose – after he had produced the single-roll typescript of *On The Road* in 1951, but very substantial revisions to *On The Road* occurred while he was evolving his spontaneous prose approach. See: Charters, *Kerouac*; French, *Jack Kerouac*, p.84.
40. See Hunt, *Kerouac's Crooked Road*. Kerouac plainly offers, of course, writing, not typing, to invert Truman Capote's glib put-down, quoted in Janet Winn, 'Capote, Mailer and Miss Parker', *The New Republic*, 9 February 1959, p.28. His writing, through, in *Visions*, becomes an exploration of *writing*, this paper argues.
41. Jacques Derrida, *Of Grammatology* (1967) trans. G. Spivak (Baltimore: Johns Hopkins University Press, 1976), p.270.
42. In this sentence, I make use of Jürgen Habermas' phrase, but I have particularly in mind the tension existing between Lyotard's insistence that we remain 'incredulous towards metanarratives' and Habermas' belief that some ground must be found on which to base critiques. See: Jean-Francois Lyotard, *The Post-Modern Condition: A Report on Knowledge*, trans. Geoff Bennington and Brian Massumi (Minneapolis: University of Minnesota Press, 1984), p.xxiv; Jürgen Habermas, 'The Entwinement of Myth and Enlightenment: Re-reading *Dialectic of Enlightenment*', *New German Critique*, No. 26 (1982), pp.18ff.

3

Journeys in the Mindfield: Gregory Corso Reconsidered
Jim Philip

The 1989 publication of *Mindfield*, Gregory Corso's selection of his poems from the mid-1950s onwards, allows us a useful vantage point from which to review not only his own work, but also that larger movement of which it is a part. According to the revered figures who have provided introductions for the volume, all is well. For Allen Ginsberg, Corso is a 'loner'[1] who, despite being 'laughably unlaurelled by native prizes',[2] has, through sheer devotion to his craft, earned his place among the greats. We are pointed also to further dimensions of Corso's career: 'His crucial position in world cultural revolution mid-XX century as originator of the "Beat Generation" literary movement, along with Kerouac, Burroughs, Orlovsky and others, grants him an experience inside history few bards or politicians have known.'[3] So Gregory has a stature in the movement, and the movement has a stature not only in the literary, but also the cultural and social history of our times. It has achieved and sustained an international audience. Moreover, it has been the herald of a world in which the authority and legitimacy of the 'bard' has risen once more to challenge that of the 'politician', in which culture opposes power in new and significant ways. William Burroughs, the second gatekeeper of this volume, offers a more ambiguous personal portrait, but concludes in similar, veritably 'up-Beat', tone. Corso has suffered 'reverses'.[4] 'But his vitality and resilience always shine through, with a light that is more than human: the immortal light of his Muse. Gregory is indeed one of the Daddies.'[5]

It would be interesting to know what Corso himself has made of these testimonies. Undoubtedly they would accord with a certain, often playfully deployed, craving for fame and status evident in performances and interviews, as well as in his written work. He, after all, has been the one to claim special attention as the favoured 'Nunzio'[6] of the Muse, the true inheritor of the mythic energies of Hermes, Mercury,

Ganesha, Toth, Moses and Loki. However, I would suspect that other retained senses, of sharp recognition and wry humour, would enable him to take a rather different view of the processes of his own canoni-sation. What has happened to these previously urgent voices? Why have they become the packagers in bland and copywritten terms of their own success and that of others? Is there not, in fact, a defeat involved here, a new complicity with the languages and practices of academic and publishing establishments? Could the occasion not have been seized as one on which to initiate a more searching conversation about the nature and fate of the movement as a whole, and the different experi-ences and emphases of its members? Certainly it is a relief to turn from one end of the book to the other, from the voices of the sponsors to that of the poet himself, in its most recent mode:

> Of what import is it I set thing aright?
> Who knoweth *niente*?
> You bring Capital Punishment to this city
> you'll have me poet of a dumb city –
> that just don't sound right –
>
> My son in my dreams is me
> the dark nurseless room
> the quick shadow
> the small innocent head safe under the blanket
> I am a father far away from his children
> but like Holderlin sayeth I am closer to god
> away from Him ...

> STOP[7]

Here at least we are in the presence of the interrogative, as opposed to the affirmative. The questions, the sources of anxiety, but also of qualifying humour, are many and varied. What gives an underlying movement to the passage is the restlessness of the older man who has found that age has brought with it not settled wisdom, but rather, as he puts it earlier in this long and interesting poem, 'a multitude of variable thought'.[8]

The experience is crucial to the later work included in this volume and is the source of many of its devices and structural features. The Muse that Corso invokes here is not the grateful bestower of gifts long-earned, but rather a mad pursuer whose demands and demolitions proceed with the rapidity of a machine-gun. It is here also that the term adopted for the title of the book emerges. But if what we are invited to enter is a 'mindfield', an area of memory and speculation, it is also a 'minefield', a dangerous territory in which the explosion of meaning and relationship is as likely to occur as its consolidation. The close and painful implications of such threatened incoherence are well evoked in the last lines of the quoted passage. Here it could be said that the sense of disturbance lies not only in the physical distance from the child but also in the feared inability to act as guide, mentor and protector. There is no easy acceptance, either in personal or wider generational terms, of the role of 'Daddy'.

If the anxieties raised and faced here are intellectual and personal, they are also, importantly, social. Paradoxically, despite the separations implied, father and son meet on the same ground of insecurity, exposure and veiled menace. The passage is set in New York, described here as the 'dumb city', and, as it moves from soliloquy to outward address, the immediate audience it seizes upon are those citizens who, in 1989, are calling for the restoration of the death penalty. What is evoked, then, is the metropolitan panorama of the 1980s with its increasing divisions between wealth and poverty and its proliferation of homelessness, vagrancy and drug-related crime. And if the city is 'dumb' in relation to the powerlessness, ignorance and demoralisation of many of its inhabitants, it is 'dumb' in another sense, in relation to the stupidities of the political Right, for whom selective recrimination takes the place of any more civilised or coherent response. It is worth recalling here Corso's own origins in metropolitan poverty and social chaos, and the way in which, perhaps to a greater extent than for any of the other Beat writers, the city of New York has operated for him as a kind of touchstone; a place to return to, after travels, successes and defeats, to test the real efficacy and advance of any so-called 'world cultural revolution'. The news from 1989 would appear to be that repetition, or perhaps regression, are the more appropriate descriptions.

The preoccupations of this passage veer, then, towards the intensely personal, and in another direction towards the broadly social. However, from the first question onwards, it is clear that what they centre upon is the literary, the rehearsing and reviewing of a range of writing strategies. The interrogative and reflective comments would appear to be addressed in the first instance to his own work. However, in their very generality they could be said to be applicable to Beat writing as a whole, to that network of lived contacts and influences that has been the context of his own career. What are raised initially are those two rather contradictory tendencies, leading on the one hand towards spiritual leadership and regeneration, and on the other towards apocalyptic nihilism, that have always characterised the movement. Such tendencies are certainly to be found within the pages of *Mindfield*, but

evident to a greater degree, surely, within the respective writings of its
two introductory figures. Corso would appear to be at once acknowledging the intensities of such a body of work, while questioning
ironically the extent of its ultimate impact upon contemporary consciousness. There is the further implication, perhaps, that this oscillation
between hope and despair, this pressure towards extreme expression of
one kind or the other, may be the deeper inheritance of anyone who
sets out to be an American poet. Behind the figures of his contemporaries it might be possible to discern the more pervasive founding
influences of Whitman, and of Poe.

The next turn of the passage is, as we have seen, towards direct intervention in social and political debate. Beyond the immediate point, what
is raised for a moment is the issue, often latent in Corso's own poetry
as in that of other Beat writers, as to whether, and if so, how, a detailed
engagement with the workings of oppressive power might be incorpo-
rated into the text. Here again there is an inheritance involved, from
the radical poets, performers and songwriters of the 1930s. However,
if their efforts have stood in one sense as a model, they have also stood
as a warning, of the dangers of ephemerality that may beset a 'protest'
literature, more reactive than pro-active in its responses to a society and
a culture in crisis. It is interesting to note in this context that Corso's
own suggestions as to how to create an American political text often
seem to owe as much to European as to indigenous sources. His aphoristic
one-liners ('you'll have me poet of a dumb city') are designed to shock
and provoke very much in the manner of the wall slogans of the Paris
Situationists of the 1960s. While this is a device of some potentiality,
there is also a way in which, as Corso suggests in the following line, it
'just don't sound right'; it is not the voice of the people, but of frustrated
intellectuals, verging on the brink of cultural terrorism.

The final lines of the quoted passage return us to a more familiar mode,
to the poetry of the fleeting, enigmatic, personal moment. Such a
mode, from Emily Dickinson to Robert Creeley, has always been a part
of American writing, and the Beats, in their different ways, have all contributed to it. Yet Corso's final ellipsis might be taken as an invitation
to submit these procedures, as others, to reconsideration. Could it not
be that poetry of pathos is always in danger of slipping into a poetry
of bathos; that the mode in question is one that may lead to a sentimentalisation of the exposed self, to a special pleading in relation to
the reader? Overall, then, what is being suggested is that one of the several
interests in this passage lies in the extent to which it submits its own
writing practices to careful reflection. Moreover the reflections are of
such a kind as to provoke review not only of the work of one author,

but of a whole generation, and indeed of that generation's participation in a wider inheritance.

Our first acknowledgement, then, has been of Corso in the present. One of the pleasures of reading *Mindfield* is to discover a writer so restless and renewed, so willing to take on currents of doubt, and to wrest from them new modes of enquiry and expression. It is a stance and practice that contrasts favourably, in ways that have already been suggested, with some other moves made by some other 'Daddies'. However, no reading of the volume, and no reassessment of the career embodied within it, would be complete without a return to the Corso of the past. What did it mean to be a Beat writer in the late 1950s and early 1960s? What particular emphases and directions did Corso himself seek to bring to the movement? What were the achievements, and to what extent, despite the range of reconsiderations that time has brought with it, were there breakthroughs of insight and expression that remain to be built upon? One useful move in this direction is to go back not all the way, but halfway, to a text that works almost as a precursor to *Mindfield* in that it records an earlier public encounter between 'poet-friends',[9] including Allen Ginsberg. This is the poem 'Columbia U. Poesy Reading – 1975'. Here, Corso already expresses some doubts as well as amused fascination at what is happening to the writing careers of some of his contemporaries. 'Al volleyed amongst Hindu gods/then traded them all for Buddha's no-god/A Guggenheim he got'.[10] Here also he contemplates a return to origins, to what for him were the founding energies of the Beat movement, as, emerging like its creators from isolation, obscurity and anxiety ...

> a subterranean poesy of the streets
> enhanced by the divine butcher: humour,
> did climb the towers of the Big Lie ...[11]

The particular emphases are interesting and valuable, and indeed the lines can be taken as having the quality not only of observation, but of commitment. For Corso, as for others, the fundamental project was that of cultural negation, the challenging of the 'Big Lie', and we should not forget what a large and daunting task that must have seemed amidst the apparently massive assents and conformities of postwar society. For some, the energies of that negation lay in personal search, in movement, in self-imposed exile, in the turning to other cultures and belief systems. Perhaps it could be said that for Corso the real imperatives and opportunities lay in the effort not so much to get outside America as in the effort to get further inside it. The lines above evoke the existence of strong currents of popular imagination, of elements of dissent, mockery, desire and aspiration only half-repressed beneath the functional surfaces of everyday life. It evokes also the liberatory role of a poetry that might draw upon such resources, creating new forms of expression, and new audiences, as it does so. Could it not be said that what we have here is a kind of manifesto, a statement of intent against which to measure Corso's distinct procedures and achievements?

Already latent in the passage quoted above is one important strategy worthy of initial consideration. Some readers may already have noted that, in evoking the possibilities of a contemporary poetry, Corso at the same time alludes playfully to a longstanding, culturally pervasive legend, that of Jack and the Beanstalk! The persistence, adaptation and extension of European folk traditions within American popular culture of the nineteenth century is a process that has been explored by several commentators, notably Constance Rourke in her definitive study, *American Humour*.[12] Other American writers, amongst them William Carlos Williams, have made use of this material, recognising within it valuable imaginative resources beyond the limits of the official culture. It would be wrong to describe Corso as a dedicated folklorist, but it would be fair to suggest that many of the earlier poems in *Mindfield* bear an interesting relation to the tradition of the American tall tale. They offer brief and powerful narratives, they make full use of the supernatural and the bizarre, they rivet our attention but refuse to moralise, creating a space for enjoyment and interpretative reflection. How, for instance, does one write a poem about the processes of labour, of economic exploitation followed by insecure and unrespected old age, that is still the lot of most American citizens? Corso's strategy is to call up from the world of pantomime and folktale (and Disneyland?) that familiar device of the talking animal. The poem in question is 'The Mad Yak', where the animal speaks in tones of fatalism, endurance, dignity and innocence that are as appealing as they are excruciating:

> I am watching them churn the last milk
>   they'll ever get from me
> They are waiting for me to die ...[13]

In a final extension to the poem, this figure of anonymous suffering is deployed to recall, in ways newly disturbing to the reader, that ultimate crime of the modern age, the Nazis' final solution, with its combination of insane purpose and technological rationality:

> Poor uncle! He lets them lead him
> How sad he is, how tired!
> I wonder what they'll do with his bones?

And his beautiful tail!
How many shoelaces will they make of that![14]

How, for instance, does one write a poem about the gigantic arena of American competitiveness, and the fantasies of success and nightmares of failure that are the individual lot within it? Corso's strategy is to transpose us to what has always seemed to him a saner place, the city of Paris, and then to replay for us certain archetypal American scenes. In the poem 'Dream of a Baseball Star', the hero/victim is Ted Williams and he leans at night upon the Eiffel Tower, weeping for the loss of his fame, his prowess and his luck (even his bat has dwindled into a 'knotted and twiggy'[15] shadow of its former self). There is one last game to be played, as the ultimate pitcher hurls flaming baseballs at him. We contemplate the moment of his humiliation:

> The umpire dressed in strange attire
> thundered his judgement: YOU'RE OUT!
> And the phantom crowd's horrific boo
> dispersed the gargoyles from Notre Dame.[16]

However, in pantomime and fairy-tale such things are not allowed to happen. To a chorus of applause, both human and divine, Ted Williams completes his final home run. The poem deploys with gusto the mythologies and rituals of baseball, but it could be said to have reference also to a longer succession of American culture heroes and the stories woven around them. From Daniel Boone onwards, the popular imagination has sought out such figures, through whom to articulate varying and ambiguous responses to the battle with nature, the battle with others and the battle with the machine.

Other perennial sources of popular humour, storytelling and image-making are those common rituals that make the passage from one condition of life to another. 'Marriage' is probably Corso's most widely known and celebrated poem, and its success surely derives from its original contribution to this established mode. There are many familiar elements here: in-law jokes, reception jokes, honeymoon jokes. However, in the poem, as in life, these are the paradoxical context for the continued and apparently untarnished vitality of the myth of marriage itself.

> Yet if I should get married and its Connecticut and snow
> and she gives birth to a child and I am sleepless, worn,
> up for nights, head bowed against a quiet window, the past behind me
> finding myself in the most common of situations, a trembling man[17]

Here the implications and the aspirations of marriage are at once both personal and public. 'I's' marriage to 'she' is not only celebrated as the fulfilment of romantic love. It is also evoked as the successful passage into 'the most common of situations', the site of respectability, status, home, family, property. To marry is also to marry the system, and to reap the benefits of such conformity. If the image has the slickness of the television advert, it also has elements of solemnity, of tradition, of Christian mystery. We are aware of the multiple investments made by establishments of various kinds – religious, political, commercial – and of their combined efforts in sustaining the institution as an ideologi-cal centre of American life. As the poem readily and humorously admits, there is still a sense in which to remain outside of all of this is to risk conditions of isolation, ostracism and freakishness:

... what if I'm 60 years old and not married,
all alone in a furnished room with pee stains on my underwear
and everyone else is married! All the universe married but me![18]

There is a wry acceptance, then, on the part of the speaker of the power of convention, of all the elements, from the sentimental to the dogmatic, that are deployed in defence of it. However, what gives the poem its tension and its sense of narrative is the extent to which, despite these blandishments and these forces, he does remain an outsider, listening with greater fascination and intensity to the parodic and anarchic voices that rise within him as he contemplates the married future. This is the voice that answers 'Pie Glue' instead of 'I do',[19] that competes with the roar of the Niagara Falls in screaming 'I deny Honeymoon'.[20] The speaker is troubled by his own perverse expressions, even as he delights in them; what emerges is his profound suspicion that these experiences, offered as the acme of personal choice and emotional fulfilment, may in fact be the site of the greatest cultural coercion.

These are poems that seek to celebrate and sustain a popular imagi-nation. Beyond and within their quizzical humour, they bear witness to a widespread response that is as wary of the processes of ideological persuasion as it is of the processes of economic and social injustice. However, it must be said that, in the body of Corso's work as a whole, they take their place alongside other texts that are a good deal more anxious in their probing of the forces of US history and the possible transformations of consciousness that have accompanied them. Of all the characters who populate Corso's poems, perhaps most memorable is the Motorcyclist Blackfoot:

> ... O he's an angel there
> though sinister sinister in shape of Steel Discipline smoking
> a cigarette in a fishy corner in the night, waiting, america,
> waiting the end, the last Indian, mad Indian of no fish or
> foot or proud forest haunt, mad on his knees ponytailing &
> rabbitfooting his motorcycle, his the final requiem the final
> america READY THE FUNERAL STOMP[21]

This figure emerges with dramatic force at the end of a poem called 'Spontaneous Requiem for the American Indian', and indeed could be said to rescue it from the questionable expectations aroused by its title. There have been many examples in American poetry of such 'requiems', that eulogise the virtues of a 'vanished' people, even as they disguise the causes and the procedures of their 'vanishing'. Here, there are survivors, but survivors whose emotional lives are deeply bound up in the history of destruction that the rest of the poem records. It is difficult to decide whether what is being evoked is a cult of escape, a cult of power, or a cult of death. Perhaps we are to assume that the figure himself does not know, and is seeking a resolution in the sounds and signs of his own violently enacted 'poesy of the street'.

Other texts of the same period bear witness to Corso's fears that structures of power and violence, always latent and evident to minority groups, now threaten to become the totalitarian condition of the nation and affect the inner and outer lives of all US citizens. In the poem 'Army', for instance, we are offered a rich and ambiguous recasting of the military triumphalism of the postwar years. There is a frenetic travelling of the battlegrounds of a generation, as if in pursuit of one image that might embody fully the deeper historical and personal consequences of these worldwide events. There are sudden disruptive voices that complicate the narrative of victory by bearing witness to unresolved issues of moral compromise or defeat:

> They said shoot the young boy and I did.
> I would like to have shot him at a distance
> They had me put the pistol to the back of his head
> I cried
> but the army summoned the brass band
> (its prestige and morale supply)
> and soon my sobs became song.[22]

In its subtlest moments, what this poem probes are conditions of psychic imbalance and unease that have emerged at every level of this

society that has discovered itself to be an army, this democracy that
has discovered itself to be a repressive and compromised empire.

> I stepped upon an old bombardment
> my path pyloned by dark meditative Generals.
> "So!" I cried, "So this is the sadness of Generals!"
> I sat awhile in the arms of Eisenhower and slept
> and dreamed a great bomb had died,
> its death rattle made stentor
> in the breast of my human bed.[23]

Here we are in an odd landscape that is as evocative of war zones as
it is of the Washington shrines of the Republic. The guardian figures
of this America are the Generals, and it is they who preside in brooding
silence over some ritual of military initiation that has become
synonymous with the gaining of citizenship. There are signs of collective
guilt here, but also, perhaps, of a widespread desire to evade the implications of it. In the strange but compelling dream logic to which Corso
commits the poem, one kind of 'passing out' is accompanied by
another. To meet Eisenhower, to meet the spirit of the nation, is also
to encounter an exhaustion, a longing for it all to be over, a desire for
oblivion to be found either in sleep, death or a return to the womb.
The lines are as evocative of a general culture based on the wish to forget
and to escape, as they are of the more fractured lives of particular individuals.

Another of the great poems of this period is built around Corso's
perception that, for many of his contemporaries, their most secret and
preoccupying relationship may not be with other humans at all, but
with an object – 'You Bomb Toy of Universe Grandest of all snatched-
sky'.[24] The irony is one that encompasses the whole course of human
history, but its intimacy to each person is established as Corso sculpts
the opening section of his text into a bomb-like shape on the page that
we may trace with our own fingers. There is a further shocking immediacy
to the poem as it leaps beyond the conventional terms of the nuclear
debate, in which strategic justification is opposed by moral indignation,
to expose more intuitive, more ambiguous responses:

> I scope
> a city   New York City   streaming   starkeyed   subway shelter
> scores and scores   A fumble of humanity   High heels bend
> Hats whelming away   Youth forgetting their combs[25]

Here there are elements both of fascination and terror. If we are in the air, we are also on the ground. We encounter the fantasy of power and control that accompanies the possibilities of such unprecedented destruction. But we encounter also the panic-stricken rushing mass and the anonymous, herded nature of death within it. Much of the rest of the poem is devoted to exploring further this secret life of the bomb; the ways, at once tragic and comic, in which it has entwined itself within the alienated dream-life of the nation. For the New York commuter, the bomb is a 'Satyr Bomb',[26] promising for a moment the anarchic dislodgement of the routines, the environment and the skyline that have dominated his life:

> The top of the Empire State
> arrowed in a broccoli field in Sicily ...[27]

For the bored and sated fan, the bomb is a 'sportive bomb', promising that ultimate competitive spectacle of nuclear war in which all will move and all will be moved:

> The billioned all-time attendance
> The Zeusian pandemonium
> Hermes racing Owens[28]

As a culmination, and as a response to other tendencies in mass entertainment, we are offered the possibilities of the following deranged movie:

> O Bomb   I love you
> I want to kiss your clank   eat your boom
>   Your are a paean   an acme of scream
>   a lyric hat of Mister Thunder
>   O resound thy tanky knees
> BOOM   BOOM   BOOM   BOOM   BOOM[29]

Here, to a soundtrack that exceeds all others, machine has become man, or man has become machine, creating the ultimate symbol of a desire that is at once sadistic and masochistic. There is a grotesque humour to these formulations, inviting us both to laugh and to cry, and reminding us that this indeed may be the ultimate, unstable defence strategy of populations trapped in a history of power and technological rationality. Yet if this loud, apocalyptic arena is the foreground of the poem, it could not be said to be without suggestions of another kind. As the reader may have noticed, it is full of pauses, spaces of silence perhaps, that invoke the great standing back that, on an individual and a social level, may also be part of this historical moment. From the start the possibility is held out, albeit in tentative ways, that the bomb may be not the 'ender' but the 'budger of history',[30] the agent of reconsiderations, of resumptions of responsibility, of new communicative ventures. If it has brought the world together in one way, it may bring it together in others; its ultimate transformation may be as the

> Bomb in which all lovely things
> moral and physical anxiously participate[31]

This is an issue that remains unresolved, of course. All that can be said is that Corso's poem retains an emotive, almost shamanistic, intensity. In its ability to take us to the edge of destruction and then to rescue us from it, it remains, perhaps, the most dramatic embodiment of his own creative strategies and of their continued relevance and potential.

It has been the purpose of this chapter to offer some fruitful terms for the reconsideration of Corso's work, in relation both to its present vitality and its past achievements. What, finally, can be pointed to by way of underlying and sustaining continuity? Perhaps the best way to recall Corso's deep concerns, and his sense of what connects him to others, is to consider that significant group of poems in which there is conversation with other writers, artists, musicians and their works. Much could be said about the selection and juxtaposition of these figures, who range from François Villon to Charlie Parker. However, what is here offered as the most interesting and informative encounter is that recorded in the poem entitled 'Uccello'. The painting to which the poem refers is a battlefield scene, probably 'The Rout of San Romano', completed about 1450, and on view in the National Gallery, London.

> You'd think it impossible for any man to die
> each combatant's mouth is a castle of song
> each iron fist a dreamy gong flail resounding flail
>   like cries of gold
> how I dream to join such a battle![32]

There is a sense of fascination here, at the uncanny, comprehensive and intimate speaking of the work of art across the boundaries of space and time. By way of a parallel to Corso's reaction it is interesting to note that the art historian, E.H. Gombrich, breaks off from his discussion of Uccello's innovatory perspectival methods to note the paradoxical power of the image: 'The whole gay picture seems very remote from the realities of war.'[33] The ambiguities briefly evoked here are explored more fully in Corso's poem. and interpreted by him as a deliberate and provocative artistic challenge. For him, the painting is remarkable for its combination of documentary accuracy and Utopian vision; it is at once about war and about peace, about conflict and conversation, about mass slaughter and individual expression. Given the linked preoccupations explored in this chapter, it is possible to understand why it appeared to him to be an archetypal work, a work as multifariously responsive to the origins of modernity, as his own has been to its culmination.

NOTES

Unless otherwise indicated, quotations in this chapter are from: Gregory Corso, *Mindfield: New and Selected Poems* (New York: Thunder's Mouth Press, 1989). The following notes give titles and page numbers, or other details.

1. 'On Corso's Virtues', Introductory note by Allen Ginsberg, p.xiv.
2. Ibid.
3. Ibid.
4. 'Introductory Notes', William S. Burroughs, p.xix.
5. Ibid.
6. See 'Columbia U. Poesy Reading – 1975', p.163.
7. 'Field Report', p.268.
8. Ibid., p.256.
9. 'Columbia U. Poesy reading – 1975', p.161.
10. Ibid.
11. Ibid., p.162.
12. Constance Rourke, *American Humor* (Garden City: Anchor Books, 1953).
13. 'The Mad Yak', p.38.
14. Ibid.
15. 'Dream of a Baseball Star', p.71.
16. Ibid.
17. 'Marriage', p.63.
18. Ibid., p.64.
19. Ibid., p.61.
20. Ibid., p.62.
21. 'Spontaneous Requiem for the American Indian', p.139.
22. 'Army', p.95.
23. Ibid., p.94.
24. 'Bomb', p.65.
25. Ibid.
26. Ibid.
27. Ibid., pp.65, 66.
28. Ibid., p.66.
29. Ibid., p.69.
30. Ibid., p.65.
31. Ibid., p.68
32. 'Uccello', p.29.
33 E.H. Gombrich, *The Story of Art* (Oxford: Phaidon Press, 1950) p.190.

4

An Anarchist Among the Floorwalkers: The Poetry of Lawrence Ferlinghetti

Alistair Wisker

Who's this bum
crept in from the streets
blinking in the neon
an anarchist among the floorwalkers
                    Lawrence Ferlinghetti: 'Director of Alienation'

Like others in this volume I first encountered the Beats, Lawrence Ferlinghetti prime among them, in the 1960s. Two volumes served in particular: the Penguin *Modern Poets 5* and *Pictures Of The Gone World* published by City Lights in the Pocket Poets Series. The view quickly, and rightly, spread that here was a poetry whose voice was direct, questioning, warning, cajoling, enjoining, irreverent and in touch with the thoughts, feelings and paraphernalia of the contemporary generation. Ferlinghetti's 'In Goya's Greatest Scenes' held a special force:

In Goya's greatest scenes we seem to see
                    the people of the world
    exactly as the moment when
        they first attained the title of
                    'suffering humanity'[1]

The poem opens with these lines and then sets off to explore the characteristics of suffering humanity caught by the 'imagination of disaster': 'they are so bloody real/it is as if they really still existed'. At that point the poem shifts directly to the contemporary world in which we find the same people, albeit in a changed landscape of false windmills, 50-lane freeways and billboards, a concrete continent which has:

74

more maimed citizens
in painted cars
and they have strange licence plates
and engines
that devour America

Here we have a voice of perception, engaged and angry at what it perceives. It is a committed voice, anxious about the way things seem to be going, determined to share that perception and to speak out purposefully.

This populist view of poetry was one Ferlinghetti has clearly shared with other San Francisco poets, among them Robert Duncan, Philip Whalen, Michael McClure and Gary Snyder. One meets it again in early lines from the following early (and untitled) poem:

Constantly risking absurdity
and death
whenever he performs
above the heads
of his audience[2]

The poet-acrobat, 'a little charleychaplin man', climbs onto a high wire which he has made and reaches towards a still higher perch where 'Beauty stands and waits'. As she starts her death-defying leap it is uncertain whether or not the poet-acrobat will catch her fair, eternal form. The poet is seen as a chancer, a perceiver, an instructor, and a performer, 'the super realist/who must perforce perceive/taut truth'. All the tricks he can muster are played, by the poet, in order to perceive and communicate this 'taut truth'. At his best Ferlinghetti is a great communicator and his fascination is, very often, with oral communication – the impact of the human voice sometimes together with musical accompaniment. He has spoken of 'street poetry':

Getting poetry back into the street where it once was, out of the classroom, out of the speech department, and – in fact – off the printed page. The printed word has made poetry so silent.[3]

Ferlinghetti's second book, *A Coney Island Of The Mind*, published in 1958, contains seven poems grouped together under the title 'Oral Messages'. These are fluid, deliberately incomplete pieces in which the speaker announces:

I am waiting for my case to come up
and I am waiting
for a rebirth of wonder
and I am waiting for someone
to really discover America[4]

One of the themes to which Ferlinghetti often returns is to be found
in the idea that there is a real America still to be discovered and, as we
shall see at the end of this chapter, this becomes the subject of a later
poem – 'After the Cries of The Birds' – in which San Francisco sets off
to become the real America. The seven 'Oral Messages' – 'I Am Waiting',
'Junkman's Obbligato', 'Autobiography', 'Dog', 'Christ Climbed Down',
'The Long Street' and 'Meet Miss Subways' – have in common a fluidity,
an atmosphere of the rebirth of wonder, and a sense of discovery.
Ferlinghetti identifies the poems as 'conceived specifically for jazz
accompaniment and as such [they] should be considered as spontaneously
spoken "oral messages" rather than as poems written for the printed
page'.[5] These poems were performed as experiments and Ferlinghetti
described them as still in a state of change. They were originally available
on a recording which he made with Kenneth Rexroth and the Cellar
Jazz Quintet of San Francisco. 'Dog' has been reprinted many times over
the years but it is perhaps 'Autobiography'[6] which most clearly represents
the character of the set of poems. The refrain has to do with 'leading a
quiet life/in Mike's place every day'. The poem is a thematic exploration
of this 'quiet life' in which the speaker watches the champs of the Dante
Billiard Parlor, gets caught stealing pencils from the Five and Ten Cent
Store, lands in Normandy, goes on watching the world walk by, reads
the Classified columns, sees Walden Pond drained to make an amusement
park and is only temporarily a tie salesman whilst waiting for a top job.
Here we have the same kind of apparently wandering narrative, the same
kind of casual, committed, faithfully recorded, fictionalised, romantic
listing of the sights and scenes of everyday life, its thoughts, dreams
and disasters that gets into the lyrics of Bob Dylan and, later, of Bruce
Springsteen. It is a world in which the old certainties, the old reverences
and the going sense of meaning are all under scrutiny, if not lost
already; a world in which the speaker, who both is and isn't Lawrence
Ferlinghetti, has 'read somewhere/the Meaning of Existence' yet has
'forgotten/just exactly where'.[7]

Another 'take' on Ferlinghetti lies in a poem like 'Summer in Brooklyn'
which begins:

Fortune
          has its cookies to give out
     which is a good thing

since it's been a long time since
that summer in Brooklyn
when they closed off the street
one hot day
and the

FIREMEN

turned on their hoses

and all the kids ran out[8]

As the poem proceeds, the kids reduce in number from a couple of dozen to six 'running around in our/barefeet and birthday/suits'. Finally the firemen stop their hoses and go back into their firehouse to continue their card game. The speaker in the poem is left with Molly who, embarrassed, looks at him and runs in herself: 'because I guess really we were the only ones there'.

'Summer in Brooklyn', like so many of Ferlinghetti's poems, has the infectious warmth of local humanity, and the intellectual honesty, which he found in the work of William Carlos Williams, and which he believes is the central characteristic of the Rutherford poet's continuing influence. This serves to remind the reader that he has been influenced by and has influenced a particular vein of American poetry. Ferlinghetti's early review of Williams' *Autobiography* identifies Williams as representing the other side of the coin in American literature:

> On one side, Europe and the expatriate writers, Henry James, Ezra Pound, T.S. Eliot; on the other side, America and Whitman and all those with their roots in American soil.[9]

Ferlinghetti makes it clear that he identifies Williams with the Whitman camp and quotes his now well-known view that the publication of *The Waste Land* in 1922 was 'the great catastrophe in our letters'. The San Francisco poet is also at pains to make it clear that this isn't a case of literary isolationism:

> This is not to say Dr. Williams never left home. He spent more than one year in Europe and knew many of the Americans there, especially in the 1920's, and was well up on all their movements. Yet he was for the most part an unhappy expatriate. By his own description, he is happiest when hard at his medical practice, letting the poetry germinate while he works, finding the resolution of medicine and poetry in the final, limitless search for poetic essence in the life he is able, because of his profession, intimately to touch.[10]

Ferlinghetti's poetry, too, germinates while he works and travels, and has its essence in the life he is able intimately to touch. Despite the blasphemy, the tendentious naïvety and the surrealism, there is a tough reasonableness about Ferlinghetti's views and works which reveals an intellectual grasp of the evolution of literature, especially American. He is aware that choice is as important as chance and this is especially apparent when he comes to compare Williams with his friend, Ezra Pound:

> Their ends are disparate: Williams in the same, snug harbour of Rutherford; Pound alienated from his country in St. Elizabeth's Hospital, Washington, D.C.[11]

Ferlinghetti's review of Williams was written during 1951, his first year as a resident of San Francisco. This was obviously a formative period in his life and his regular visits to 250 Scott Street, where Kenneth Rexroth had his spacious six-room, book-filled apartment, undoubtedly played a part. By all accounts Ferlinghetti was quiet at this time: 'Rexroth was the great master, and I was just a kid', he is quoted as saying.[12] The same accounts make it clear that the great master was ready to fill any silence being seldom short of a word; the point of the gatherings at his apartment seemed to Michael McClure to be 'to exercise his own genius':

> We would listen, and we'd ask him questions. Kenneth was like Godwin was to early nineteenth-century England – an anarchist, teacher, political figure, *literateur*. He was a very brilliant man and put many of us on our feet with a stance we could grow with.[13]

There is no doubt that Kenneth Rexroth helped Ferlinghetti to grow, as did Robert Duncan, whom he met at Rexroth's soirées. Meanwhile Ferlinghetti was pursuing his literary career in other directions. He had persuaded the book review editor of the *San Francisco Chronicle* to let him try some unpaid reviews. In July 19521, the then Lawrence Ferling began a series of poetry reviews, the piece on Carlos Williams being published in October of that year.

The circumstances of Ferlinghetti's life perhaps make him particularly sensitive to the influence of both choice and chance, which he has seen at work in his comparison of Pound and Williams. A parenthesis at the opening of a recent biography emphasises that both his parents had gone before he was two, he was abandoned at six, then as a teenager he was sent away by his caretakers after leading his gang into petty crime. It is argued that he subsequently raised himself out of these circumstances, not just to salvage an ordinary life with a decent job, wife, kids, car and the rest, but:

to other circumstances a as extreme as those beginnings: to become Lawrence Ferlinghetti, publisher, poet, novelist, painter, spokesman of his time.[14]

I don't want to proceed with a 'life' in this way, nor have I the space to do so. I do, however, want to sketch in just a few episodes because I believe that this helps to focus an author's work – even if the reader has been born in an age which celebrates, in the famous phrase, the death of the author. Ferlinghetti was born in Yonkers, New York, in March 1919. He gained a first degree from the University of North Carolina and an MA from Columbia University. He saw active service in the Second World War and late in 1943 he assumed command of his first ship. Ferlinghetti remembers the approach of D-Day with both clarity and drama:

> The night before the invasion started we were in Plymouth, and the side lanes leading up to the harbor were choked with transport – weapons, wagons, lorries jammed with troops – American, French, British, all lined up silent. And there was a blackout, so you'd go along these roads just packed with troops and all kinds of equipment and everything was in the dark. It was like the night before Agincourt – small campfires and men huddled around them and everything very silent, like the description in *Henry V*.[15]

After his Navy service Ferlinghetti, as he put it, emptied wastebaskets at *Time* for a while, before living in Paris between 1947 and 1951. There he added to his qualifications a Doctorat de l'Université from the Sorbonne. His dissertation was on 'The City as Symbol in Modern Poetry: In Search of a Metropolitan Tradition'. It involved studies of a number of authors including Eliot, Walt Whitman, Hart Crane, Mayakovsky, Lorca, Francis Thompson, André Breton and Djuna Barnes. The method was, as Ferlinghetti describes it, to go through the works of the selected writers and summarise what they had to say about the city, identifying which works in particular embodied it. His life and art are clearly associated with cities and with San Francisco in particular, and this association, this fascination, is there throughout Ferlinghetti's work. The poem and essays in *Literature and the American Urban Experience* are the papers of a conference on literature and the urban experience held at Rutgers, the State University of New Jersey, in 1980. Out front, as it were, is Ferlinghetti's 'Modern Poetry is Prose (But it is Saying Plenty)', which was composed for presentation at the poetry forum during the conference. The poem takes the shape of a history of modern poetry as seen through Ferlinghetti's eyes – naming and thus celebrating Whitman, Emerson, Sandburg, Vachel Lindsay, Wallace Stevens, Langston Hughes, Blake, Allen Ginsberg, D.H. Lawrence, Kerouac, and others:

poetic strummers and wailers
in the streets of the world
making poetry of the urgent insurgent Now[16]

The poem, as it continues, speaks of poets turning inwards to record their personal graphs of consciousness – Robert Creeley and Charles Olson are there, as are Whitman and Ginsberg, who had taken poetry almost singlehandedly in new directions. The process of renewing poetry is to be traced in the San Francisco poets, of course, the New York poets, the objectivists, the projectivists and the constructivists. The still wild voice 'inside of us' is present in the 1980s of the poem (and don't we need it in the 1990s):

a still insurgent voice
lost among machines and insane nationalisms
still longing to break out
still longing for the distant nightingale
that stops and begins again[17]

On 25 August 1944, the day Paris was liberated, Ferlinghetti and a junior officer took an abandoned jeep to the city. The vehicle broke down and the two officers stopped at a café in Saint Brieuc in Brittany for wine. Ferlinghetti noticed that a paper tablecloth had something scrawled on it, which inspection revealed to be a poem bearing the signature of Jacques Prévert. This incident began one of Ferlinghetti's fascinations. Prévert had become popular in the 1930s for his straight-talking, irreverent and often satirical view of French life and its figures of authority – a view which suited Ferlinghetti well. He took the tablecloth with him and very soon began on his translations of *Paroles* which were issued by City Lights, his own imprint, late in the 1950s and by Penguin Books in Britain in the mid-1960s. As Ferlinghetti puts it:

What Prévert means to us is naturally quite a different thing from what he has meant to the French. Many of the poems in *Paroles* grew out of the Second World War and the Occupation in France ... Prévert spoke particularly to the French youth immediately after the war, especially to those who grew up during the Occupation and felt totally estranged from Church and State. Since then we have had our own kind of resistance movement in our writers of dissent – dissent from the official world of the upper middle class ideal and the White Collar delusion and various other systemized tribal insanities.[18]

Of course, Ferlinghetti himself is part of the 'resistance movement' which he describes – and speaking to the same postwar generation worldwide. As he began writing, Ferlinghetti was undoubtedly influenced by Eliot, Thomas Wolfe, Kenneth Rexroth and others, but in his early work the tone and some of the subject matter of Prévert is most apparent. This can be clearly identified in Ferlinghetti's own translation of 'Pater Noster' which begins:

> Our Father who art in heaven
> Stay there
> And we'll stay here on earth
> Which is sometimes so pretty
> With its mysteries of New York
> And its mysteries of Paris[19]

The poem develops into a catalogue of the world's mysteries, which are as attractive, paradoxical and curious as any that heaven can offer. It is reminiscent in its comic-irreverent tone and treatment of hallowed material of the fifth section of *A Coney Island Of The Mind* which begins:

> Sometime during eternity
> 　　　　　　　some guys show up
> and one of them
> 　　　　who shows up real late
> 　　　　　　　　is a kind of carpenter
> 　　from some square-type place
> 　　　　　　　like Galilee
> 　　and he starts wailing
> 　　　　　　　and claiming he is hep
> 　　to who made heaven
> 　　　　　　　and earth
> 　　　　　　　　and that the cat
> 　　who really laid it on us
> 　　　　　　　is his Dad[20]

Ferlinghetti's poem is more complex, more mischievous and more dramatic than the Prévert, both in its structure and its meaning. Much of the impact is visual, the lines disturbing and breaking expectations and patterns, just as the meaning is interrogating the projected tone, complacency, and implicit righteousness of Christian belief. As Ferlinghetti has said, Prévert is at his best when he 'simply shows you something and lets you draw your own conclusions'.[21] When he goes beyond this 'showing', we are sometimes, as in 'Human Effort', treated to triteness. The importance of Prévert, according to Ferlinghetti, is that at his best he is:

one of those who hold on to your sleeve and say:
'Don't go for it ... keep out of it.'[22]

The influence of Prévert is helping the American poet to shape what is
essentially a poetry of dissent.

Ferlinghetti returned to the United States and, after an unsuccessful
stay in New York, which he said was just too tough and avaricious for
him, he went to San Francisco early in 1951. The city which was to
become his home and a central factor in his inspiration 'had a
Mediterranean feeling about it. I felt it was a little like Dublin when Joyce
was there. You could walk down Sackville Street and see everyone of
any importance on one walk.'[23] Early in 1953, Ferlinghetti and his wife,
Kirby, moved into an apartment in a hillside house with a view of the
Bay. Here the poet began the poems which were to form the centre of
Pictures Of The Gone World. These poems make reference to Brancusi,
Picasso, Dada and Sarolla and the Spanish Impressionists amongst the
painters and art movements, and Dante, Yeats and Rimbaud amongst
the writers. But the collection is most remarkable for the painterly
treatment of Ferlinghetti's immediate subject matter. Characteristic of
this is his first completely San Francisco poem, as he described the piece
which opens the collection:

> Away above a harborful
>
> of caulkless houses
> among the charley noble chimneypots
> of a rooftop rigged with clotheslines
> a woman pastes up sails
> upon the wind
> hanging out her morning sheets[24]

Ferlinghetti believes that style is a feeling for the weight and arrangement of words on a page. In 'Away above a harborful', it is clear that
he is using the page as a canvas, as he develops his style in which the
page is analogous to the open form of the abstract expressionist painters.
Meanwhile he was also sending off his Prévert translations and it was
through this activity that he came across Peter Martin's *City Lights*
which has been named after a Charlie Chaplin film:

The hero of the film ... was the perennial outsider – dispossessed, alienated,
victimized by the immense mechanism of the modern world. It was a figure
with whom Ferlinghetti instinctively sympathized. Though he didn't see
himself as a victim like Charlie, he clearly felt himself one of the 'common

men,' threatened by the massed forces of the bureaucratic, materialist, conformist world.[25]

Pete Martin and Ferlinghetti met and, in June 1953, they opened the immediately successful City Lights Pocket Book Shop. The following year Martin sold his share in the store to Ferlinghetti and went back to his native New York to open a bookstore in Manhattan. Straightaway Ferlinghetti set about realising one of his plans, which was to base a publishing venture in the bookstore. He got together the 27 poems which became *Pictures Of The Gone World* – number one in the pocketbook series, published by City Lights Press on 10 August 1955. City Lights very soon became one of the major imprints in the history of American literature, and Ferlinghetti began to publish William Carlos Williams, Allen Ginsberg, Kenneth Patchen, Kenneth Rexroth, Denise Levertov, Gregory Corso, Neal Cassady, Jack Kerouac and many others – most of the writers needed for a course in the new American literature, postwar, have appeared from City Lights. The press was one of the major catalysts for the arrival and output of the Beat generation. Around 1955, poetry went public in San Francisco, based on the bringing together of the East Coast Beat writers – Ginsberg, Kerouac and Corso – with the West Coast writers – Rexroth, Ferlinghetti himself, Snyder, McClure, Whalen, Lamantia and others. One of the most inspiring outcomes of this meeting was a reading which Ginsberg organised at the Six Gallery in San Francisco, to which he invited McClure, Snyder, Whalen and Lamantia – with Rexroth as master of ceremonies. The Six Poets at the Six Gallery reading was given in October 1955. It was on this occasion that Ginsberg gave the first reading of his long poem *Howl*, which launched his career as a poet at the same time as it celebrated the inauguration of the San Francisco poetry renaissance; the event brought a new awareness to the audience of the large group of talented poets in the city; it also brought to the poets themselves a new sense of belonging to a community. What was emerging was something more than the 'New York poets' or the 'San Francisco poets'. The sum of the parts was a literary movement that was to become a national and international phenomenon.

This phenomenon turned out to be enigmatic, simultaneously a celebration and a condemnation of the postwar world, a rich compound of nihilistic, committed, romantic, modernist and existentialist impulses. Getting Ferlinghetti, Ginsberg, Kerouac, Corso, Burroughs and Cassady grouped together under an umbrella labelled 'Beat' has always been difficult; there is always a stray philosophy, an infectious idea, a broken ideal, an individuality and a commitment which has defied any such attempt. The label 'Beat' has often been used but seldom defined;

indeed, one of its characteristics is that it is an embattled position which is resistant to definition. The contradictory, dialectical, tendentious character of the Beat generation has been its critical downfall; it has often seemed confused because there has been an obsession with the lifestyle rather than the works of the generation. The characteristic preoccupations of the Beats have to do with art, and particularly abstract expressionism, popular music, particularly some forms of jazz, drugs, sex, community and communal living, travel, anarchistic politics, religious experimentation, a fascination with criminality, being on the offensive against society whilst at the same time acknowledging alternative kinds of society.[26] These characteristics, which are not intended to be exhaustive, are exhibited in different measure and different combinations by the different writers who were fashioning their particular literary aesthetics in the culturally repressive America of the Cold War era. They sought to oppose its philistine and repressive mores by exploring and exploiting the extreme potential of the individual self. Not surprisingly, these characteristics become the subject of the art produced, and hence the focus on lifestyle in the contemporary critical response. It is not surprising, either, that the Beats professed close allegiances with some of the great figures of the romantic movement, and particularly with the Romantic ideology expressed by Blake, Shelley, Whitman and Lawrence. However great the debt to European Romantic ideology and indigenous American Transcendentalism, it is without doubt mediated by post-Romantic thought:

> It is hardly possible to read a classic Beat text without being aware of the way in which its Romanticism is continued, qualified and interrogated by the Modernism of Stein, Pound, Eliot, Williams (who wrote the introduction to *Howl*), Faulkner, Hart Crane, Thomas Wolfe and Henry Miller (who wrote the preface to *The Subterraneans*); the Surrealism of Apollinaire, Prévert (whose *Paroles* Ferlinghetti has excellently Englished), Eluard, Reverdy and Lorca; and the Existentialism of Hemingway, Céline, Artaud (whose *In Order to have finished with the judgement of God* Ginsberg has proclaimed a major influence on his early works), Sartre and Camus (whose *The Myth of Sisyphus* has been a touchstone for Ferlinghetti).[27]

It is precisely as a result of the containment, qualifications and interrogation of specific characteristics of Romanticism by specific characteristics of Modernism that the energy, tensions, and volatility of the best Beat writing arises. Ferlinghetti is in no way a disengaged writer; in fact, a powerful sense of commitment is evidenced in a great deal of his writing. He was incensed, whilst writing about his 'Tentative Description of a Dinner Given to Promote the Impeachment of President

Eisenhower', by those he described as Beat natives who said he could not be both Beat and committed at the same time:

> all the tall droopy corn about the Beat Generation and its being 'existentialist' is as phoney as a four-dollar piece of lettuce. Jean-Paul Sartre ... would give the horse laugh to the idea of Disengagement and the Art of The Beat Generation. Me too. And that Abominable Snowman of modern poetry, Allen Ginsberg, would probably say the same. Only the dead are disengaged. And the wiggy nihilism of the Beat hipster, if carried to its natural conclusion, actually means the death of the creative artist himself. While the 'non-commitment' of the artists is itself a suicidal and deluded variation of this same nihilism.[28]

Ferlinghetti's sense of commitment became very clear after the Six Poets at the Six Gallery reading when he sent a telegram to Ginsberg offering to bring out *Howl* as a City Lights publication. He used the words which Emerson had used in writing to Whitman about his *Leaves of Grass* – 'I greet you at the beginning of a great career'. He added, 'When do I get the manuscript?' Ferlinghetti and Ginsberg worked together, supplementing *Howl* with some other poems, including 'A Supermarket in California', which wonderfully realises a dream encounter with Walt Whitman. Ferlinghetti sent the manuscript to William Carlos Williams, who wrote an introduction to the volume describing Ginsberg as a poet who 'sees through and all around the horrors he partakes of in the very intimate details of his poem. He avoids nothing, but experiences it to the hilt.'[29] In September 1956, City Lights took delivery of the first fifteen hundred copies, but it was when the second printing arrived the following March that the trouble started.

On 25 March 1957, the Collector of Customs, Chester MacPhee, ordered the second printing to be seized. This was reported in the *San Francisco Chronicle*:

> collector of Customs Chester MacPhee continued his campaign yesterday to keep what he considers obscene literature away from the children of the Bay Area. He confiscated 520 copies of a paperbound volume of poetry entitled *Howl and Other Poems* ... "The words and the sense of the writing is obscene," MacPhee declared. "You wouldn't want your children to come across it."[30]

Ferlinghetti was prepared for this. He demonstrated a real grasp of literary, social and political affairs over the following months. On 3 April, the American Civil Liberties Union (to which he had submitted the manuscript of *Howl* before it went to the printers) informed MacPhee that it would contest the legality of the seizure. The first printing had been done by Villiers in Great Britain, chosen by Ferlinghetti because they were both experienced and reasonable. Now he announced an entirely new edition to be printed within the United States, and thus removed from the jurisdiction of the customs. This photo-offset edition was for sale at the City Lights bookstore, while the customs held on to the few copies from Britain.

The ensuing events did much to bring together and advertise the work of the Beats. Both the customs and the police, albeit unintentionally, did much to aid this development:

> I recommended a medal be made for Collector MacPhee, since his action was already rendering the book famous. But the police were soon to take over this advertising account and do a much better job – 10,00 copies of *Howl* were in print by the time they finished with it.[31]

On 19 May 1957, the book editor of the *San Francisco Chronicle*, William Hogan, gave his Sunday column over to an article by Ferlinghetti who viewed *Howl* as without doubt the most significant long poem to be published since the Second World War, and perhaps since Eliot's *Four Quartets*. As Ferlinghetti himself says, many added 'Alas' to this:

> Fair enough, considering the barren, polished poetry and well-mannered verse which has dominated many of the major poetry publications during the past decade or so, not to mention some of the 'fashionable incoherence' which has passed for poetry in many of the smaller, avant-garde magazines and little presses. *Howl* commits many poetic sins; but it was time.[32]

The unswerving commitment which Ferlinghetti revealed throughout the trial of *Howl* is characteristic. He challenged critics to identify another single long poem which was as resonant of its time and place and generation. The central part of his *Chronicle* article emphasises his own concerns and his response to Ginsberg:

> It is not the poet but what he observes which is revealed as obscene. The great obscene wastes of *Howl* are the sad wastes of the mechanized world, lost among atom bombs and insane nationalisms. Ginsberg chooses to walk on the wild side of this world, along with Nelson Algren, Henry Miller, Kenneth Rexroth, not to mention some great American dead, mostly in the tradition of philosophical anarchism.[33]

As Ferlinghetti suggest, Ginsberg's best personal defence of *Howl* appears in another poem of his, 'America', where he asks:

> What sphinx of cement and aluminium bashed open their skulls
> and ate up their brains and imagination?

Moloch! Solitude! Filth! Ugliness! Ashcans and unobtainable
    dollars! Children screaming under the stairways!
Boys sobbing in armies! Old men weeping in the parks![34]

There is no doubt that Ferlinghetti identifies with this view, and with
the idea that by exhibiting the obscene wastes of the mechanised world
a process of improvement may be begun. He turns Collector MacPhee's
words back on himself in describing what Ginsberg exposes as:

A world, in short, you wouldn't want your children to come across ... Thus
was Goya obscene in depicting the Disasters of War, thus Whitman an exhi-
bitionist, exhibiting man in his own strange skin.[35]

As it turned out, collector MacPhee was only the first skirmish in a war.
The customs released the books it was holding at the end of May. Then
('They were terrible nice, really', said Kirby Ferlinghetti) the police arrived
and the fun really started. Captain William Hanrahan of the Juvenile
Department took MacPhee's accusation about the likely corruption of
children seriously. Ferlinghetti described the Juvenile Department as
'well named, in this case'. Two officers turned up at City Lights while
Ferlinghetti was out and Kirby met these well-groomed college students:

I would have sworn they were just out of Yale. They said it was all in the line
of duty, ma'am, and I guess I got a little emotional about the whole thing
and told them there were a lot more obscene things in books you can buy
every day at any bookshop.[36]

Kirby noticed that the officers were a little embarrassed about the whole
thing. Shortly afterwards, Ferlinghetti was being fingerprinted in San
Francisco's Hall of Justice. He describes this as 'a dandy way for the city
officially to recognize the flowering of poetry in San Francisco'. One
newspaper reported all this as: 'The Cops Don't Allow No Renaissance
Here'.[37] Both Ferlinghetti and Shigeyoshi Murao, who was tending the
cash register when one of the police officers purchased a copy of *Howl*
from City Lights, were charged with publishing and selling obscene
literature.

The trial in San Francisco was widely publicised, bringing a great deal
of attention to both Ferlinghetti and Ginsberg and selling thousands
of copies of the book. The Beats and the San Francisco poets, represented
respectively by Ginsberg and Ferlinghetti, joined forces and the literary
cluster of the Beat generation was ready for orbit. Ferlinghetti's own
account of the trial emphasises some of the great voices in support of
Howl – Henry Rago, editor of *Poetry (Chicago)*, Robert Duncan and Ruth

Witt-Diamant for the San Francisco (State College) Poetry Center, James Laughlin from *New Directions*, Kenneth Patchen, Barney Rossett and Donald Allen (editors of the *Evergreen Review* in which *Howl* was reprinted during the trial), Mark Schorer, Leo Lowenthal, and Kenneth Rexroth who spoke for many others in concluding that the simplest term for describing Ginsberg's books is 'prophetic'. He argued that *Howl*, Ferlinghetti's *Pictures Of The Gone World*, and other key works of the Beat generation by Kerouac, Cassady, Snyder, Corso and others are based in a tradition of prophetic writing:

> There are the prophets of the bible, which it [*Howl*] greatly resembles in purpose and in language and in subject matter. The theme is the denunciation of evil and a pointing out of the way out, so to speak.[38]

There is no space here to explore the debate which was raised by the trial, a debate which was just as extreme and paralleled by the trial of D.H. Lawrence's *Lady Chatterley's Lover* in London in the autumn of 1960. Both acquittals led to vastly increased sales, and both were based on the evidence given by many of the critical and creative geniuses of the day. In many ways the aura which became attached to the question of the worth of *Howl*, as of *Lady Chatterley's Lover*, has to do with the significant context of such cultural moments, not in terms of a disputation with the great tradition, but in terms of their insertion into the domain of popular literature.[39] Ferlinghetti was justifiably pleased with the outcome of all this. He emerged as a master of confrontation based on commitment, and the *Chronicle* reported the happy, curious scene in which 'the Judge's decision was hailed with applause and cheers from a packed audience that offered the most fantastic collection of beards, turtle-necked shirts and Italian hair-dos ever to grace the grimy precincts of the hall of Justice'.[40] The Judge's decision was subsequently seen as a landmark in law, and Ferlinghetti believes that, since Judge Horn was re-elected to office, the People were in agreement that it was the police who had committed an obscene action. The scene was rather like the one depicted in Ferlinghetti's novel, *Her*, in which the Poetry Revolution is growing in Paris:

> The Poetry Revolution was growing, the Poetry Revolution was shaking, transforming existence and civilization as it rolled down around the corner of the Boule Miche and down the Boulevard Saint-Germain toward Odéon where Danton watched over a Metro entrance and pocket-watches hung from trees each with a different time swinging in the breeze but all of them indicating it was later than you think, while crowds of black berets and herds of sandals came floating and staggering out of the Café Mabillon and the Pergola to join the much-belated Poetry Revolution, while three thousand

nine hundred and forty-two alumni of the Académie Duncan came streaming out of the Rue de Seine combing their hair with Grecian lyres.[41]

Over the years Ferlinghetti has published a number of plays, travel journals, translations, and two novels – *Her* and *Love in the Days of Rage*. Perhaps the best known of these is the novel *Her*, which he had begun in Paris, much influenced by *Nightwood* by Djuna Barnes, a copy of which had been given to him by two friends – Mary Louise Barrett and Mary Birmingham – who were living in the same street in Paris as the women in *Nightwood*. *Her* was published by New Directions in 1960. The passage quoted above is characteristic of the style which Ferlinghetti adopted, which echoes the tripartite structure and interior monologue of Djuna Barnes. The novel was given a mixed critical reception but it sold very well – 100,000 copies had been sold by 1988 when the novel was in its thirteenth printing. Despite the range of his writing, it is in his poetry that Ferlinghetti's reason for writing exists and he describes himself as a poet against his will, with no alternative in life – 'I was only interested in writing ... too selfish to spend much time on other people.'[42] He has travelled widely giving readings, and made a number of recordings of his poetry. One of the ageless radicals and a true bard, his poetry creates its own style and shape on the page. It is sometimes whimsical, sometimes unsettling, always committed to an honest rendering of his basic motivation to be an agent provocateur and, as he puts it, subversive, anarchistic and prophetic. His third book of poetry, *Starting From San Francisco*, emphasised these points in a number of poems which are in effect broadsides, alive to geography and politics, to the sadness of a world seemingly shrunk and bereft of its dreams. The sadness is caught in the figure, the portrait of the brakeman who haunts the final lines of the title poem:

> this world shrunk
> to one lone brakeman's face
> stuck out of darkness –
> long white forehead
> like bleached skull of cow –
> huge black sad eyes –
> high-peaked cloth cap, grey-striped –
> swings his railroad lantern high, close up,
> as our window whizzes by –
> his figure splashed upon it,
> slanted, muezzin-like,
> very grave, very tall,
> strange skeleton –[43]

Having presented this haunting portrait, the poem asks, 'Who stole America?' The question reminds me of one of the shorts fired off by another American poet who is fully conscious of the centrality of both political and human geography – Ed Dorn. In 'What Will Be Historically Durable', our ear is bent by the opening statement that 'About Nixon there was/Something grandiose' and then bent again, towards perception, by the concluding statement that 'Nothing illustrates this/More than/When he stole the post office.'[44] It is the corruption that it itself engenders that steals America. In 1860 Walt Whitman had written 'Starting from Paumanok ... I strike up for a New World' and, a hundred years later, Ferlinghetti starts up from San Francisco and explores parts of America, South America, Europe, and the 'obscene boundaries' created by the Cold War.

At this time, his first two volumes, *Pictures Of The Gone World* and *A Coney Island Of The Mind*, were being read in many languages around the world – in England, France, Italy, Germany, Finland, Sweden, Denmark, Czechoslovakia, Japan, Canada, Mexico, Cuba, Argentina, Peru, Chile, Puerto Rico, and the former USSR. Barry Silesky, in the most recent exploration of Ferlinghetti's life and work, makes it clear just how long is the shadow that his poetry has cast in our times:

> Unparalleled in popularity, it has been read by more people, in more countries, than that of any living American poet. Countless numbers who may have read no other contemporary poetry – and maybe no poetry at all besides what was forced on them at school – have read Ferlinghetti.[45]

Apart from his writing, since the late 1940s Ferlinghetti has been a serious and obsessive painter and, in spring 1990, the University of California mounted a large retrospective exhibition of his work.

It is not surprising, therefore, that painting and responses to paintings are often his subject matter. There is a visual quality to much of Ferlinghetti's work and this is clear in a number of the poems explored earlier in this chapter – 'In Goya's Greatest Scenes' for instance, or 'Away above a harborful'. The painterliness and the response to individual paintings is present right from the start of the poetry. Section eight of *Pictures Of The Gone World*[46] begins with the lines: 'Sarolla's women in their picture hats/stretched upon his canvas beaches/beguiled the Spanish/Impressionists', and section twenty-four opens with a characteristically challenging declaration: 'Picasso's acrobats epitomize the world'. Other poems in direct response to individual paintings include 'Short Story on a Painting of Gustav Klimt', 'Monet's Lilies Shuddering', 'Returning to Paris with Pissarro', 'Seeing a Woman as in a Painting by

Berthe Morisot', and the spirited, sharp and witty evocation of Chagall's 'The Equestrienne' in 'Don't Let That Horse':

> Don't let that horse
> > > eat that violin
> > cried Chagall's mother
> > > > But he
> > > kept right on
> > > > > painting
> > And became famous[47]

The tone of voice in Ferlinghetti's poetry varies from the humorous, as in 'Don't Let That Horse', to the angry, as in a tirade like 'One Thousand Fearful Words for Fidel Castro', or the mischievous and blasphemous, as in section five of *A Coney Island Of The Mind*. What characterises his work is his openness and honesty of response, guided by a relentless and unstinting creativity and inventiveness. If you believe, as Ferlinghetti does, that art and poetry in particular presuppose the independence of the artist, then it is likely that such necessary independence will involve dissidence of one kind or another. The first thing that the poet has to do is to live that type of life which doesn't compromise. When Ferlinghetti got hold of his FBI file through the Freedom of Information Act, he found a note written on it by J. Edgar Hoover which said, 'Ferlinghetti is a beatnik rabble-rouser who also may be a mental case'. The poet commented, 'In my opinion you couldn't ask for a better calling card than that.'[48] Ferlinghetti believes that taking government grants and living on them is to compromise even before you start writing. It is a purist view and there is no doubt that it has become an embattled position in recent years, but it is one which he has held from the beginning, and which he expressed with special effect during the 1960s. Ferlinghetti quoted Herbert Marcuse and the notion of repressive tolerance – the policy of tolerance as self-protection against subversion or violence. Susan Sontag brilliantly described this as the process of defusing unsettling or subversive ideas by assimilating them. As Ferlinghetti puts it in *Tyrannus Nix*:

> Many American poets do in fact help the government in sanctioning a status quo which is supported by and supports WAR as a legal form of murder ... The State, whether Capitalist or Communist, has an enormous capacity to ingest its most dissident elements.[49]

Ferlinghetti's poetry derives from the way in which his honesty and creativity mix with his responses to actuality, be it life in San Francisco, social inequality or oppression, politics or travel. In July 1966, Ferlinghetti, who was much travelled in the external world, took an internal journey by taking LSD for the first time. There might well be a relationship between this event and his long poem 'After The Cries Of The Birds'; it is plain enough that the poem is a response to both interior and external voyages and discoveries. It was published in December 1966 in both *The Village Voice* and the *San Francisco Oracle*, which perhaps indicates both Ferlinghetti's grasp of literary affairs and the simultaneous 'overground' and 'underground' status of the poetry. When it was published in book form by Dave Haselwood Books in 1967, Ferlinghetti had added 'Genesis of "After the Cries of the Birds"', which was written for presentation at the Berlin Literarisches Colloquium and read on a programme with Andrei Voznesenski. In his essay Ferlinghetti offers an exploration of the genesis of the poem and a homage to San Francisco, of which he says that its physical characteristics and its location, perched as it is high on the northern tip of its low peninsula, contribute to the city not feeling like the rest of America:

> Its political face may look the same. The same Fuzz are present in its City Hall and in its Hall of Justice built in the most advanced style of Mussolini Modern. Servants of the People armed with real guns (in the best tradition of the Wild West) still roam the streets. But its students in Black Friday City Hall riots against Congressional Committees on UnAmerican Activities, and its Berkeley Student Movement, and its Free Speech Movement, and its Sexual Freedom Movement, and its free bookstores, and its peace marches, and its Poets Peace Fasts, and its Buddhist temples and its Zen Centres and its Chinatown and its Japan-town and its psychedelic communities and its Poets Outside still telling America to go fuck itself with its atom bomb ... all these panic ephemera creating some illusion of what San Francisco might possibly become apart from the rest of America, what San Francisco might someday become as it finally becomes detached or detaches its Self from what America still wants to be, from what the dominant material mechanical militarist Mammon money America will always still want to be.[50]

This view of San Francisco carries over into 'After The Cries Of The Birds'. The poem has a refrain which marks off episodes based on the lines with which it opens:

> Hurrying thru eternity
> > after the cries of the birds has stopped
> I see the "future of the world"
> > > in a new visionary society
> > > now only dimly recognizable
> > > in folk-rock ballrooms
> > free-form dancers in ecstatic clothing
> > > their hearts their gurus[51]

It is a visionary work in which the form represents the speaking voice on the page. As it continues we share a vision of the city with the speaker hurrying through eternity 'to a new pastoral era'. For a moment, we are in the Berkeley Rose Garden 'looking West at sunset to the Golden Gate/adrift in its Japanese landscape' and, a moment later, the island of the city has floated free – 'never really a part of America'. By the end of the poem, San Francisco has become the capital city of an envisioned new New World guided by Ferlinghetti, 'anarchist among the floor-walkers'. His city becomes the model of an improved future, demonstrating that Ferlinghetti is a poet, ultimately, of place – in a distinctly and distinguished American tradition. A poet of place in such a thoroughgoing manner that he reaches us all, his San Francisco becoming a San Francisco of all our minds. His version of life and art in the second half of the twentieth century is one which we may or may not share, but which we cannot ignore.

NOTES

1. Lawrence Ferlinghetti, *Endless Life: Selected Poems* (New York: New Directions, 1981) p.27. Previous publication includes *Penguin Modern Poets 5: Gregory Corso, Lawrence Ferlinghetti, Allen Ginsberg* (Harmondsworth: Penguin Books, 1963).
2. Ferlinghetti, *Selected Poems*, p.43.
3. Ferlinghetti, quoted in *American Poetry of the Twentieth Century* (London: Longman, 1990), p.292.
4. Ferlinghetti, *Selected Poems*, p.59.
5. Ferlinghetti, quoted in Barry Silesky, *Ferlinghetti: the Artist in His Time* (New York: Warner Books, 1991) p.91.
6. Ferlinghetti, *Selected Poems*, pp.47–55.
7. Ibid., p.55.
8. Ferlinghetti, 'Summer in Brooklyn', in *Children's Poetry* (San Francisco: Kingfisher Books, 1985) p.80.
9. Ferlinghetti's review of Williams' *Autobiography* reproduced in Charles Doyle (ed.), *William Carlos Williams: The Critical Heritage* (London: Routledge and Kegan Paul, 1980) p.248.
10. Ibid.
11. Ibid.
12. Silesky, *Ferlinghetti*, p.47.
13. Ibid.
14. Ibid., p.1.
15. Ibid., p.20.
16. Ferlinghetti, in *Literature and the American Urban Experience* (Manchester: Manchester University Press, 1981) p.5.
17. Ibid., p.9.

18. *Prévert: Selections from Paroles*, trans. by Ferlinghetti (Harmondsworth: Penguin Books, 1965) p.9.
19. Ibid., p.19.
20. Ferlinghetti, *Selected Poems*, p.31.
21. *Prévert*, p.9.
22. Ibid.
23. Silesky, *Ferlinghetti*, pp.43–4.
24. Ferlinghetti, *Selected Poems*, p.3.
25. Silesky, *Ferlinghetti*, p.55.
26. This brief list of characteristic preoccupations is developed in an extremely helpful essay by John Osbourne and Peter Easy, 'Wanted: A Good "Beat" Critic' in *Over Here*, Autumn 1984, pp.16–17.
27. Ibid., p.19.
28. Ferlinghetti, in *The New American Poetry* edited by Donald M. Allen (New York: Grove Press, Inc., 1960) pp.412–13.
29. Silesky, p.67.
30. Ferlinghetti, in the *Penguin Book of the Beats* (Harmondsworth: Penguin Books, 1992) pp.254–5.
31. Ibid., p.255.
32. Ibid.
33. Ibid., p.255–6.
34. Ibid., p.256.
35. Ibid.
36. Silesky, p.70.
37. Ann Charters, op. cit., p.256.
38. Ibid., p.260.
39. This point is developed in Stuart Laing, 'Authenticating Romantic Fiction – Lady Chatterley's Daughter' from *It's My Party: Reading Twentieth Century Women's Writing*, Gina Wisker (ed.) (London: Pluto Press, 1994).
40. Ferlinghetti, in *The Penguin Book of the Beats*, pp.262–3.
41. Ferlinghetti, *Her* (London: MacGibbon & Kee, 1966) p.45.
42. Ferlinghetti, quoted in Silesky, p.50.
43. Ferlinghetti, *Starting From San Francisco* (New York: New Direction, 1967) p.8.
44, Ed Dorn, 'What Will Be Historically Durable', in *Hello, La Jolla* (Berkeley: Wingbow Press, 1978) p.19.
45. Silesky, p.254.
46. Ferlinghetti, *Selected Poems*, p.7.
47. Ferlinghetti, *A Coney Island Of The Mind* (New York: New Directions, 1958) p.29.
48. Ferlinghetti, *When I Look at Pictures* (San Francisco: Peregrine Smith Books, 1990), quoted on back cover.
49. Ferlinghetti, quoted in Silesky, p.197.
50. Ferlinghetti, 'Genesis Of' in *After The Cries Of The Birds* (San Francisco: Dave Haselwood Books, 1967) unpaginated.
51. Ibid.

5

William Burroughs and Language

David Ingram

Not the least part of William Burroughs' status as a major American writer is his profound concern with language itself. Burroughs' writings have offered an ongoing, radical critique of the habitual structures of Western languages. His most significant resource for this has been the work of Alfred Korzybski, whose seminars he attended at the University of Chicago in 1939. Korzybski's system of General Semantics explores possible links between human language structures and the pathology of the human mind–body in society. Burroughs shares several assumptions with 'the Count', including an interest in language as affectivity, and a distrust of abstraction, binary opposition and totalisation.

Burroughs' essay 'Electronic Revolution' (1968) addressed these issues by proposing the need 'to build a language in which certain falsifications inherent in all existing Western languages will be made incapable of formulation'. The notion that a language may falsify reality suggests the empiricist tendency in Burroughs' explorations of language and semantics. These 'falsifications' arise from linguistic-conceptual practices dating back to Aristotle, and are centrally manifested for Burroughs, following Korzybski, in three specific instances of language misuse: 'is', 'the' and 'either/or'. As alternatives, Burroughs argues for linguistic practices that are spatialised, non-linear and concrete, finding models for such procedures in hieroglyphic and pictographic languages, especially those of ancient Egypt and China.

The Aristotelian 'IS of identity' (e.g. 'he *is* my servant') 'always carries the implication of that and nothing else, and it also carries the assignment of permanent condition. To stay that way.'[1] Phenomena are thereby simplistically represented as singular, finite and static, rather than as multiple, complex and in processual movement. Burroughs observes in 'The Book of Breeething' that the 'is of identity' is rarely used in Egyptian

95

pictorial writing, where instead of saying 'he is my servant they say he (is omitted) *as* my servant: a statement of relationship not identity'.[2] Through this spatialised juxtaposition of different elements, Egyptian pictograms constitute a more open and provisional language structure than that made possible by Western assumptions of singular identity.

'Electronic Revolution' also criticises misuse of the definite article as a perpetuation of dogmatism and authoritarianism, in that alternative possibilities become excluded. The word 'THE' 'contains the implication of one and only: THE God, THE universe, THE way, THE right, THE wrong. If there is another, then THAT universe, THAT way is no longer THE universe, THE way.' To rectify this problem, the definite article 'THE' 'will be deleted and the indefinite article A will take its place' (p.154).

Burroughs' third Korzybskian challenge to Aristotelian linguistic habit rejects the act of reducing complex phenomena to binary oppositions ('EITHER/OR'): 'Right or wrong, physical or mental, true or false, the whole concept of OR will be deleted from the language and replaced by juxtaposition, by *and*. This is done to some extent in any pictorial language where the two concepts stand literally side by side.' Binary opposition, by polarising simplistic and mutually exclusive positions, is a 'conflict formula', providing a linguistic-conceptual basis for competitive aggression and war 'from here to eternity' (pp.155–6).

In *Science and Sanity*, Korzybski articulated his central assertion, which forms the basis of Burroughs' explorations of language:

> A map *is not* the territory it represents, but, if correct, it has a *similar structure* to the territory, which accounts for its usefulness ... If we reflect upon our languages, we find that at best they must be considered *only as maps*. A word *is not* the object it represents ...[3]

Language is regarded as a provisional mediation of a fundamentally nonverbal and processual reality, and as such is a process of selection and abstraction from the world to which it refers. Korzybski argued for the 'adjustment' of the 'structure of language' to the 'structure of the world and ourselves, as given by science at each date ...'.[4] Consequently, the world as revealed by Einsteinian science will require different forms of representation than those provided by the 'AEN trilogy' of Aristotelian, Euclidean and Newtonian structures. Language is therefore evaluated in terms of its correspondence to a world of facts, but not in a naïvely positivist or empiricist way, for 'no "facts" are ever free from "doctrines": so whoever fancies he can free himself from "doctrines," as expressed in the structure of the language he uses, simply cherishes a delusion ...'.[5] It should be stated, in addition, that Korzybski's system does not exclude 'AEN' structures completely; rather they are included in the non-linear system 'as a particular case'.[6]

Geoffrey Leech has criticised General Semantics for its 'over-optimistic faith in the curative powers of semantics', arguing that the system makes the mistake of 'assuming too readily that "bad" language is a cause, rather than a symptom, of human conflict'.[7] Yet this argument falls into the very either–or exclusivity that Korzybski was opposing. Nevertheless, by concentrating on language as a main determinant of social and individual pathology, General Semantics does tend to elide the reciprocal determination of social, historical and political forces on language itself.

In *The Job*, Burroughs cites Korzybski's re-examination of the apparently simple sentence, 'this *is* a chair'. 'Now, whatever it may be,' observes Burroughs, 'it's not a chair, it's not the word chair, it's not the label chair. The idea that the label is the thing leads to all sorts of verbal arguments, when you're dealing with labels, and think you're dealing with objects.'[8] This emphasis on the difference between word and object is in contrast to the structuralist approach of Saussure, whose definition regards the 'linguistic sign' as 'not a link between a thing and a name, but between a concept and a sound pattern'.[9] Yet, despite this disparity on the issue of referentiality, which will be discussed in more detail later, there are important areas of overlap between Korzybski and recent post-structuralist researches into language.

For example, Julia Kristeva has argued that repressive mechanisms are inherent in the cognitive-grammatical structures of Western languages. The Greek (Indo-European) sentence, which 'begins as subject–predicate and grows by identification, determination, and causality', is fundamental to the way in which discourses of rationality and scientific abstraction establish systems of hierarchy and law. Moreover, Kristeva counters the reductiveness of binary codification, the 'one or zero', according to which the 'linguistic, psychic, and social "prohibition" is 1 (God, Law, Definition)'. As a resistance to binary closure, she proposes Bakhtin's notion of the 'double' of poetic language, in that it allows for 'an infinity of pairings and combinations'. This notion of *double* is not a binary or dialectical system, but rather 'denotes "spatialization" and correlation of the literary (linguistic) sequence'.[10]

Burroughs' interest in spatialised linguistic forms is further recalled in Deleuze and Guattari's theory of the 'rhizome' as a multiple, non-totalisable system. *On The Line* also advocates use of the conjunction 'and' as a linguistic-cognitive action that produces non-hierarchical, spatialised juxtapositions, and ruptures the fixities of singular identity: '"and

... and ... and ..." In this conjunction there is enough force to shake up and uproot the verb "to be".'[11]

Burroughs' interest in non-linearity beings together ancient pictographic and hieroglyphic languages with twentieth-century forms of montage and collage, as strategies of resistance to anachronistic verbal controls. Non-linearity occurs both at the level of the sentence, in his use of 'cut-up' and 'fold-in' procedures, and at the larger level of book layout and narrative procedure.

The Naked Lunch enacts these techniques of spatialised organisation in that, as suggested in its '*atrophied preface*' (significantly placed towards the end of the book), the reading process itself can be non-linear: 'You can cut into *The Naked Lunch* at any intersection point.'[12] The novel nevertheless places this multiplicity in play with an appeal to overall unity and coherence: 'The Word is divided into units which can be all in one piece and should be taken so, but the pieces can be had in any order being tied back and forth, in and out fore and aft like an innaresting sex arrangement. This book spills off the page in all directions, kaleidoscope of vistas ...' (p.226).

The techniques of 'cut-up' and 'fold-in' with which Burroughs experimented mainly in the 1960s, in collaboration with the painter Brion Gysin, are mechanisms that include randomness and non-linearity in the processes of textual production.[13] As such, they are considered appropriate to twentieth-century experiences and conceptions of reality. This desire to respond to the discontinuity and multiplicity of life in an urbanised society places Burroughs' writing with earlier techniques such as Cubism and Dada, including the work of Tristan Tzara, an early experimenter with a version of 'cut-ups'. In America, Dos Passos drew on newsreels as a resource for the 'Camera-Eye' sections of his novel *U.S.A.* (1938). The work of Marshall McLuhan explores connections between the forms of electronic mass media and artistic innovation, asking the question, 'How does the jazzy, ragtime discontinuity of press items link up with other modern art forms?'[14]

In his essays, Burroughs interprets the discontinuous techniques of montage in quasi-empiricist terms as forms homologous to processes of human mind–body perception. Cut-ups 'make explicit a psychosensory process that is going on all the time anyway'.[15] Describing the act of human perception in 'The Fall of Art' as a 'montage of fragments', he goes on to assert that collage techniques in twentieth-century painting are therefore 'actually much closer to the facts of perception, than representational painting'. Yet writing has been slow to acknowledge this need for non-linear forms:

Writing is still confined in the sequential representational straitjacket of the novel, a form as arbitrary as the sonnet and as far removed for the actual facts of human perception and consciousness as that fifteenth-century poetical form. Consciousness *is* a cut-up; life is a cut-up. Every time you walk down the street or look out the window, your stream of consciousness is cut by random factors.[16]

This desire to invent literary forms that correspond to processes of thought and experience raises important issues of mimesis and referentiality. Burroughs' arguments in his essays tend to be more in keeping with, though not identical to, an Anglo-American field of linguistic theory that includes Korzybski, Charles Peirce, and I.A. Richards and Ogden's *The Meaning of Meaning*. As such, he explores a more empirical area of research than that of the currently hegemonic Saussurean line of structuralist linguistics.

Burroughs' interest in ancient languages further demonstrates this tendency. Like Fenellosa and Pound earlier in the twentieth-century, he admires written Chinese for both its non-linearity of structure and its imagistic concreteness. Chinese is 'already cut-up', and is open to multiple interpretations, in that 'there are many ways that they can read any given ideograph'.[17] Burroughs again makes referential accuracy a vital criterion of value, describing Chinese in 'Electronic Revolution' as 'closer to the multi-level structure of experience, with a script derived from hieroglyphs, more closely related to the objects and areas described ...'.[18]

Similarly, Egyptian hieroglyphics are regarded in terms of resemblance to their object:

The written word is of course a symbol for something and in the case of a hieroglyphic language like Egyptian it may be a symbol for itself that is a picture of what it represents. This is not true in an alphabetic language like English. The word leg has no pictorial resemblance to a leg. It refers to the *spoken* word leg. So we may forget that a written word *is an image* and that written words are images in sequence that is to say *moving pictures*.[19]

The emphasis on 'resemblance' in the relationship between an iconographic sign and its object may be compared to the tendency in structuralist-based linguistics to emphasise differences, whereby iconic signs are regarded as not motivated by nor naturally linked to their object. As Umberto Eco puts it, iconic signs are a transformation of their object, a notion that 'does not suggest the idea of natural correspondence; it is rather the consequence of rules and artifice'.[20]

Eco's semiotic theory stresses the conventional, culturally determined aspects of referentiality. Meaning is a product of codes shared by a particular linguistic community, so that 'an expression does not, in principle, designate any object, but on the contrary *conveys a cultural content*'.[21] 'Similitude' in iconic signs is therefore '*produced* and must be *learned*'.[22] Closeness to the object, in Burroughs' sense, will therefore be a relativistic meaning-effect assigned by cultural convention.

This structuralist critique of referentiality is further developed by Derrida, for whom the problems of a naïve realism, which ignores the ways in which reference and representation are effects constructed by language in the absence of the referent, are symptoms of a myth of 'transparence' or the 'presence of the signified'.[23] Hence his critique of representation, based on the need to 'suspend or at any rate to complicate, with great caution, the naive opening that once linked the text to *its* thing, referent, or reality, or even to some last conceptual or semantic instance'.[24]

Although Burroughs' writings on language do not argue for the social conventionality of meanings and reference in the explicit way of structuralist linguistic theory, he is nevertheless no naïve realist. For the notion of 'reality' in his work is an ongoing problematic, never simply regarded as objective and external to the perceiving mind (the 'realist' or 'materialist' position), nor as a simple projection of mind ('idealism'). Instead, Burroughs moves beyond such age-worn binary oppositions, recognising no 'clear-cut difference between inner and outer'.[25] For him, 'all phenomena are both subjective *and* objective'.[26] The real is thus posited as an existential process of mental–physiological acting in the world. In the *Paris Review* interview, Burroughs gave a Korzybskian definition of 'reality' as a 'more or less constant scanning pattern'. Reality is constructed by a process of selecting and excluding particular perceptual data. There is therefore no stable, fixed nature or reality, rather a 'biologic film' which can be altered.[27] Reality is never simply a pre-existent given in Burroughs' work, but must be constantly recreated in an ongoing struggle for the power of meaning-production: 'The scanning pattern we accept as "real" has been imposed by the controlling power on this planet ....'[28] That such constructions are culture-specific, as argued by Eco and earlier by Benjamin Whorf, is implied in Burroughs' awareness of alternative language-perceptive systems to those of Aristotelian-based Western controls.

Burroughs' assertion that 'written words are images in sequence' seems to blur the distinction made earlier in the same quotation between alphabetic (phonetic) languages and pictographic languages. Clearly, a phonetic word, that is, a linguistic sign, cannot be construed as an 'image' in the same way that an iconographic sign may be. What Burroughs is mainly concerned with, in this nostalgia for iconographic signs, is a writer's recognition of the need to concretise language, recalling manifestations of a similar desire in T.E. Hulme's *Speculations* (1924) and Pound's 'Imagisme'. As Burroughs puts it, the 'ability to think in concrete visual terms' is 'almost essential to a writer'.[29] Such 'concreteness' will be a relativistic effect of language, produced through the selection and combination of those signifiers whose conceptual signifieds (to use Saussurean vocabulary) are relatively concrete rather than abstract. Korzybski's awareness of the processes of generalisation and abstraction in language provides Burroughs with his theoretical protocol. Korzybski offers the writer 'precision of thought and expression' by pointing out that 'generalities without a clear referent are misleading and meaningless'.[30] Burroughs cites his mentor again in arguing that a 'word that has no referent is a word that should be dropped from the language, and I would say certainly from the vocabulary of the writer'. Burroughs gives as his example the word 'fascism': 'we have so many different phenomena lumped under this word that the use of the word can only lead to confusion. So we can drop the word altogether and simply describe the various and quite different political phenomena.'[31] There is a continual need to oppose widespread addiction to the false securities of generalised labels and totalising categorisations.

The desire for imagistic concreteness relates to the interest that Burroughs has shown in magic as a myth of origin for language and art: 'Perhaps the most basic concept of my writing is a belief in the magical universe, a universe of many gods, often in conflict.'[32] Art is 'magical in origin', in that the artist is 'trying to make something happen in the mind of the viewer or reader'.[33]

In Burroughs' Manichean universe, journalism is also a 'magical operation designed to bring about certain effects', but, for 'operators' like Hearst and Luce, it is 'mostly black magic'.[34] The mass media are a main enemy in Burroughs' novels, abusing language to reduce human beings to passive consumer-addicts, and thereby reinforcing obedience to centralised authorities. The novels explore, without sentiment or complacency, the workings of a system of addiction and manipulation that is, as Barthes put it, 'simultaneously imposed and demanded'.[35]

Mr Hart, as an exemplar of this monopolistic, tyrannical media control in *Ah Pook Is Here*, prevents any possibility of a mutual, genuinely participative system of communication: 'The basic formula on which Hart's control machine rests is *unilateral* communication. Everyone must be forced to receive communications from the control machine' (p.49). Such language is parasitical, in the way defined by Michel Serres, whereby a 'human group is organized with one-way relations, where one eats the other and where the second cannot benefit at all from the first'.[36] There is no place in Burroughs for reassuring, fundamentally conservative 'post-modernist' alibis of consumer 'reappropriation' or 'creativity',[37] predicated as they are on unexamined capitalistic assumptions of unlimited economic growth, and evading thereby issues of addiction and irreversible ecological damage and waste.

Burroughs considers not 'creative consumption' but subversive counter-production as a means by which people may become active participants in a culture. 'Electronic Revolution' proposed experimentation with tape-recorder cut-ups, to explore 'illusion' as a *long-range weapon to scramble and nullify associational lines put down by mass media*' (p.126). Written in 1968, the essay argues for continual experimentation with forms of countercultural revolution, based in oppositional modes of production, including the 'underground press' as the 'only effective counter' to the power of the 'establishment mass media' to 'falsify, misrepresent, misquote, rule out of consideration as *a priori* ridiculous or simply ignore and blot out of existence: data, books, discoveries that they consider prejudicial to establishment interest' (p.127). Burroughs here recalls Marcuse's analysis of contemporary society as a one-dimensional system in which 'ideas, aspirations, and objectives that, by their content, transcend the established universe of discourse and action are either repelled or reduced to the terms of this universe'.[38]

The idea towards which Burroughs' acts of resistance are directed is an anarchist individuality, the production of a self that transcends imposed power. His concern is the invention of new forms of self-control within non-authoritarian structures. Conditioning by others within a power relationship will be replaced by deconditioning, and then reconditioning under one's own terms, to produce what Burroughs refers to in *The Job* as a 'self that one is, apart from imposed thinking' (p.24).

As a novelist, Burroughs is concerned with the ways in which the production of this self is prevented by authoritarian language structures. His exploration of comic myths of origin for language, such as ventriloquism and viral infection, are probes into the enemy's field, exploring forms of invasion and possession against the will of the human being who acts as host. In *Ah Pook Is Here*, Mr Hart's agent, the Whisperer, 'can imitate any voice and make Jones whisper out the dirtiest sex words from ten feet away' (p.37). In the essay 'On Coincidence', Burroughs' comedy challenges such authoritarian centres: 'In the beginning was the word and the word *was* God. And what does that make us? Ventriloquist dummies. Time to leave the Word-God behind. "He atrophied and fell off me like horrible old gills" a survivor reported. "And I feel ever so much better."'[39] Language as absolutist power is decentred. This 'logocentrism' is not so much Derrida's version (the assumed priority of speech over writing in Western culture, as a binary opposition which deconstruction reverses), but rather tends to include both oral and written language as potential forms of power and manipulation by the 'word'. The essay also gives a version of Burroughs' most recurrent myth of origin for language, that of parasitical invasion as an embodiment of power relationships based on authoritarian exclusivity:

> The theory set forth in *2001*, that stranded space travelers took over a tribe of apes, in this way teaching them at the same time to understand and obey the spoken word, seems to me as probable as any other theory I have heard on the origin of language. According to Jaynes' hypothesis, language derived not from practical necessities but from the religious experience. Religious truth is always of a categorical and dogmatic nature. 'I am *the* way and *the* light.' Use of the definite article conveys the concept of one and one only. *The* way. *The* universe. *The* truth. (p.98)

Viral infection, the 'prototype of hostile invasion',[40] is a variation on the stealing of energy from unwilling hosts that has been the basis of fictions of vampiric possession since at least the so-called Gothic novels of the late eighteenth century. It may also be seen as an extrapolation from Korzybski's pathologisation of language as the passing on of 'contagious semantic disturbances'.[41] Somewhat disconcertingly, Burroughs has reiterated the literalness of this notion, beyond the figurative or allegorical: 'I have frequently spoken of word and image as viruses or as acting as viruses, and this is not an allegorical comparison. It will be seen that the falsifications in syllabic Western languages are in point of fact actual virus mechanisms.'[42]

In Burroughs' conception, word-as-virus originates outside the body, and reproduces behavioural structures based on habit and repetition, rather than on creativity and innovation: 'The Word clearly bears the single identifying feature of virus: it is an organism with no internal function other than to replicate itself.'[43] Exogenous, invasive power treats the body as a machine for inscription, imposing automatic, habitual behaviour patterns which, as Korzybski argued, keep human beings at the level of animals. Possibilities for creative innovation and difference are suppressed, as *Nova Express* puts it: 'Have written connection in The Soft Typewriter the machine can only repeat your instructions since it can not create anything' (p.76). (For Burroughs, cybernetic languages, based on binary codification, perpetuate models that over-simplify the complexity of the human being in order to facilitate authoritarian control.) Virus is a self-replicating machine that manipulates the victim's emotions, in particular the capacity for fear and hate, as areas of special vulnerability to dependency and control: 'the virus power the fear hate virus slowly replaces the host with virus copies – Program empty body –' (p.66).

Extrapolating from Reich's research into sexuality and language, Burroughs further locates the bases of authoritarian verbal controls in eroticism. *The Place of Dead Roads* explores this area by parodying science fiction quests for origins, as Kim undertakes a mission to find the 'link, the beginning of human speech', to gather evidence for Doc Schindler's hypothesis on the 'erotic factor in language':

> "It must be something inherent in the nature of language itself ... After all, language is communication – that is, getting to know someone all over like in the altogether ... There is in fact strong evidence that at one time the larynx was a sexual organ ... The first words were not warning cries or exchanges of information ... The first words were obscenities ..."[44]

Speech originated amongst a species of deadly red monkey, the 'larynx fuckers ... throwbacks in remote valleys who still use the larynx as a sexual organ ...' (p.244). Instead of Rousseau's paradisal state of innocent song, primordial language is already fallen, its scene of origin marked by perversion and obscenity: 'The first words were unspeakably foul ... And that is why they have not been uttered for a million years except in those remote valleys ...' (p.242). The monkeys are carriers of language as virus, 'Talk Sickness' or 'the Yacks', a parody of deathly addiction to automatic speech habits. Infected Americans rehearse everyday clichés and banalities: 'They will swarm out of a derelict building and yack in the faces of pedestrians: "We love New York!" or stick their heads into car windows and yack out: "Have a good day!"' (p.258).

The Ticket That Exploded explores the link between eroticism and language in terms of invasion by the 'Other Half':

> The 'Other Half' is the word ... The presence of the 'Other Half' a separate organism attached to your nervous system on an air line of words can now be demonstrated experimentally ... The human organism is literally consisting of two halves from the beginning word and all human sex is this unsanitary arrangement whereby two entities attempt to occupy the same three-dimensional coordinate points giving rise to the sordid latrine brawls which have characterized a planet based on 'the Word', that is, on separate flesh engaged in endless sexual conflict –[45]

Sexuality and language are connected by a form of parasitism that imposes on sexual relations the restricting duality of masculinity and femininity as universal essences, based, as Eric Mottram puts it, 'on the semantic history of sexual addictions to what "authority" decrees is correct ...'.[46] 'Operation Rewrite' counters this power structure by challenging the notion of the 'human' as unchangeable with a redefinition in terms of an artefact that can be redesigned.

However, this politicised reading of Burroughs should be put in play with a contradictory tendency towards an abiding essentialism that regards word and flesh as irredeemably flawed, beyond the transformational potentiality of history and politics. The desire to transcend language and the body, to leave both behind in a movement of evolutionary advance, informs much of Burroughs' writing. The ultimate desire to 'rub out the word forever'[47] moves far beyond Korzybski's demand for a renewed language and society based on notions of sanity and improved communication. In *The Ticket That Exploded*, the act of writing itself even becomes subject to addictive impulses: 'Yes sir, boys, it's hard to stop that old writing arm – more of a habit than using ...' (p.146). More constructively, Burroughs posits silence as a refusal to perpetutate conflicts, as at the end of *Nova Express*: '– Shut the whole thing right off – *Silence* – When you answer the machine you provide it with more recordings to be played back to your "enemies" keep the whole nova machine running – The Chinese character for "enemy" means to be similar to or to answer – Don't answer the machine – Shut it off –' (p.155). Silence is thus an ideal state beyond imposed control, a starting-point for self-regulative creation: *Naked Lunch* 'demands Silence from The Reader. Otherwise he is taking his own pulse ...' (p.222).

In *Writing Degree Zero*, Barthes refers to the final 'agraphia' of Rimbaud as a sign that 'there is no writing which can be lastingly revolutionary, and that any silence of form can escape imposture only by a complete abandonment of communication'.[48] Yet, for Burroughs, the silence of writing is an ongoing necessity, a permanent revolution for survival and health. His work therefore offers several models for the role of the writer in society, countering the pathology of language with provisional techniques for health.

'WORD' (1958) is one of Burroughs' most extreme statements of writing as an heroic transgression of limits and a loosening of repressive self-controls, related to expressive noise rather than silence: 'Brothers, the limit is not yet. I will blow my fuse and blast my brains with a black short-circuit of arteries, but I will not be silent nor hold longer back the enema of my word hoard ...'.[49] The writer is an adventurer, who risks breaking taboos to enter areas of evil and the previously unsayable. If the somewhat arch emphasis on writing as competitive performance and self-display is unusual for Burroughs (and suggests an association with Lautréamont), this does not distract from the ferociousness of the attack on the euphemistic repressions of liberal, genteel writing.

In the 1985 Introduction to *Queer*, writing is signified as an exorcism, a confrontation between the writer's persona, his memory and experience, and the fact of possession:

> The event towards which Lee feels himself inexorably driven is the death of his wife by his own hand, the knowledge of possession, a dead hand waiting to slip over his like a glove ...
>
>   I live with the constant threat of possession, and a constant need to escape from possession, from Control. So the death of Joan brought me in contact with the invader, the Ugly Spirit, and maneuvered me into a lifelong struggle, in which I have had no choice except to write my way out. (p.18)

The link between writing and inoculation against viral infection is also made explicit: 'As soon as something is written, it loses the power of surprise, just as a virus loses its advantage when a weakened virus has created alerted antibodies. So I achieved some immunity from further perilous ventures along these lines by writing my experience down' (p.12).

This connection between writing and human biology is a model common to much of Burroughs' work. *Nova Express* defines writers as 'Biologic Counselors', who play a crucial role in restoring health by intervening in human evolutionary development. These 'must be writers that is only writers can qualify since the function of a counselor is to *create* facts that will tend to open biologic potentials of his client ...' (p.121). Fiction-making and imaginative creation are thus seen as necessary means of fulfilling human potentiality. An emphasis on creative transformations of reality is also explicit in Burroughs' space traveller, a figure of open-minded, innovative, non-ideological exploration and experimentation: 'Artists and creative thinkers will lead the way into space because they are already writing, painting and filming space ... *We are not setting out to explore static pre-existing data*. We are setting out to *create* new worlds, new beings, new modes of consciousness.'[50] This space traveller is not to be confused with that all-American hero, the astronaut, who merely transfers into space the existing state of affairs on Earth. Rather, Burroughs recalls those concerns with 'perceptual and mental experimentation, the shifting of frontiers, the rhizome ...' that Deleuze and Guattari find as a 'line of flight' typical of radical American art.[51]

In arguing for the indispensability of the creative writer, Burroughs does not repeat Romantic assumptions of originality. On the contrary, the essay 'Les Voleurs' celebrates the potentialities of creative theft, whereby words, phrases, characters or 'sets' from a multiplicity of prior texts can be stolen and transformed. He records his sense of shock when Gysin, writing *The Process*, copied verbatim an entire section of dialogue from a science fiction novel: 'You see, I had been conditioned to the idea of words as *property* – one's "very own words" – and consequently to a deep repugnance for the black sin of plagiarism.' Yet it is possible to abandon the 'fetish of originality', so that the 'whole gamut of painting, writing, music, film, is yours to use'.[52]

This attack on the notion of originality may be placed with Barthes' description of a text as a 'multi-dimensional space in which a variety of writings, none of them original, blend and clash'.[53] This argument is developed further by Derrida's notion of 'scission', a mechanical action (the cutting of a book by a letter-opener) which may be compared to Burroughs' use of scissors to cut-up pre-existing texts. Both actions reveal and produce a text that is multiple, fragmentary and non-original: 'Scission is necessary because of the fact (or as a consequence of the fact, as you will) that the beginning is plied and multiplied about itself, elusive and divisive; it begins with its own division, its own numerousness.'[54]

However, in Burroughs' own statements on his writing, it is clear that he considers the author neither dead nor totally absent. Nor is there a place for deconstructionist hyperboles ('the reader is co-creator of the text' or 'the writer is only another reader') – approaches which seriously underestimate the work and value of the artist, and serve as alibis for a pseudo-egalitarian levelling downwards. In firm contrast, Burroughs' work insists on the creative role of the writer, who, when involved in producing cut-ups, will consciously select, edit and transform the pre-written materials: 'somebody has to *do* the cutting up. Remember that I first made selections. Out of hundreds of possible sentences that I might have used, I chose one.'[55] The 'selection and arrangement of materials is quite conscious …'.[56] The need to acknowledge the exceptional creative figure, and to take the risk of evaluating art, remains crucial for Burroughs: 'Anyone can use scissors, but some can use them better than others … It takes a master.'[57]

I will now go on to discuss cut-ups in more detail. Burroughs' own interpretation of cut-up activity asserts its subversive and revolutionary potential. Gysin described their experiementation in Paris in the 1950s as follows:

Painters and writers of the kind I respect want to be heroes, challenging fate in their lives and in their art. What is fate? Fate is written: "Mektoub", in the Arab world, where art has always been nothing but abstract. "Mektoub" means "It is written". So … if you want to challenge and change fate … cut up the words. Make them a new world.[58]

The artist is conceived in broadly Romantic terms, as an heroic challenger of limits, with an ongoing, experimental task to liberate human time-structures (consciousness, memory, perception, the body, history) from determinism and law-bound closure:

> It seems like our entire sensory input in pre-preprogrammed. Mektoub. It is written. Snip. Snip. Cut it up ...
> Remember that your memory bank contains tapes of everything you have heard, including of course your own words ...
> Could you, by your cutting up, overlaying, scrambling, cut and nullify the prerecordings of your own future? Could the whole prerecorded future of the human race be nullified or altered? I don't know – let's see.[59]

The conceptualisation of 'reality' in Burroughs' work in terms of analogies from technology – computer program, recording tape, film-strip, typewriter, adding machine – tends to suggest human potential subordinated to a reductive mechanistic determinism. However, these models also challenge such determinism by implying that reality is complex and alterable, rather than unconditional and therefore inevitable. Burroughs' concern to include randomness in notions of the real may thus be placed within the larger context of the critique of determinism in contemporary science. As Prigogine and Stengers argue: 'We find ourselves in a world in which reversibility and determinism apply only to limiting, special cases, while irreversibility and randomness are the rules.'[60]

In Burroughs' notion of cut-ups, however, assumptions of linearity and irreversibility in human time-structures are themselves challenged. The fold-in method, like a flashback in film, enables the writer to 'move back and forwards on his time track ...'.[61] This is a Bergsonian or Proustian view of time as a non-linear structure, in which past and future are involved in a complex present. As Derrida writes in *Disseminations*, in language remarkably similar to that of Burroughs: 'If account be taken of what divides it, cuts it up, and folds it back in its very triggering, then the present is no longer simply the present.'[62]

So the writer becomes for Burroughs a time-traveller, exercising renewed faculties for imaginative meaning-creation. Cut-ups 'establish new connections between images', so that 'one's range of vision consequently expands'.[63] In literary terms, there is a strong resemblance here to Russian Formalist notions of 'defamiliarisation'. Within the apparent randomness, an active mind perceives order and significance, creating 'intersections' between juxtaposed events so that '*seemingly* random factors ... on examination turn out to be highly significant and appropriate'.[64]

Typically, Burroughs often pushes these theoretical speculations into areas where they become themselves unsettling and unfamiliar, and a challenge to rationalist mindsets: 'When you experiment with cut-ups over a period of time, some of the cut and rearranged texts seem to refer to future events.'[65] Given Burroughs' stated interest in possible 'connections between so-called occult phenomena and the creative process',[66] the literalness for him of this notion of prognostication should be taken seriously.

In political terms, Burroughs and Gysin conceived cut-up experimentation as a counter-technology to authoritarian and tyrannical control, questioning and disrupting mass media representations of reality by revealing new, ironic areas of signification in the habitual and formularised 'messages' of monopolistic power. In *The Ticket that Exploded*, tape recorder cut-ups lead to new discoveries, 'as if the words themselves were called in question and forced to give up their hidden meanings' (p.21). Language is shown to operate on the lines stated by Korzybski's theory of the 'multiordinal, infinite-valued, and *non-el* (non-elementalistic) character of meanings'.[67]

Burroughs' interpretations of cut-ups tend to emphasise this level of 'meaning', the area of the signified. But what is also brought out in such writing is the materiality of language, what Jacobson calls the 'palpability of signs'. This 'poetic' function of literary language draws attention to itself as language, and deepens 'the fundamental dichotomy of signs and objects'.[68]

The cut-up sections of Burroughs' novels challenge habitual linguistic and narrative structures, transgressing in particular the normative rules of prose syntax based on the linear sentence. Reading such material is therefore to be made aware of habitual processes of meaning-construction, as well as shifting areas of indeterminacy and asignifying opacity, which appear to move beyond signification into areas of unconscious psychic affect. Jackson Mac Low, writing in connection with aleatory techniques in so-called 'language-centred' poetry, argues that the attention of the reader in such works may be 'centered on such language elements in themselves rather than on anything the authors wish to "say" or "imitate"'. The act of reading is therefore participative, in that 'all or the larger part of the work of giving or finding meaning devolves upon the perceivers'.[69] Mac Low's further speculation that the perceiver's mind may be the 'object of imitation' in aleatoric works can be placed with Burroughs' own theory that non-linear, montage techniques correspond to processes of human consciousness and perception.

It may be argued that the critical power of cut-ups derives from their parasitical relationship with the very forms of mass media they contest. Burroughs makes these connections clear in the *Paris Review* interview, where television is described as a '*real* cut-up'.[70] Moreover, advertisers are 'doing the same sort of thing' as the writer, being similarly concerned with 'the precise manipulation of word and image to create an action'. However, the two activities are seen as crucially different in both intention and effect, in that the 'action' Burroughs intends is 'not to go out and buy Coca-Cola, but to create an alteration in the reader's consciousness'.[71] Again, there is an important emphasis on the conscious intention of the writer as a crucial factor in artistic production. As *The Ticket That Exploded* puts it: 'It would seem that a technique a tool is good or bad according to who uses it and for what purposes' (p.23).

If to cut-up a given text is to introduce noise (a parasite) into a system of communication, then this action is ambivalent, tending, as Michel Serres points out, to both subvert and renew that system: 'the noise temporarily stops the system, makes it oscillate indefinitely ...' yet 'chance, risk, anxiety, and even disorder can consolidate a system'.[72] Yet the argument that non-linear forms such as cut-ups and montage have been already appropriated by mass media systems and thereby made to dissipate their revolutionary potential is overstated.[73] Similarly, the issue as to how a revolution in artistic discourse and socially established signifying practices may connect with changes in social, economic and political structurations should perhaps most usefully be left as an open, ongoing question, simplistic theories of the 'end' of history, art, politics, etc. notwithstanding. If the temptation to overstate the subversive and revolutionary potential of any strategy, cut-ups included, may derive from feelings of despair and impotence that generate bad faith, the opposite danger of denying the importance of art and the artist in contemporary society should also be questioned.

The central problem of such 'post-modernist' approaches tends to reside in their continuing to signify cultural issues in terms of binary oppositions, which deconstructionist reversals of hierarchy do nothing to abolish. For the complexity of the situation moves beyond a simple polarisation: *either* a work is negative *or* affirmative. As Sartre put it, a work of art is both 'negative' and 'a creation'.[74] Burroughs' activity of mimicking, parodying and redirecting mass media techniques does not therefore necessarily suggest a defusion of his works' critical or oppositional potential. For it is precisely the connections that twentieth-century artworks make with mass media forms that give them their power and effectiveness as what McLuhan calls 'antienvironments' that make contemporary culture visible.[75] By exploring industrial, mass-produced forms in a fresh way, artists challenge the 'strictly inside or unconscious consumer point of view of industrial folklore'.[76] Artists articulate their culture, and create thereby real alterations in consciousness, in an ongoing process of renewal that makes totalising, either–or security-labels such as 'avant-garde' and 'postmodernism' misleading and simplistic.

As Burroughs argues in 'The Fall of Art', the 'influence of art' has a 'long-range cultural effect', and is 'no less potent for being indirect'.[77] Writers are 'in a way, very powerful indeed. They write the script for the reality film ....'[78] Nevertheless, the possibilities of subversive resistance in Burroughs are tempered by a recurrent sense of irreversible damage, summed up with unsettling terseness in *The Western Lands*: 'We lost!'[79]

The constant presence of such black humour and irony in Burroughs' writing disrupts easy, categorical interpretations. Rather, his work recalls McLuhan's assertion: 'I am an investigator. I make probes. I have no point of view. I do not stay in one position.'[80] As an explorer of questions of language, Burroughs draws on many different hypotheses, theories and unsupported assertions to address the complexity of the field of enquiry without the limitations of a singular, static 'position'. His theoretical formulations are therefore frequently disorientating, and work to undermine the formation of fixed orthodoxies by playing with received distinction between truth and fiction. There is no aspiration to what Derrida calls a 'white mythology', which would efface its own fictiveness in an assertion of transcendental, immutable truth.[81] As Burroughs puts it, in *The Place of Dead Roads*: 'The mark of a basic shit is that he has to be *right*' (p. 155).

NOTES

1. W.S. Burroughs, 'Electronic Revolution' in *Ah Pook Is Here and other texts* (London: John Calder, 1979) p.153.
2. W. S. Burroughs, 'The Book of Breeething', ibid. p.65.
3. A. Korzybski, *Science and Sanity*, 4th edn (Clinton, Mass: Colonial Press, 1941) p.58.
4. Ibid., p.59.
5. Ibid., p.87.
6. Ibid., p.97.
7. G. Leech, *Semantics* (Harmondsworth: Penguin, 1974) p.57.
8. W.S. Burroughs with D. Odier, *The Job* (London: Cape, 1970) pp.39–40.
9. F. de Saussure, *Course in General Linguistics* (London: Duckworth, 1972) p.98.
10. J. Kristeva, *Desire in Language* (Oxford: Basil Blackwell, 1980), p.70.
11. G. Deleuze and F. Guattari, *On The Line* (New York: Semiotext(e), 1983) pp.57–8.
12. W.S. Burroughs, *The Naked Lunch* (London: John Calder, 1982) p.222.
13. See E. Mottram, *William Burroughs: The Algebra of Need* (London: Marion Boyars, 1977) pp.37ff; E. Mottram and W.S. Burroughs, *Snack!* (London: Aloes Books, 1975) pp.77ff.
14. M. McLuhan, *The Mechanical Bride* (London: Routledge & Kegan Paul, 1951) p.3.
15. W.S. Burroughs, *The Third Mind* (New York: Viking, 1978) p.4.

16. W.S. Burroughs, 'The Fall of Art' in *The Adding Machine: Collected Essays* (London: John Calder, 1985) p.62.
17. Burroughs, *The Third Mind*, p.6.
18. Burroughs, 'Electronic Revolution', *Ah Pook Is Here*, p.153.
19. Ibid., p.66.
20. U. Eco, *A Theory of Semiotics* (Bloomington and London: Indiana University Press, 1976) p.200.
21. Ibid., p.61.
22. Ibid., p.200.
23. J. Derrida, *Of Grammatology* (Baltimore and London: Johns Hopkins University Press, 1976) p.286.
24. J. Derrida, *Disseminations* (London: Atholone Press, 1972), p.43.
25. W.S. Burroughs, *Queer* (London: John Calder, 1985) p.16.
26. Burroughs, 'It Belongs to the Cucumbers', in *The Adding Machine*, p.55.
27. 'William Burroughs: an Interview', with Conrad Knickerbocker, in *Paris Review* no. 35 (New York, 1965) pp.17, 30.
28. W.S. Burroughs, *Nova Express* (London: Panther, 1969), p.52.
29. W.S. Burroughs, 'Technology of Writing', in *The Adding Machine*, p.36.
30. W.S. Burroughs, 'Who Did What Where and When', ibid., p.159.
31. Burroughs, 'Technology of Writing', ibid., p.35.
32. W.S. Burroughs, 'My Purpose Is to Write For the Space Age', in J. Skerl and R. Lydenberg (eds), *William S. Burroughs At the Front* (Carbonale, Illinois: Southern Illinois University, 1991), p.268.
33. 'The Fall of Art', in *The Adding Machine*, p.61.
34. W.S. Burroughs, 'Ten Years and a Billion Dollars', in *The Adding Machine*, p.49.
35. R. Barthes, *The Fashion System* (London: Cape, 1985) p.215.
36. M. Serres, *The Parasite* (Baltimore and London: John Hopkins University Press, 1982) p.5.
37. For example, D. Hebdige, *Hiding in the Light* (London: Routledge, 1988).
38. H. Marcuse, *One Dimensional Man* (London: Sphere, 1968) pp.26–7.
39. W.S. Burroughs, 'On Coincidence', in *The Adding Machine*, p.103.
40. Burroughs, *Ah Pook Is Here*, p.38.
41. A. Korzybski, *Science and Sanity*, p.83.
42. Burroughs, *Ah Pook Is Here*, p.155.
43. Burroughs, 'Ten Years and a Billion Dollars', in *The Adding Machine*, p.48.
44. W.S. Burroughs, *The Place of Dead Roads* (London: John Calder, 1983) p.208.
45. W.S. Burroughs, *The Ticket That Exploded* (London: Paladin, 1987) pp.43–5.
46. E. Mottram, *William Burroughs: The Algebra of Need*, p.91.
47. *Nova Express*, p.10.
48. R. Barthes, *Writing Degree Zero* (London: Cape, 1978) p.75.
49. W.S. Burroughs, *Interzone* (London: John Calder, 1989) p.144.
50. Burroughs, 'On Coincidence', in *The Adding Machine*, p.102.
51. Deleuze and Guattari, *On The Line*, p.64n.
52. W.S. Burroughs, 'Les Voleurs' in *The Adding Machine*, p.20.

53. R. Barthes, 'The Death of the Author' in S. Heath (ed.), *Image–Music–Text* (London: Fontana, 1977) p.146.

54. Derrida, *Disseminations*, p.300.

55. Burroughs, *The Third Mind*, p.8.

56. Burroughs, *The Job*, p.15.

57. Letter to Dick Seaver in T. Morgan, *Literary Outlaw* (New York: Henry Holt, 1988) p.425.

58. Interview in *Rolling Stone* (1972), in E. Mottram, *The Algebra of Need*, p.38.

59. W.S. Burroughs, 'Creative Reading' and 'It Belongs to the Cucumbers', in *The Adding Machine*, pp.45, 59–60.

60. I. Prigogine and I. Stengers, *Order Out of Chaos* (London: Flamingo, 1984), p.8.

61. Mottram and Burroughs, *Snack!*, p.7.

62. Derrida, *Disseminations*, p.303.

63. Burroughs, *The Third Mind*, p.4.

64. Burroughs, 'Creative Reading', in *The Adding Machine*, p.43.

65. Burroughs, 'It Belongs to the Cucumbers', in *The Adding Machine*, p.53.

66. Burroughs, 'Technology of Writing', p.37.

67. A. Korzybski, *Science and Sanity*, p.84.

68. R. Jakobson, 'Linguistics and Poetics' in R. and F. DeGeorge (eds), *The Structuralists from Marx to Lévi-Strauss* (Garden City, NY: Doubleday, 1972) p.93.

69. J. Mac Low, 'Language-Centred; in R. Silliman (ed.), *In the American Tree* (Orono: University of Maine, 1986) pp.493–4.

70. *Paris Review*, No. 35, p.42.

71. Ibid., pp.39, 40.

72. M. Serres, *The Parasite*, p.13.

73. See, for example, F. Jameson, 'Postmodernism and Consumer Society; in H. Foster (ed.), *Postmodern Culture* (London: Pluto Press, 1983).

74. J.P. Sartre, *What is Literature?* (Bristol: Methuen, 1986) p.174.

75. M. McLuhan and H. Parker, *Through the Vanishing Point* (Evaston and London: Harper and Row, 1969) p.252.

76. M. McLuhan, *The Mechanical Bridge*, p.4.

77. Burroughs, 'The Fall of Art', in *The Adding Machine*, p.61.

78. Burroughs, 'Remembering Jack Kerouac' in *The Adding Machine*, p.180.

79. W.S. Burroughs, *The Western Lands* (London: Picador, 1987) p.254.

80. M. McLuhan, 'casting my perils before swains' in G.E. Stearn (ed.) *McLuhan Hot and Cool* (Harmondsworth: Penguin, 1969) p.16.

81. J. Derrida, 'White Mythology' in *Margins of Philosophy* (Brighton: Harvester, 1982).

6

The Prisoner of Self:
The Work of
John Clellon Holmes

Cynthia S. Hamilton

John Clellon Holmes' place in literary history was assured when, in 'This is the Beat Generation' (1952), he named, and in naming constructed a generation. Beatness, he explained, 'implies the feeling of having been used, of being raw. It involves a sort of nakedness of mind, and, ultimately, of soul; a feeling of being reduced to the bedrock of consciousness.'[1] The Beat generation were, he emphasised, a postwar generation: 'Brought up during the collective bad circumstances of a dreary depression, weaned during the collective uprooting of a global war ... They grew to independent mind on beachheads, in gin mills and USOs, in past midnight arrivals and pre-dawn departures.'[2] In a later essay, 'The Name of the Game' (1965), Holmes explained, 'There was a feeling in the first years after the Second World War that is difficult to evoke now. It was a feeling of expectation without reasonable hope, of recklessness without motivation, of uniqueness seeking an image.'[3]

Although it was the restlessness and recklessness of the Beat generation which attracted the notice and censure of the 'Square' world and the press, their clucking commentary often missed the full dimensions of the Beats' rebellion. The surface movement, Holmes argued in 'This is the Beat Generation', was symptomatic of a deeper quest, a quest for spiritual values within a world of status seekers and other-directed men and women, a quest pursued out of desperation because 'the valueless abyss of modern life is unbearable'.[4] The result, said Holmes, is 'a *will* to believe, even in the face of an inability to do so in conventional terms. And that', he adds, 'is bound to lead to excesses in one direction or another.'[5] For the Beat generation, the search for meaning could not be directed outward, for both political and religious orthodoxies had been discredited. Instead, the journey turned inward, into the depths

114

of the self, using alcohol, drugs and sex to escape from rationality and reach a level of more transcendent meaning.

Holmes was an articulate interpreter of a particular Beat perspective, as his two seminal essays, 'This is the Beat Generation' and 'The Philosophy of the Beat Generation' (1958) show, and these essays deservedly stand beside Norman Mailer's 'The White Negro' (1957) as classics of the period. *Go* (1952), the first of the Beat novels, is Holmes' full-length portrait of his generation. However, he was not a spokesman for his age or his literary crowd. His perspective on the Beat scene was unique. Seymour Krim, introducing 'The Philosophy of the Beat Generation' in his anthology, *The Beats* (1960), commented that Holmes 'brings a New England temperament to Harlem, so to speak – conservativeness to a frantic scene ...'.[6] Holmes himself recognised his aloofness and his rather ambivalent allegiance in the way he characterises himself in *Go*, his first novel. In 'The Great Rememberer' (1966), one of several portraits of Jack Kerouac, he contrasts Kerouac's temperament with his own: 'He is freely contradictory, I tend to be trapped by my own consistencies; he absorbs, I analyze; he is intuitive, I am still mostly cerebral; he muses, I worry; he looks for the perfection in others, and finds existence flawed; I am drawn *toward* the flaw and believe in life's perfectibility.'[7] Holmes could act as an interpreter of the Beat perspective because of his somewhat distanced partisanship and because he made the Beat worldview comprehensible to a wide audience, placing the Beats historically by comparing them with their immediate predecessors and successors. In 'The Game of the Name' (sic), he carefully sets the Beats apart from the Beatniks and Hippies who followed. Throughout 'This is the Beat Generation', Holmes distinguishes the worldview of the Beat generation from that of the 'Lost Generation' which had preceded it.

Here, as elsewhere, Holmes displays a talent for selecting the revealing and significant detail:

> But the wild boys of today are not lost. Their flushed, often scoffing, always intent faces elude the word, and it would sound phony to them. For this generation conspicuously lacks that eloquent air of bereavement which made so many of the exploits of the Lost Generation symbolic actions. Furthermore, the repeated inventory of shattered ideals, and the laments about the mud in moral currents, which so obsessed the Lost Generation, do not concern young people today. They take these things frighteningly for granted. They were brought up in these ruins and no longer notice them. They drink to 'come down' or to 'get high,' not to illustrate anything. Their excursions into drugs or promiscuity come out of curiosity, not disillusionment.[8]

Holmes depicts both generations through their attitudinal stances, selecting the significant and evocative detail to help him make his point. He uses the occasional word or phrase which one might expect to hear from the lips of the groups portrayed; he presents people in a way which offers a convincing approximation of the way they would tell their own story. It is this approach to his material which links Holmes' journalistic essays and portraits with those of the New Journalists. In the Preface to *Representative Men* (1988), Holmes comments that, like a number of imaginative writers, he had explored the possibilities of what he calls 'Creative Non-fiction', using 'the impressionist techniques and the first person point of view of modern fiction ...'.[9]

The line dividing Holmes' 'Creative Non-fiction' from his first novel, a *roman à clef*, is very fine. In the Preface to a later edition of *Go* (1976), Holmes expresses some qualms about this literalness: 'These were the places we lived in, the events that occurred, the way we talked, and the things we talked about. In this sense, the book is almost literal truth, sometimes a truth too literal to be poetically true ... .'[10] *Get Home Free* (1964) can be seen as a sequel to *Go*, though the characters here, Holmes says, have become wholly imaginary. *The Horn* deals with the jazz scene in the 1950s, with Geordie based on Billie Holiday, and Edgar Pool on Lester Young and Charlie Parker. In these later novels, Holmes moves beyond literal truth and, in *The Horn* especially, he achieves a rich and resonant complexity.

The journalistic writings and the novels are complementary endeavours which can usefully be read in tandem. The problem of belief, a major preoccupation of his essays, also haunts Holmes' fiction, most strikingly in *Go* where the narrator Hobbes (Holmes), is motivated by the same craving for meaning as his friends, but is unable to accept uncritically their answers to the problem of living, and so is perfectly placed to expose contradictions, ironies and equivocations. 'At the extremity of life', wrote Holmes in 'The Broken Places: Existential Aspects of the Novel' (1959), 'there are really only three choices open to a man: madness, suicide, or faith.'[11] These are explored in *Go*, as the characters hover uncertainly between choices which can look very much alike. Stofsky's (Ginsberg) visionary faith looks like madness. Pasternak's (Kerouac) life-affirming hunger is as destructive as Agatson's (Cannastra) denial of life's worth. Indulgence in booze, sex and drugs may be used as hedonistic affirmation, transport to a glimpsed mystery within, confirmation of a cynical apprehension of life's meaninglessness, or some blurred combination of the three.

As Hobbes becomes involved in the boozy bohemian lives of the group of wild, young fellow writers and their friends, he is drawn into their frenetic, destructive lifestyle. Although he finds their ideas compelling and their freedom attractive, his married existence, his dutiful work on his novel, and his more cautious and analytical temperament keep him somewhat apart despite his attempts to keep pace. Hobbes finds Kennedy's (Cassady) uncritical affirmation of all experience unacceptable. He is made uneasy by theft and criminal associates. He finds Stofsky's visions unbelievable, and is embarrassed by his friend's passionate need for belief, a need he shares.

Returning from a party in the small hours of the morning, drunk and dizzy from drink and marijuana, and momentarily deprived of his intellectual defences, Hobbes thinks he glimpses life's meaning. But in the end, Hobbes is not drawn toward faith by a positive experience. It is the senseless death of Agatson, a member of the group, which takes Hobbes to the brink from which he retreats. After Agatson's death, Hobbes has a vision of the living Hell which he imagines made Agatson so hungry for oblivion. Leaning against a toilet wall in a seedy bar he reads the graffiti:

> ... even the wall he leaned against was crowded with an illiterate testament to the barrenness of the heart. There loneliness scribbled a lewd invitation; desire chalked out a vulgar sketch; frustrate tenderness turned cruel with mockery; ungiven love became a feverish obscenity. All, all ... blunt confessions of longing, words as would be written on the walls of hell. He was paralyzed by a vision of unending lovelessness.
> 'This, *this* was what drove Agatson so wild!'
> Certainly somewhere, some time this fatal perception must have entered him like a germ and corrupted his heart and mind. And Hobbes suddenly knew that someone who believes this vision is outraged, violated, raped in his soul, and suffers the most unbearable of all losses: the death of hope. And when hope dies there is only irony, a vicious senseless irony that turns to the consuming desire to jeer, spit, curse, smash, destroy.
> 'I must get out of here!' he groaned aloud. 'I must get out!'[12]

The book ends with a qualified affirmation of life, but the need for meaning is made clearer than the nature of meaning. Holmes makes the need for belief, for meaning, palpably apparent by depicting the hollowness and hopelessness of material existence devoid of some form of spirituality. Here as in his other novels, his main character glimpses hope from the depths of despair. Holmes sketches the pattern in 'The Broken Places': '... at the bottom of human life is meaninglessness; at the bottom of meaninglessness is anxiety; at the bottom of anxiety is despair. But at the bottom of despair is faith.'[13]

The main protagonists of *Go*, *The Horn* and *Get Home Free* all follow this pattern. But they make the leap to faith with difficulty for they see themselves as intellectual sophisticates, and it is hard for them to relinquish their cynicism and their irony. Their moments of epiphany therefore have a tentative appearance, and are often unconvincing. Indeed, they almost appear more sentimental, happy-ending hopes than real conversions. So, at the end of *Go*, when Hobbes turns back from the brink, he looks towards a home he hopes for, but cannot see beyond the Chrysler building. The dominant commercialism which has blocked more humanistic values in the postwar world makes it impossible for Hobbes to see his home. And the home for which he searches is an impossible dream; his relationship with his wife is disintegrating, held together not by love, but by loneliness, lust and longing. The ironies evoked are stronger than the hope held out.

Even Stofsky's belief is a desperate act of will, not the product of conviction or conversion:

> 'You see? You see? If *that* were all,' and he gestured out the window *widely*. 'If that were all there was – motion, chaos, terror – I'd give up, right now! I'd walk out this window on the air. Just walk out and trust to luck, take my chances, die! ... But I will believe, I tell you! I've decided to believe.'[14]

The chaos Stofsky motions toward is the same chaos Hobbes searches for some sign of home.

When Holmes wrote an introduction for a new edition of *Go* in 1976, he explained that writing the book developed his ideas about the problem of belief: 'Gradually, as the book went on, I came to understand that passionate involvement in life, on any level, held out the only hope, and that lovelessness (what Ginsberg later called "tenderness denied") was the ultimate sickness of the age, and that its source was in all of us who refused to take the risk of vulnerability.'[15] It is not the cautious Hobbes, a younger version of Holmes himself, with his commonsense scepticisms and his over-reliance on rationality, who is the hero of the novel, but the concerned and sensitive Stofsky, the Ginsberg figure, who, in Holmes' words, 'alone seems capable of the future evolution in the spirit that I had come to feel was essential by the time I finished the book'.[16]

Get Home Free covers a longer time span than *Go*, allowing its characters to mature significantly. At the beginning of the novel, the two main characters are in retreat from the ruins of their doomed, destructive relationship. Both Verger and May retire to their homes to lick their wounds and to search for solid ground. He heads for New England, then to Europe; she heads South. Both make their peace with the past and with their world. At the end of the novel, they meet again.

May's voyage to the brink takes the form of a long night, during which she realises that she can neither retreat back into the shallow, callous world of Southern belles, beaux, snobbery and racism, nor into a primitive world of pure sensuality. She can accept neither the socialites' demands for conformity, nor the outcasts' urgings that all taboos be broken. Exhausted after a night of rotgut booze, marijuana and raw emotional experience, she walks up the path to her aunt's house barefoot, her inappropriate New York gown dirty and dishevelled, her shoes lost. But she has survived intact, and is able to recognise something of value. For the first time she realises 'how desperate and beautiful is the urge in all living things to survive life, and enter into reality at last; to reach that surpassing understanding that is held out, beyond the hangover and the orgasm, to all those who are exhausted by excess – the single understanding I know about, that need not be bitter simply because it is bleak'.[17] Because of this awareness, to which both Verger and May have awakened on their separate journeys, the book can end with the possibility of rebuilding their relationship on fresh ground, and with diminished expectations.

The Horn also ends with expressions of hope, faith and affirmation, but in a more convincing way, because the epiphany comes less through excess than through art. When Edgar Pool, the dying pioneer of jazz, hears his own music played as a tribute by the young musician who has beaten him in a musical duelling match, it rebuilds his shattered belief in his music. Edgar is able then to shed his sneering cynicism and bitterness:

> Edgar felt that quick lift in the heart that occurs only when everyone, inexplicably, miraculously, has found the same pure groove; the good, hopeful lift of jazz (which is always deeply on God's side, after all); the lift forward and up. And just as he felt it his eyes lit on two young white men transfixed at a table right before him, their faces full of ecstasy and music, and all at once, staring and shivering, he seemed to *know* them, their very souls ... 'It's all the same,' he thought, staring at them. 'It's just the same for them as me,' black or white – no matter how they shouted at him now, no matter what they said; in spite of bitterness and irony and scars. They loved the thing he loved, and it had spoken to all of them alike, and that generous, eager, joyful softness of anticipation in their faces had been in his face, too.[18]

As Chris Challis has convincingly argued in 'The Recognizable Pseudonym in the Novels of John Clellon Holmes', one of the jazz aficionados transported by the music is Holmes himself, making a cameo appearance, moved to transcendence by the power of art.[19]

Transcendent insight allows Edgar to cast off the mask of irony and cynicism and to accept tenderness and vulnerability. He is able, finally, to acknowledge his love for Geordie, and his last word, spoken to the young man who has cared for him during his last drunken day, is one of hope, not bitterness: 'Celebrate', he says.[20] But tenderness is as difficult to accept as belief, as Holmes continually demonstrates, and lust and the need for love can become as muddled as self-indulgent excess and the need for transcendence. All Holmes' characters are preoccupied with *self*-fulfilment, making relationships with others both potentially useful and fraught with dangers: 'Short of murder, sex might be said to be the ultimate existential act', writes Holmes in 'The Broken Places'. 'The participant swings perilously back and forth over the abyss of absolute Merging on the one hand and absolute Contingency on the other. Loss of ego or loss of bliss ... .'[21] The selfish, voracious individual makes demands as he attempts both to construct and to escape from himself. The uniqueness of Holmes' work lies in the extent to which he exposes and laments the cost exacted from others in the name of self-fulfilment.

In *The Horn* we see the lengths to which the unregenerate Edgar is prepared to go to re-establish a relationship, on his terms, with Geordie. While she has successfully and agonisingly kicked the heroin habit, he has not. Feeling deserted, he tries to turn her on again, and she wakes suddenly to find him 'preparing the needle, a confused secretive giggle in his throat as he stared at her bare arm lying motionless along the blanket'.[22]

Get Home Free is a study of individuals who use one another to make themselves feel whole, or at least better. Verger escapes from feelings of inadequacy by holding May absolutely responsible for her inability to achieve orgasm. May humiliates him, in turn, by flaunting her new lover. When they retreat from this increasingly bitter and destructive relationship, going in opposite directions to their homes, both go slumming, participating in the dissipations of others while remaining aloof. This allows them to use the misfortunes of others to descend vicari-ously into the abyss. When they have had their fill, they escape, leaving others to bear the cost of the excursion. Verger's memory of his time with Old Man Molineaux is telling: 'And so when I think of those weeks now I am almost always tagging along with him, perversely enjoying the spectacle we made – the dissolute old swamp-yankee toper, and the only son of a shabby-genteel family. I am tieless, and unpressed, and always a little high. I am listening to some fantastic monologue, and laughing a little too hard.'[23]

The significance of May's excursion to the swamp, to a house which exists 'beyond all eyes at last, all restraints, all codes, all dreary neces-sities' is recognised by Hobbes, who has gone there for the same reason.[24] '"You have to say 'no' before you can say 'yes'"', he tells May. '"In our day, you have to keep looking for new boundaries to cross, new taboos to rifle for experiences nothing has prepared you for ... ."'[25] He recognises that breaking taboos does not help one escape a puritanical nature, however. '"Perhaps we're the last moralists"', he comments, glimpsing the truth that this descent into degradation is a perverse moral quest.[26]

Hobbes is also aware of the destructive self-centredness which prevents meaningful relationships, telling May, '"we're either trying to die ourselves, don't you see, or to annihilate the other, never to fuse."' May remembers Hobbes' wife, with 'her grieved eyes on him, his guilty eyes on her, and all the abysses in between they'd tried to cross with words, with mere knowledge', and understands. The answer, Hobbes tells May, is touch, 'just touch'.[27] But the removal of self-restraint does not mean that Hobbes has escaped his insularity. Although his need to touch is as imperative as his need to sin, isolation is as difficult to escape as the need for moral boundaries. Even in the swamp house, sexual fulfilment remains oddly and selfishly individual. 'Not yet, please,' pleads Billie as Hobbes tries to arouse her. Hobbes pays no attention as he repeatedly asks her to 'sin' with him.[28]

It is a black woman Hobbes desires. May dances seductively with Willie. And it is Willie, the angry Black Muslim, who recognises that both Hobbes and May display their racism when they choose black partners, as if making this choice makes their degrading descent into primitive sensuality complete. A deeper, unthinking cruelty lurks behind their egalitarian masks. They can afford to go slumming, to attempt to 'forget' their white skin; he can't. 'Man, the minute I believe you, the *next* minute I get myself lynched', he says, recognising his 'otherness' when told to forget the race issue.[29] Holmes shows that constructing an 'other' in terms of race or gender or both is a manipulative and divisive act which invites destructive relationships.

Holmes' sensitivity to racism masquerading as liberalism sets him apart from the other Beat novelists. His depiction of women is also noteworthy. While he never challenges traditional gender roles, Holmes' more nuanced portrayal of women and his recognition of self-serving male behaviour sets him apart, especially from Kerouac. In *On The Road* (1957) Dean's (Neal) desertion of Camille (Carolyn) is recounted with jocularity. Understandably, in her memoir, Carolyn Cassady is much less amused by Neal's announcement of the purchase of a car with their savings and of his imminent departure for the East. For Kerouac, Dean's flight across the country is a life affirming existential act; to Carolyn Cassady it shows Neal's selfish irresponsibility.[30]

These are extreme, opposite reactions. Holmes is more subtle in his analysis in *Go*. Information about Kennedy's (Neal) irresponsible actions accumulates as Kathryn, Hobbes' wife, and Dinah, Kennedy's first wife, discuss the trip to New York. Kathryn has difficulty understanding why

Dinah would accompany Kennedy to New York after he had divorced her and married someone else. Dinah tries to explain:

> She laughed confidingly, almost with nostalgia, glancing fondly at Hart's gyrations over the music. 'Oh, he's still in love with me ... but it's really all over for *me* anyhow. I just couldn't take it, I mean caring about him and living with him too. When I went back to Denver and he married Marilyn was when I got to be a real lush. I drank a quart or more each day ... I still love him, you know, but I don't want him or care any more. You can't *care* for him, it gets to be too awful and unbearable ... Now I'm having fun with him again. It's been so much better this time.'[31]

Dinah tries to articulate her ambivalence; her guilt, her own need for freedom, her love, and her hurt. The range of emotion depicted is much richer than that allowed to women in *On The Road*. Holmes shows that women can be drawn to irresponsible freedom too, breaking away from the standard equation of women with entrapment or as mere adjuncts who fulfil male needs.

Holmes also exposes the way men use women, projecting onto them rejected duties or attributes of self, thus distancing themselves from responsibility while maintaining their right of judgement. When Hobbes criticises his wife's nervousness over the theft of some petrol, Stofsky comments, 'What odd gentility!' and laughs.[32] Later he elaborates, telling Hobbes, 'Kathryn said what you were really feeling all the time. I mean below your shrewd smiles and your Machiavellian agreements.' Hobbes angrily attempts to defend his action, but Stofsky replies, 'You don't accept her. You always squash her in the name of protecting her from other people ... that's how you justify it!'[33] Stofsky tries to make Hobbes see that he cannot accept Kathryn as she is because he cannot accept himself, and so uses Kathryn, criticising her for possessing attitudes he is ashamed of in himself.

The destructive and demeaning relationships depicted in Holmes' fiction show that self-serving personal relationships do not enable one to escape from the prison of the self. The more distanced and ostensibly disinterested relationship between the artist and his audience offers another means of defining and escaping the self. All three of Holmes' novels contain artist figures, but only one explores the functions of art in a significant and extended way. *Go* merely reflects the insecurities of the young, highly self-conscious writer whose experience it depicts. *Get Home Free* contains the portrait of a writer who has exhausted his resources and is seeking to renew them through excess and the appropriation of another's innocent awe.

The Horn explores the way art enables the artist to define and transcend the self, and depicts a variety of responses on the part of the artists themselves to the self-discoveries and exposures encouraged by the creative venture. *The Horn* is Holmes' most original and most significant experiment with the novel form. It is a jazz novel not just because jazz musicians are the protagonists and the jazz scene its setting, nor because it deals with the development of jazz, but because it is built from the formal structures of jazz, the riff and the chorus. The riff sections provide the underlying structure, giving the novel continuity. These contain the main plotline; we follow Edgar Pool's progress from venue to venue as he drinks and attempts to borrow money to return home while his young protege offers companionship and tries to protect him from his self-destructive impulses. The chorus sections contain the reactions, reminiscences, and feelings of musicians who have known and been influenced by Edgar. They are solo performances in which the musicians define their commitment to their art as they react to Edgar's defeat and downfall. Each soloist has a different attitude to his art, to his audience and to Edgar's art and personality, thus placing them in relation to one another.

Holmes' use of jazz musicians to explore the role of the artist in the postwar world seems fitting, for not only was theirs an art of irony and improvisation, an art of exploration rather than commercial slickness, but it was this art more than any other that spoke to Holmes and his contemporaries: 'In this modern jazz, they heard something rebel and nameless that spoke for them, and their lives knew a gospel for the first time', Holmes comments in *Go*. 'It was more than a music; it became an attitude toward life, a way of walking, a language and a costume; and these introverted kids ... who had never belonged anywhere before, now felt somewhere at last.'[34]

Holmes also relates the main characters of *The Horn* to the great nineteenth-century American writers. In the Introduction (1976), Holmes explains his conception of the novel:

> I wanted the book to function on three levels: fictional characters – Edgar Pool, Geordie Dickson, Wing Redburn, plus the musicians whom rumor and hearsay had already made fabulous to those of us who cared – Lester Young, Billie Holiday, Diz and Bird; and the writers of the great American Renaissance of the nineteenth century, who had defined, in their personalities and their works, the situation of the artist here – Melville, Whitman, Poe, Dickinson. The epigraphs to each chapter, added with some trepidation after the fact, are clues to who is who.[35]

By pairing these nineteenth-century writers with the twentieth-century musicians, Holmes appropriately suggests a deeper rhythmic pattern, an extended tradition; both groups were working in a distinctly, self-consciously American mode. And, with the exception of Geordie

(Dickinson), the fictional characters are strikingly well matched with their forebears. Edgar Pool (Poe) is a musician who brings art out of the tortured depths of himself; for whom the process of artistic creation becomes an act of destroying the self. At the end of his life he must face 'the ghastly knowledge he had fought all day with drink and mockery and self-delusion, that his life and his work had betrayed him somewhere, long ago perhaps, and he had gone on refusing to see it, his pride swelling like a boil around the dark suspicion of the truth ...'.[36] Edgar feels betrayed by the audience who did not give him the recognition he craved. He turns his bitterness into irony and mockery directed at his colleagues, his audience and himself, alienating himself still further.

Wing Redburn (Melville) understands the dark depths of Edgar's vision, but is saved from 'that dark, sour look of Edgar's in his own heart' because he does not take the human predicament personally.[37] His realisation of a shared humanity makes him tender, and he searches for 'the same song, the one song – to know which suddenly, was worth to him whatever life might take away'.[38] But his tenderness does not stop him from articulating the hard truth of humanity's relative insignificance. In his ambitious music, which leaves 'everyone gaping and dumbstruck', he is unable to 'forget what he knew, even though Edgar Pool had blown his poor head against his ingrown life ...'.[39] This music, with its powerful momentum, its dark knowledge, its tenderness, and its search for ultimates, is now the only way Wing can play.

Edgar also touches a dark chord in Junius (Hawthorne), but Junius pulls back into the safe preserve of his mother's domesticity, and into an art that has a disturbing impersonality: 'he communed with the music, as if he were alone there, but gave no hint of what it cost him in either agony or joy. He played, but he would not perform ... Something about his face proclaimed too clearly to those who watched that they had no reality to him, and this was somehow infuriating to all those who had no other life but jazz.'[40]

Metro (Whitman) has known Edgar for many years. Moved by Edgar's commitment to music more than by his message, Metro takes up the horn and plays his message of wild, uncritical affirmation. His music is 'like a chant wrenched from a mouth out of which all the thwarted joy of the body pours at once – crude as the flesh most naturally is when the mind lets go; loud, wanton and repetitive the way a chant must be ...'. Metro howls 'his idiot-truths like the first prophet of joy who dared to say there was no sin ...'.[41]

The pairing of nineteenth-century writer and soloist resonates well on the three levels Holmes describes, but there is a fourth layer present as well. Holmes saw the Beat writers as the new Romantics, the participants in a new American Renaissance. In his essay on 'The Beat Poets'

(1975), he commented that these writers 'linked up again with the oldest American literary tradition – the rolling combers of Melville, the bardic inclusiveness of Whitman, the October tang of Thoreau, the lapidary apothegms of Emerson. And the westward-looking, open-souled, who-reads-this-encounters-a-man stance of these ancestors was their stance too.'[42] Holmes had specific pairings in mind: Melville with Kerouac, Ginsberg with Whitman; it seems likely that if he paired himself with anyone, it was with Hawthorne.

The giants of the American Renaissance with their passionate belief in the power of the individual and the need for the individual to achieve self-fulfilment, with their conviction that intuition could take them closer to the truth than logic, with their search for some form of transcendence and their sceptical regard for the social values of their day, with their re-evaluation of the role of the artist and their experimentation with artistic forms – these transcendental explorers spoke to and informed the Beat writers, who knew their work well. The resulting dialogue, spanning the century between, suggests that for Holmes, art was not only a means of creating and exploring the self, but was also the key to escaping the prison of self. 'The truth seems to be', Hawthorne wrote in 'The Customs House', 'that, when he casts his leaves forth upon the wind, the author addresses, not the many who will fling aside his volume, or never take it up, but the few who will understand him, better than most of his school mates and life mates.'[43] And in 'The Broken Places', Holmes responded: 'I say to a man whose book I open: give me something peculiar to yourself, and thus news to me ... Communicate across the void, the sense of your reality to my reality.'[44]

NOTES

The essays and prefaces by John Clellon Holmes referred to can be found in *Passionate Opinions: The Cultural Essays* (Fayetteville: University of Arkansas Press, 1988). The portrait of Kerouac is reprinted in *Representative Men: The Biographical Essays* (Feyetteville: University of Arkansas Press, 1988). These are two of the recently compiled three volume set of *The Selected Essays by John Clellon Homes*. The first volume, not referred to, is *Displaced Person: The Travel Essays* (Fayetteville: University of Arkansas Press, 1987). The first edition of *Go* was a censored version of Holmes' intended book. I have used the author's preferred version, published in 1980 by New American Library (New York). I also used reissued versions of *Get Home Free* (New York: Thunder Mouth Press, 1988) and *The Horn* (London: Penguin, 1988).

Norman Mailer's 'The White Negro' first appeared in *Dissent*, Summer 1957. The essay is reprinted in Mailer's *Advertisements for Myself* (London: Andre Deutsch, 1961). Also referred to in the text are: Seymour Krim (ed.), *The Beats*

(Greenwich, CT: Gold Medal Books, 1960); Chris Challis, 'The Recognizable Pseudonym in the Novels of John Clellon Holmes', *Moody Street Irregulars: A Jack Kerouac Magazine*, 12 (Fall 1982), pp.7–8; and Carolyn Cassady, *Off The Road* (London: Flamingo, 1991).

1. John Clellon Holmes, 'This is the Beat Generation', *Passionate Opinions: The Cultural Essays* (Fayetteville: University of Arkansas Press, 1988), p.58.
2. Ibid., p.59.
3. Holmes, 'The Name of the Game', *Passionate Opinions*, p.51. Both 'The Name of the Game' and 'The Game of the Name' first appeared in *Nothing More to Declare* (New York: E.P. Dutton, 1967).
4. Holmes, 'This is the Beat Generation', *Passionate Opinions*, p.63.
5. Ibid., p.61.
6. Seymour Krim, ed., *The Beats* (Greenwich, Ct: Gold Medal Books, 1960), p.13.
7. Holmes, 'The Great Rememberer', *Representative Men: The Biographical Essays* (Fayetteville: University of Arkansas Press, 1988), p.116.
8. Holmes, 'This is the Beat Generation', *Passionate Opinions*, p.60.
9. Holmes, 'Preface', *Representative Men*, pp.xiii, xiv.
10. Holmes, 'Introduction', *Go* (New York: New American Library, 1980), p.xvii.
11. Holmes, 'The Broken Places: Existential Aspects of the Novel', *Passionate Opinions*, p.166.
12. *Go*, p.310.
13. Holmes, 'The Broken Places', p.162.
14. *Go*, p.69.
15. Holmes, 'Introduction', *Go*, p.xxii.
16. Ibid., p.xxiii.
17. Holmes, *Get Home Free* (New York: Thunders Mouth Press, 1988), p.239.
18. Holmes, *The Horn* (London: Penguin, 1988), pp.231–2.
19. Chris Challis, 'The Recognizable Pseudonym in the Novels of John Clellon Holmes', *Moody Street Irregulars: A Jack Kerouac Magazine* 12 (Fall 1982), pp.7–8.
20. Holmes, *The Horn*, p.240.
21. Holmes, 'The Broken Places', p.168.
22. Holmes, *The Horn*, p.107.
23. Holmes, *Get Home Free*, p.74.
24. Ibid., p.187.
25. Ibid., p.216.
26. Ibid., p.217.
27. Ibid., p.218.
28. Ibid., p.219.
29. Ibid., p.209.
30. Carolyn Cassady, *Off The Road* (London: Flamingo, 1991), pp.74–7.
31. *Go*, pp.148–9.
32. Ibid., p.147.
33. Ibid., p.151.
34. Ibid., p.161.
35. Holmes, 'Preface', *The Horn*.

36. *The Horn*, p.213.
37. Ibid., p.47.
38. Loc.cit.
39. Ibid., pp.47–8.
40. Ibid., p.59.
41. Ibid., p.154.
42. Holmes, 'The Beat Poets', *Passionate Opinions*, p.227.
43. Nathaniel Hawthorne, 'The Customs House', *The Norton Critical Edition of The Scarlet Letter*, Second Edition, Ed. Sculley Bradley, et al., (New York: Norton, 1978), p.6.
44. Holmes, 'The Broken Places', p.163.

7

'Why do we always say angel?': Herbert Huncke and Neal Cassady[1]

Clive Bush

'It seems anyway that I am wrong in everything I think so I might as well believe everybody and be a saint and make money in television.'

Allen Ginsberg to Neal Cassady[2]

'The innaresting thing about Cocteau is his ability to bring the myth alive in modern terms.'
"Ain't it the truth?" said Allerton.

William Burroughs, *Interzone*[3]

Assuredly we bring not innocence into the world, we bring impurity much rather: that which purifies us is triall, and triall is by what is contrary. That vertue therefore which is but a youngling in the contemplation of evill, and knows not the utmost that vice promises to her followers, and rejects it, is but a blank vertue, not a pure; her whitenesse is but an excrementall whitenesse.

John Milton, *Areopagitica*[4]

In the America of the 1950s the literary tradition appeared to many to have run out of steam, and a dullness policed by the New York literary set ensured that approved literature was as polite as it was dead, as academic and class-bound as it was minimally inventive in form.

There were parallels in political life because the American society in which the Beat writers came to public attention was the society of 'hidden persuaders', the 'power elite', the 'organisation man', the 'mechanical bride' and 'the feminist mystique', to choose among many of the decade's descriptive epithets. These suggestions of largely hegemonic controls were matched by, and based upon, the actual politics of the era of unchallenged American mid-century power which produced McCarthyite witchtrials, the Korean War, the Dulles–Eisenhower manipulation of foreign governments, not to mention the virtually feudal oppression and ghettoisation of black people. America's once magnificent Englightenment conceptions of freedom were being co-opted to promote a market-driven, ever-increasing productivity which promised to destroy nature itself: a veritable logic of historical reason which out-Hegeled Hegel.

At the personal level, the ambition of the Beat writers was to recover a sense of self which married a visionary tradition to a recovery of individual worth which challenged the historic, normative values of postwar America. At the artistic level, the ambition was to create new American forms of prose and poetry out of a deep and wide-ranging reading (from the Vedic texts to Dostoevsky), and to free them from academic categories and the abstract banalities of most then-current academic criticism. At the political level (and the practice, as will be shown, varied widely from 'social' challenge to actual 'political' practice), the aim was to subvert the apparent consensus of the suburban American dream.

Yet there was another peculiarly American strain, the need for a religious metaphysic to underwrite personal authenticity. Whitman had reinforced the romantic and visionary tradition from the texts of Indian religions. In early American literature, religious Eastern texts were classically given romantic attention by Emerson and Thoreau in their different ways. The Beats, too, would variously embrace Buddhism, Catholicism, forms of Zen and Taoism, and, in the case of the Cassadys, for example, religious cranks like Edgar Cayce and his followers. At best the resources of non-Western religions (meditation techniques especially, certain drug experiences) enabled the writers to steady themselves for creative work at the heart of the frantic chaos of urban America. At worst, the Beats were in danger of sometimes forgetting Camus' warning: 'There is no compromising between the literature of apologetics and the literature of rivalry.'[5] William Burroughs was one of the few in the circle to be intensely sceptical about the sacred. When his Tibetan Holiness, Chögyam Trungpa Rinpoche, got so drunk that he fell down the stairs and suffered concussion, and then claimed it was his karma, Burroughs inwardly exclaimed with one of his mocking parodies, 'O excellent foppery of the world! As if we were fools and drunkards by heavenly compulsion.'[6]

How did Neal Cassady and Herbert Huncke fit into this? What models on every level did they provide for the great writers of the Beat generation: for Ginsberg and Kerouac? Their actual written works are, after all, minimal. The first and most obvious fact is that their lives, on and off the record, posed a challenge to the specifically personal and social values of Cold War America. In 1961 (oddly enough, when the initial radicalising sexual and drug-related iconoclasms of the movement were being safely commercialised), J. Edgar Hoover stated publicly that the beatniks were one of the three greatest threats to America.

On the positive side, Huncke and Cassady were more than survivors. At best they lived with wit, grace and flair; at worst they succumbed to that careless, driven egotism of the human being trapped in situations where society left few choices but psychopathic revenge. Cassady's excessive jail sentence for 'possession' compounded by a vicious judge's definition of his 'attitude' only serves as an exemplary instance.[7] They served the writers they befriended, not always willingly, with models of how to survive without material goods, and they confirmed continuously, in Olson's words, that 'man is larger than/his social reformation'.[8] Huncke and Cassady could provide living instances of 'rebels without a cause' (a phrase reeking with a massive evasion of political and social definition) and of the 'white negro', Mailer's attempt to theorise a post-existentialist model of behaviour to counter emotional plague.[9]

Yet the very term 'psychopathic' poses problems. In essence, it transfers legal and political and social definitions to a medicalised discourse, with all the dangers that implies. By the end of the 1950s in America, it had been replaced by the term 'delinquent'. The word 'psychopath' was just too convenient for the kinds of replacement of legal by the professionally expert judgement outside the courtroom and of which Thomas Szasz gave so brilliant an account throughout the 1950s. Mailer's effort to reclaim the term for his 'white negro', as a means for the subject to get to a position where choice and a capacity for risk and courage in a deadened society might again become possible joins the radical psychologists' attempt of the same period to reclaim desire as an ally rather than as an enemy of freedom.

Yet another term must be added. Cassady and Huncke provided American instances of what Kerouac called the 'fellaheen': a word borrowed from Spengler (massively influential in the ideology of the Beat movement) and applied by them, in the first instance, to the inhabitants of a Utopianised Mexico experienced as pure Other. Carolyn Cassady saw the 'construction' of this particular 'subject' as legitimation for a type of irresponsible male behaviour.[10] But for Kerouac it was at least as much a construction which helped him to articulate a sense of cross-cultural global solidarity with oppressed and deprived peoples who could be romanticised as being without nationality, as primitive, instinctual, cunning and in tune with the 'cosmos'.[11] Ginsberg saw it as a biblical perception, the Bible being the only text educating the American perception of 'the primaeval earth-conscious non-machine populace that inhabits 80 per cent of the world'.[12] Ruling out descriptive accuracy, the 'primitivism' proposed countered heuristically the logics

of the bureaucrat; the connection with the cosmos challenged, by pure
dissent, the belief in legitimations of pure racial difference and the secret
metaphysics of those who thought they had none; and, finally, the pan-
nationalism of the image helped to confirm Zukofsky's observation that
'If there must be nations, why not/Make it clear they're for business?'[13]

Via Rilke and Lorca, the angel-headed hipster of the poetic imagination defeated the categorisations of liberal sociologist, academic
criminologist, worn-out teacher, parent, indeed any authority figure,
whether despairing wives, mothers, fathers, or powerful old men. How
to account for the beauty of the young men who come into being
programmed into poverty, urban blight, conscription and death, labour
that would insult an animal, and into hunger and unemployment?
Within a largely homophilic perspective, the celebration of a brief
angelic flowering already corrupted within a fateful universal wastage
was not the least of the Beat writers' achievements. 'Allen accepted Jack's
notion that there were "fallen angels" full of secret love, who loved even
if they didn't show it.' And yet the dreamers of angels were challenged
by the angels themselves: 'Why', wrote Cassady to Ginsberg, repeating
Kerouac's question, 'do we always say angel?'[14]

Why indeed? Part of the answer can be suggested in Sartre's great work
on Genet. The aura of the sacred haunts Huncke and Cassady, whose
roles as life-models, friends, lovers, destroyed writers, thieves, wastrels,
jailbirds and drug suppliers were both succoured and sucked dry by the
writers who had not lived very similar lives.

Citing Eliade, Sartre states: 'Genet has no profane history. He has only
a sacred history, or, if one prefers, like so-called "archaic" societies, he
is continually transforming history into mythical categories.'[15] Modern
commentators only tend to emphasise the dangers, but the transformations of mythic thinking may not be simply posed as pure opposition
to reality: 'In the light of mythological, events and persons can seem
true or false to the true story of who I am.'[16] Thus Cassady's joyriding
2000 cars in two years turns him into a hero, but the precise lineaments
of the intelligibility of the fact have all the complexity that mythic
thinking requires. Was it a case of the 'true pleasure of the thief [being]
the fictive pleasure of the fake owner'?[17]

Huncke will embrace the designation of thief to a far greater extent,
but without Cassady's intellectual sensibilities. Cassady will choose
among his contrary actions. He will stop stealing cars, but not fucking,
and he will choose a religion to support the distinction.[18] His sexual
conquests are of a kind: a number of his partners have declared the
encounters as machine-like, demonstrating a violent one-sided pleasure,
ending in exhaustion. Like his society, Cassady wills his own nothingness:
the final dereliction of himself as a sanctification of instinct. The society

whose psychological goal is homogeneous repetition, within the desire
that nothing will happen, needs a perverse fiction of itself as super-active
outside the law of its own reality. *Exhaustion* is the goal of both states.
Huncke and Cassady, but more especially Cassady, are mythic heroes
of exhaustion. Thus, their beauty is as real and compelling as any
sacrificed hero; the transactions become: my fiction for your fiction,
my sex for your bed and board, my drug for your money, your witness
to my destruction to preserve your tranquillity, my satisfaction (as
victim) of your need for power to preserve the fiction of the freedom
of my fateful luck. Yes indeed they are 'angels' – human beings with
wings, with all the freedom of air: 'the phenomenon of saintliness
appears chiefly in societies of consumers'.[19]

The saint and hero merit social approval by practising on themselves
the 'magnificent destruction which represents the ideal of their society'.[20]
The aim is pure activity without reflection, what Paul Goodman called
'an action, not a reflection or comment'.[21] The pragmatic tradition of
America favours action before reflection, or attempts, as Goodman
does, to equate it with a religious (here Taoist) legitimation of 'living
with independent integrity'. How you know integrity without reflection
he doesn't say. The practical and the mystical tended to remain only
absolute options. Plummer comments that embracing the doctrines of
Cayce led Carolyn Cassady to 'positive thinking', while it led Neal to
'Gurdieff and P.D. Ouspensky'.[22]

Other Beat figures were more actively and politically engaged. Carl
Solomon at Columbia was a member of the American Youth for
Democracy (known as the Tom Paine Club at CCNY), which later
became the Communist Political Association. Solomon argued with
Ginsberg over the legacy (political versus sexual) of Whitman.[23] Ginsberg
himself, as Carolyn Cassady noted, somewhat astonished his friends by
telegraphing Eisenhower over the Rosenbergs' execution in 1953.[24]
Presumably they had forgotten, or did not know of, Ginsberg's youthful
dream of being a labour leader as well as a poet. As a reporter on the
Labor Herald, the official journal of the New Jersey AFL, he had gotten
to know Paterson better than ever, as he reported to William Carlos
Williams.[25] Eric Mottram noted that his picketing in the San Francisco
anti-Madame Nhu demonstration of 1963 had Ginsberg stating that this
was the first time 'I've taken a political stand', and commented that
Ginsberg, to a certain extent, wards off that easy co-option by the state
of a familiar American anarchism by 'the intelligence of his body's convictions for freedom'.[26] Mottram's criticisms necessarily harden later,
while praising Ginsberg as a witness to his times.[27]

In the later 1960s, many Beat writers were active in the anti-Vietnam
war movement. For Gary Snyder, the attitudes of some of the Beat

writers changed when Castro took over Cuba, and when Martin Luther King's movement got off the ground.[28] To a degree these facts challenge Goodman's comment: 'Considered directly their politics are unimpressive.'[29]

But it was the literature that challenged the more social and personal preconceptions and prejudices of a generation. The Beat writers ransacked many literary traditions in truly American style and created a staggeringly impressive new art, which struck at the heart of American consensual deadness. The younger writers were fortunate in their mentors. Justin Brierly, Denver lawyer and high school counsellor, encouraged Neal Cassady to report to him on his reading of Kant, Schopenhauer, Nietzsche, Santayana, Shakespeare, Dostoevsky and Proust.[30] Burroughs was mentor to Kerouac and Ginsberg, introducing them to Céline, Genet, Kafka, Wilhelm Reich, Cocteau, Spengler, Korzybski, as well as Herbert Huncke, his morphine connection.[31] A few academics also assisted the reading list. John Clellon Holmes and Kerouac sat in on Alfred Kazin's classes on *Moby Dick* at the New School for Social Research. Raymond Weaver, Mark Van Doren's office colleague and the discoverer of the manuscript of Melville's *Billy Budd*, read sympathetically Kerouac's Wolfean outpourings, *The Sea is my Brother*, suggesting readings also in Gnostic literature, Chinese and Japanese Zen and the American transcendentalist tradition.[32] The reading list included Melville's *Pierre* and *The Egyptian Book of the Dead*.[33]

In their different ways, the Beat writers would draw strength from the most challenging European literature from the Romantics onwards, freely intermingled with Gnostic texts and Eastern religious texts in a project familiar to America writers since the transcendentalists. With the exception of Burroughs and Huncke, there is always a visionary strain mingling the sacred and the profane, employing anything that came to hand – including radio shows, popular fiction and comics.

For Cassady, as for the others, Proust was key. The long sentences provided the vehicle for a recall of detailed memory and, structured within an American-Denver working-class speech, resulted in a prose which had profound effects on Cassady, Ginsberg and Kerouac.[34] Spengler was of equal importance. His *Decline of the West* was in the mode of the grand epic narrative of civilisation which has always appealed to Americans. Cycle, fatality, destiny and heroic, historical pessimism made Spengler as American as a John Ford Western; here could be enacted a drama promoting an aesthetics of the will to power, without alibis of historical, scientific or religious salvation in which civilisation itself performed the last act of manifest destiny. Céline, Genet, Kafka and Cocteau could be seen in their various ways to write footnotes to the results of the unholy bargains of Faustian man. In Spengler's words, science had failed, it was the 'soul of the culture that [had] had enough'.[35]

Spengler led back to Nietzsche, to the recovery of myth to be hurled against the *Irony* of the historical and scientific consciousness alike. Hayden White long ago pointed out that the Nietzschean concepts of memory, time and history were more complex than their interpreters in the twentieth century had reckoned with. Crippled by 'the ironical self-consciousness' of conventional historical scholarship, art and religion offer themselves as a means to forget and to turn away from the consciousness of becoming: 'The unhistorical and the superhistorical are the natural antidotes against the overpowering of life by history; they are the cures of the historical disease.'[36] It is in this sense that Dean Moriarty (Neal Cassady) is the pupil of Chad (Brierly), the 'Nietzschean anthropologist' and that 'western kinsman of the sun', whose character is 'Western, the west wind, an ode from the Plains, something new, long prophesied, long a-coming (he only stole cars for joy-rides)'.[37]

In Nietzsche's *Genealogy of Morals*, the conditions for the self are laid down: 'To be oneself is to deny the obligations which both past and future lay upon one, except for those obligations that one chooses for oneself and honors simply because one finds them "good".'[38] Activity is more important than adaptation. White points to the anti-communal nihilism of Nietzsche's thought; it is not surprising that a postwar generation of American writers would have been attracted to him, given the profound disquiet of the years following 1945. Indeed, they were in a sense returning to the writers of sixty years before, for whom Dostoevsky and Nietzsche had been the heroes of historical pessimism and that new world of the 'id', with its theory of natural drives, rationalisations, sexual masochism and sublimation, of guilt as a product of cultural thwarting – so close, as Hughes points out, to Freud's own work.[39]

The Beats' 'holy fools' are to be less self-reflexive and, to a degree, less socially engaged than Dostoevsky's. With Dostoevsky's Prince there is always that enormous chasm of doubt as to the sincerity and precise motives of the teller of the tale: 'But what sort of an idiot am I now when I know myself that people take me for an idiot?'[40]

Dostoevsky makes his Idiot appear withdrawn, yet deeply social. He catches his holy fool in a network of sexual, class and ethical fictions which structure the responses of those who encounter him. No less than with Nietzsche, traditional ethics (and their accompanying moral fables and melodramas) become chips in a game of aesthetically passionate manipulation. This less-than-holy innocent ends up in a Swiss clinic, delivering himself of a few happy and intelligent truisms; a fate which, while it avoids the malign erotics of crucifixion and transfiguration, scarcely holds out hope for a life in which ecstatic and imaginative intuition is a primary moral requirement.

The hope of the Beats to the contrary was that through breakdown was the hope of breakthrough.[41] Ginsberg survived his clinic, and, with varying degrees of skill, both resisted and transformed his role, but as a poet of an American tradition of visionary experience, not as a psychologist or philosopher.

Yet the dangers were that the holy fool could not but feed on the thing he opposed: that suicidal arsenal of his own anxieties. The contortions of difficulty (of one holy fool to another) are most complexly recorded, though not resolved, in a letter from Neal Cassady to Ginsberg of 3 August 1948 and in Ginsberg's reply, later that same month:

> I've long ago escaped admiration – as such – however, you stimulate whatever degree of hero-worship I've left. But beyond all this, you stand head and shoulders above any one man I've ever known – that, in itself, is love – calls for love. Again, look at yourself as Prince Mischkine – the idiot – you manifest more of the mystic, the Dostoievskian religious, the loving Christ, than does anyone else. Or, even as young Faust, you show more of these supposedly virile, masculine ... However, off the intellectual now, you are not an abstract symbol to me; nor quite a personal love which I must combat, fear – or flee. Rather, (at last I reach the point) I have a new vision to add to our collection – you are my father ... The above paragraph is a beginning of sincerity, and the vision of the father – a good *partial* one – ...[42]

The subtext is that Ginsberg found himself more in love with Neal than the reverse. But it would be cheap to simplify the complex issues in such a way. Cassady is painfully ransacking his reading as a means of articulating his own difficulties and confusions. Thus, the Nietzschean hero is democratically refused though his temptations remain. The ambivalent erotic feelings are sentimentalised into a simplistic reading of Mischkine. Unable to find a middle way of characterising his relation with Ginsberg between a less than whole personal love and the abstract symbol of the master, 'father' becomes a tropological term for creating an emotional distance under pressure. It is less the pyschological father, for the relation is unsubtly equalised with 'wife' (Carolyn) and 'brother' (Jack Kerouac). Ginsberg naturally was stung enough to reject the equalisation. The lover does not want to be admitted into the family on equal terms.

Ginsberg's own reply is a narrative which combines confession and the conversion experience, with its transcendental personal moment, directed both to fend off his feelings for Cassady and promote a practical poetics. Here is one moment in this important letter:

I am glad you at last recognise in me the elements of Myschkin; it has taken me this long to recognise them and to be able to affirm them myself, at least the true elements. My intuition before led me into a presumption of love, where there was no true love (of world) but nonetheless, these phantasies were shadows of the truth that is within me and which will one day emerge in all its power and intensity. I cannot be your father: you putting yourself in a false situation, perhaps, apropos; Jack & Caroline: but that is none of my affair except as your fellow human & your lover. As to young Faust and the 'enigma problems' that you speak of, that is perhaps also true, that I contain or show, rather more than they ... However, I cannot speak of their souls, nor yours, for I do not know them as well as I do my own. How I am learning to know my soul in relation to itself, not to others; and to know it in relation to 'god'.[43]

Ginsberg deliberately plays on the traditional and special sense of 'father' used here and, with Whitman-like blitheness, insists on the equation of 'fellow human' and 'lover'. There is a retreat here and it is a religious one with its Thoreauvian echoes of the greater importance and conviction of self-knowledge in contradistinction to the knowledge of others. Myschkin is then to be declared true and false – not because of *his* complex relation with others – but because of the partiality of his truth along some ineffable transcendental way. Ginsberg's unhappinesses are patent: 'I long more to go to God than to you, and perhaps you are a temptation rather than an angel', and the final PS outlines a reading list of the visionary texts of Blake, Yeats, Eliot and St John of the Cross.

The postscript is important, for what Ginsberg is doing here under intense emotional pressure is attempting to articulate intimations of his precise poetic role and strength. The homiletic and imaginatively moral aspects of the Prince (the story of Marie, the brilliant inveighing against the death penalty) will also provide part of a poetic persona in a tradition which stretches back to Whitman. He will 'contain or show' *more* than they.

Cassady's treatment of the 'soul', however, is to a degree less transcendental than Ginsberg's and, in the following passage, he takes up the Emersonian themes of language, nature and poetry. He speaks here of the 'physicist of the inner world':

But the very words that he selects, to notify to others the results of his intellectual labors, betray him. The word as utterance, as poetic element, may establish a link, but the word as notion, as element of scientific prose, never. Easier to break up a theme of Beethoven with a knife than break up the soul by methods of abstract thought. Images – likenesses, are the only way for spiritual intercourse yet discovered.[44]

In a tradition going back via the symbolists (Rimbaud especially) to Emerson and beyond, Cassady creates a prose in which the juxtaposing of abstract and concrete terms turns philosophy into an aesthetics of creativity, the image into a rival (at the semantic level) of syntax, science into a handmaiden of theory, whose validations are predicated on a metaphysical psychology.

Relying on a theory of Emersonian correspondences, the word is declared both divine and available, inseparable from utterance and obliterating the distinction between the world of science and the world of art. In so doing, it appeals to what Barthes called the 'something beyond language', which for Americans is less 'the threat of a secret' than a *confidence* in an intuited set of correspondences.[45] For the Beats it became intimately connected with Eros itself. Benjamin's comments on Kraus' language are of assistance here in looking at this cluster of problems in another way. He said of Kraus' language, 'It has done away with all hieratic moments. It is the theatre of a sanctification of the name', and cites Kraus' words which are close in spirit to the dialogue between Cassady and Ginsberg: 'The more closely you look at a word the more distantly it looks back.'[46]

The transcendentalist disposition toward aphorism is also evident: 'Easier to break up a theme of Beethoven with a knife than break up the soul by methods of abstract thought'; its imperfect dualism combines the New Testament homiletic prophetic style ('It is easier for a camel etc. ...') with Old Testament psalmic poetic parallelism. The Platonism of the argument is obvious, but the association of 'image', 'likeness' and that 'gesture' of 'imperceptible movement' have their roots deep in an American Puritan visionary tradition.

In February 1952, Ginsberg was supplying Cassady with further huge book lists. He had been reading Balzac, Hesse, Kafka, Faulkner, William Carlos Williams, Robert Lowell, Goethe, Lawrence, Hardy, Gogol, Stendhal, Anson on Auden, and Genet. He was reading and translating Genet's 'Un condamné a mort'. For Ginsberg, the 'golden-obscene poetry' of Genet turns the Dostoevskian terror of those who *know* they are already dead into an erotics of a love forbidden by those who clamour for state murder. Like Genet, Ginsberg will speak *as* the homosexual lover not *on his behalf*. Unlike Genet, however, neither Ginsberg nor Cassady claim evil as their good, not because they do not know that evil will escape their embrace of it, but because they have the ultimately liberal hope that they can transcend or escape it. They lack ultimately the radicalism of de Sade, even though they too 'made the brutal discovery that there was no conciliation possible between social existence and private pleasure'.[47] Protesting, yet somehow less conscious of evil, they never quite transform transgression into glory.[48] A certain depth of mockery is absent from Cassady and Ginsberg, though perhaps for slightly different reasons.

For Ginsberg, Cassady had the simplicity of a Blakean angel, the redeemed man of the visionary experience with its simple poetic truth that it is possible to imagine things other than they seem to be:

> I sometimes see you afresh, a great erotic and spiritual existence, after all the dross of history is washed down the drain and you emerge pristine as I first knew you shining and triumphant like an angel rejoicing in the strength of your own imagination, your own self-creation fostered in the sweetness of naked idealism.[49]

The relation of 'the dross of history' and that 'great erotic and spiritual existence' was managed poetically, not ideologically. The debate, however, between the two possibilities was intense. While Raymond Weaver, for example, instructed Kerouac in Melville's *Pierre*, Plotinus, Zen and the Gnostics, Alfred Kazin at the New School for Social Research brought a greater sense of socialist analysis to the courses he taught. When, however, Kerouac bombarded Kazin with pages of *Dr Sax* the latter thought him crazy.[50]

The great twentieth-century classic which deals with the claims of the sacred against the political logic of the powerful is unquestionably Genet's *The Thief's Journal* (1949), and it is a work of especial interest for this essay because it was read intensively by the Beat writers in the 1950s. Its greatness lies less in the abstracted content of what it reveals – the banality of petty betrayal, sexual manipulation and violence among men who never had a chance – than in its capacity through tone and structural/aesthetic consideration to mock the moralising legitimations of law, police, petty officialdom and bureaucracy. The mockery is all the more powerful because Genet insists, radically, that it is a condition to which both sides have given their consent. The world Genet depicts is without compassion and invokes the absolute pride of solitude.

The work provides a benchmark for looking at Huncke and Cassady. Not only is it the work of the genre most self-conscious of its procedures, but it will here also provide a crucial sense of difference between the European and American texts. The immediate difference is in the question of *glory*. The European angel-headed hipster glories to a greater extent in punishment, cruelty, and self-abnegation as the part of the necessary confirmation and support of 'our world'.

The difference is one of culture. America had no formally adopted Church. The Italy, France, Germany and Spain of Genet's wanderings are dominated by an unbroken tradition of Catholic tradition and

morality. The choice of religious explanatory discourse is a preoccupation of the Beats; in Genet's work, it could be assumed as given.

> I knew the formula, as I had already begged for others and myself: it mixes
> Christian religion with charity; it merges the poor person with God; it is so
> humble an emanation from the heart that I think it scents with violet the
> straight and light breath of the beggar who utters it.[51]

In parallel with the holy fool in Russia, the beggar, covered with lice,
filthy and degraded can be inscribed paradoxically within a narrative
of extreme self-control, and victory: 'Poverty made us erect. All across
Spain we carried a secret, veiled magnificence unmixed with arrogance'
(p.20). Loss, defeat, victimisation, poverty, degradation, suffering have
high visibility within the traditional culture of Catholic Europe. Not
so in America.

For Genet, the difference is that religious discourse is too inscribed
in the given meanings to give any hope of transcendence, or of breaking
the vicious circle. In Cassady and Ginsberg, the hope has not been given
up. One cannot imagine any of the Beats adopting a stance of 'being
good' as a lucky charm to commit a crime, (p.24) nor seeking love in
order gain the power to destroy it (p.36).

Except, perhaps, for Burroughs. Like Burroughs' fictions, Genet's are
essentially those of melodrama: the genres and topics of rightwing
newspapers. They are narratives of spies, outlaws, diamonds, drugs,
smugglers, police, murderers, crooks, Legionnaires, prostitutes, cross-
dressing homosexuals. The narratives act out their crypto-realities on
national borders, in ports, in slums, in jails. Sardonically and actually,
Genet insists on the perfect order his fictions represent for they reach
deep into a betrayed romantic psychology of individual freedom. In this
world the palace *is* the prison, mirroring it in its rituals and in the
sumptuous destitution of its solid ruins. The alliance of aristocrat and
sentimentalised criminal is directed against the actual power of the
moralistic bourgeoisie.

Further, necessity, like the power of money, does not differentiate
between its objects: objects themselves become a nexus of human
relations under a condition of hierarchies of power to which the vengeful
discipline of self-abnegation gives its consent. Genet combines the
insights of Nietzsche and Marx as he moves through a world of nightmare
in which he claims an ever more innocent expertise: 'Yet I was not going
through Europe but through the world of objects and circumstances,
and with an ever fresher ingeniousness' (p.94). In writing this world,
legibility and legend converge to provide a new emotion: that of poetry
itself (p.98). Here the very agency of perception itself is claimed by the

power of objects. The panic of theft (the inverse of the pleasure of buying, as adultery is to marriage) creates an hallucinatory consciousness by breaking the taboo of ownership in which reified nature again asserts its own power: 'The trees were surprised to see me. My fear bore the name of panic. It liberated the spirit of every object, which awaited only my trembling to be stirred' (p.105).

Thus the saint, the creator and criminal are of a piece in Genet's work: individuality, renunciation, destruction, loss of self, 'forcing the Devil to be God', underwrite what these roles have in common (p.170). Genet differs from the Beats in that he struggles to be what the crime has made him, and caught, 'I shall perform with slow, scrupulous patience the painful gestures of the punished' (p.214).

The aloneness of the European hoodlums and pimps is in their beauty. Yet, as Sartre points out, this beauty has its own categorical imperative: 'the aesthete's will must be not only a will to Beauty but a beautiful will; needs, life, death itself must be consumed in beautiful, blazing gestures which all at once transform their authors into actors, the spectators into extras and the place into a stage set'.[52] Thus, the aesthetic, which detaches itself from the world of the purposeful, and the legitimations of the political order combine to re-enter it as a validating tone of the ritual. It is more than tone, however; it is foundation of the symbolic eroticism of sovereignty itself: that absolute desire for a once for all sovereignty in Genet that Bataille correctly criticised Sartre for not emphasising enough.[53] Norman O. Brown once commented: 'The drama enacted in the sex act is the ritual drama of divine kingship. Sex is *le theatre des pauvres* [Talleyrand]; every man a king; King Oedipus ... The phallic personality and the receptive audience are in coitus; they do it together, when it comes off.'[54]

If I can't be king, I'll be a magnificent beggar is the tragic cry of those who realise they will not make it in the ludicrously banal world of capitalist imperatives for 'work'. 'Poverty', said Genet, 'makes us erect' (p.20). The conjunction of punishment, sovereignty and sexual display is inscribed in the elaborately fetishistic and grubby apparel of every unemployed and briefly defiant streetkid in Europe. In London, postcards displaying their faces are sold alongside portraits of diamond-bestrewn Queen Mothers and Princesses by newsagents in the neighbourhoods of tourist hotels. Together they constitute the interlocked sovereign icons of the nation.

In an early published journal of 1965, Huncke's 'Song of Self' immediately shows the more detached nature of the American criminal. Uttering his own name 'creates an almost weary and loathsome feeling in me'.[55] The emphasis is on impending insanity, accompanied by thoughts of suicide. Unlike Genet, Huncke does not adopt his loath-

someness, he passively regrets it. Seduced when fifteen years old by a
Russian Jew in his late twenties, he also seduces the Russian's lover in
order to celebrate his power over his seducer. Immediately he regrets
this action: 'I was filled with a sudden sense of loneliness – which I have
never lost.'[56]

When Huncke, and he has clearly been reading Genet, declares
himself a thief, the differences become even more apparent:

> As I became a thief and less concerned with surface evaluations – the opinions
> of the majority – recognizing only a few friends – and not always sure of them
> – learning at the same time of the world of the spirit – linking me – all of us
> – together – it not mattering our outer husk – only in this world – this life –
> beginning to secure the oneness of the inner force – observing the drive and
> what became to me the direction of the individual entity toward the 'is' of
> life – feeling instinctively – and with assurance – all becomes the one God –
> the one indestructible force – power – energy – drive – call it what you
> choose – or by any word – I became more fully aware of a sense of peace.[57]

In Genet, surface and depth are not separate but locked in a static
mirror reflection of each other. The world of thieves endlessly betrays,
there is no transcendental 'is' transforming the existential moment, and,
while there is a similar sense of a vitalistic force, there is no notion of
'peace'. God appears to Genet in the monstrousness of his lovers; God
for Huncke is a hopeful transcendental nothingness. Genet earns his
solitude; Huncke fears it. Genet sees his guilt as simplifying the path
to sainthood; Huncke just suffers.

Nostalgia is the first and last mood of Huncke's autobiography, *Guilty
of Everything*, published only recently, in 1990. Today's, as opposed to
yesterday's drug scene, the milieu of the saint, is cold-blooded and rapid,
mirroring the impersonal world of the corporation and take-over wars,
and the contingent interchanges of the city. There is a sense that the
book's groundbass theme is a 1930s, or even 1920s sense of the glamour
of the carnivalesque (Harlem Renaissance) alternative scene, associated
with drugs and linked to the demi-monde through fashion and dealing.
It involved manfacturing a style (Huncke is as obsessed with clothes as
Dreiser) to hurl at the centrist compromises of the bourgeoisie:

> In the old days, believe it or not, a junkie used to be a role model of a sort.
> He'd be on the corner draped down with his Italian silk suit, his handmade
> shoes, his Stetson or his specially-made hat that had to be handled just so
> and tilted just right; and with his new car, and his old lady by his side
> wearing just this side of Bergdorf Goodman.[58]

Though Huncke lacked Kerouac's literary skills and his guilt-strewn Catholicism, he could cope with his drug habit better, and was mercifully unencumbered by the damage of Oedipal relations. *Guilty of Everything* is a combination of confession, personal narrative, and cautionary tale. It feeds into and plays with major American anxieties. For example, an early incident involves being shaken down by 'the biggest, blackest man you ever saw in your life with the longest blade you've ever seen' (p.2) and stripped naked. The difference between 1980s New York, say, and prewar Amsterdam, is the impersonality of that threat. Genet, who dreamed of being fucked by a black man, would have had in an actual encounter other multiple links with his would-be attacker in a sociality of underclass liaisons. He might also have imagined his delicious crucifixion at such a person's hands.

Huncke's take on the situation has all the humour of the mumbling, grumbling *practical* victim, built over the absence of any moralistic, guilty, or even panicking response. The humour is the distance between the high drama of the death threat and the inability to summon up anything but a low key (not even deadpan) response. Consequently there is neither guilt nor panic in his response. There's a practical 'sauve qui peut' which constitutes part of the humour, but nothing else:

> They took the coat. I happened to have good clothes. (I always tried to keep myself fairly well groomed.) Here was a good winter coat that I'd just bought – gone. Then my gloves went, my suit – the suit didn't fit either one of them but they figured they might be able to get in hock. In those days you could hock clothes in hock shops for money. (p.3)

The humour of the response mixes the sentimental with the Gothic. Huncke is a pundit in the grand American tradition, his tone edges into the archness of a Huckleberry Finn.

For the upper-middle-class school boy (no less than for Burroughs), there was nonetheless a searching curiosity about the urban underworld, then a string of jobs to support developing habits with varieties of drugs. For six years from roughly 1934–40 he 'didn't do anything but float around the country' (p.37), presumably with a lot of other unemployed men, though no sense of the world of the Depression comes through at all, just as any wider sense of political life is absent in Genet. Here, the details are tantalisingly brief (as throughout the book), but what comes across is a life of adventures initially prompted by fury at the betrayals of the bourgeois world and its limitations.

Huncke is a radical Utopian anarchist: one extreme of that complex individualism. He is unremittingly curious about his fellow human beings, but placed under the necessity of cheating them in order to survive. The absence of moral judgement parallels that of Genet, and enables him to survive by cruising, busting cars, dealing, shipping out (one time getting over to Wales in war time and slipping the ship's sugar and bananas to the people of the Rhondda valley), doing time: 'It turned out to be my first prison experience and although in many respects unpleasant, at the same time very interesting' (p.46). The difference between Huncke here and the later Timothy Leary is crucial. Huncke has an absorbing curiosity about the world *outside himself*. He earns through deviance and courage the absolute right to his own quiet self-confidence.

Huncke's sense of reality was born of necessity. One major difference between a Huncke and a Burroughs was that he always risked, in a tight fix, *not* having family or friends to bale him out. The winter of 1948 is an exemplary moment for the kind of isolation and class discrimination Huncke could face on his way to ending up in Sing-Sing. Busted for robbery with Allen Ginsberg (who had been naïvely receiving and hoarding stolen goods), Jack Melody, and Vickie Russell, their immediate respective fates expose the legal and punishment system in the US in very clear ways. Ginsberg had at this point to his credit literally pulled Huncke out the gutter and had been naïve and generous to the point of confusion in his dealings with the three petty thieves as the episode is told in Miles' biography of Ginsberg.[59] Told from Huncke's side, however, it's clear he took the rap: 'I ended up doing a bit. Somebody had to do it' (p.108).

The hierarchy of punishments had everything to do with personal relations with the 'straight' world. Ginsberg had a lawyer brother who pulled him clear. His distinguished poet and labour-leader father and Lionel Trilling got him to the Psychiatric Institute rather than to Sing-Sing. He had the support of famous men like Van Doren of Columbia who, however, told him that if he thought Huncke an 'illuminated saint' he should go to jail for his beliefs. Meyer Schapiro was more sympathetic for he had once been 'arrested and put in jail for being a "stateless bum" in Europe as a young traveler'.[60] Jack Melody got off with psychiatric treatment for a year. He was the son of the Secretary Treasurer of the eastern seaboard Mafia, and his wife, Jackie's mother, 'looked like soneone out of a wild gypsy story – an old crone with henna-red hair that stood out like a halo round her face' (p.103). Mama Melody 'knew everybody ... Jackie was her baby and she wasn't going to stand for him being put in jail' (p.104). Vickie Russell's father was a magistrate judge from a respectable family in Grosse Point, Michigan. In Huncke's words, 'he flew to New York and got his darling daughter' (p.108).

A more delightful display of the discreet charm of the bourgeoisie would be hard to imagine: The University, The Law, and The Mafia in cahoots, clucking over their children. Huncke at least had the dignity – and the misfortune – not to have institutional deals legitimated by the natural morality of the family, done over his head in defiance of equality before the law. Naturally, though, they tried. The parole board summoned his parents against Huncke's express wish – he was 33 years old – thus depriving him of his rights as a citizen. His father (whose truth is legitimated *a priori*) incriminated his son by speaking of the defiance of parental love (a lie). So armed, family and parole board prejudged him together. The one bright spot in the entire shoddy episode is that the actual judge (acting strictly on legal considerations and on a plea from the prisoner) gave him only half the maximum sentence.

Huncke quickly learnt the ritualistic moves of his oppressors, making distinctions between police and detectives, manipulating the hierarchies of power within the system, and getting wise to the psycho-theatre of arrest, charge and prison. Once inside the prison, Huncke is both wise to and naïve about the way the prison functions as a inner microscopic space of the world outside. There is no glory in Huncke's mood in the prison world, just a slightly world-weary and fatalistic acceptance of the way things are. The prison moment, however, created feelings of abandonment. Little given to self-pity Huncke remarks: 'I was cut off completely from the outside world I knew. It was a funny feeling not hearing from anyone. I admit I felt very bitter when I came out, I really did' (p.117).

He refused, however, the 'help' of offical state psychiatric hospitals, and that moment produces one of the few declarations of his own values and standards in the book:

> If I had to die a lingering death I did not want it to include personality and behavior adjustments at the hands of bureaucratic psychologists and their cohorts – the do-good social service types, conscientious and specialized in psychiatry. I believed myself far too old and settled in my ways for rehabilitation and had no desire to join the so-called society of present standards, nor to concede for one moment that it is other than maladjusted ... If I take drugs it is most certainly my business, and if it is against the law and I am caught that becomes my loss and I must pay in their coin. But they have no right to force me into a position where I must submit to mental probing and investigation under the guise of what is supposedly best or right for me. (p.181)

The strength of Huncke's book is his commitment to disengagement and dissent. Death by expert judgement as Szasz writes is a function of 'the increasing complexity of our artifical environment', a situation in which 'democracy may easily become technocracy'.[61] Huncke does not glory in his punishment, but he wants to take it on terms which preserve and acknowledge his transgression, to preserve the dignity of his antagonism to the state. Therapeutic intervention, declares Szasz, has two functions: 'one is to heal the sick, the other is to control the wicked'.[62] Huncke refused to see the two as synonymous.

Nonetheless Huncke lives, given his habit, from an early age that alternating ecstasy and despair of the absolute consumer. In that sense, his life is central to the contemporary world. But the saint, ever in need and without possessions, is caught in a permanent state of flux, which is only a delirium of freedom. Huncke wishes to escape the material world, but is caught again nonetheless when the drug itself becomes the universal equivalent of value. The moment of possession vicariously transcends the need and reproduces it. The roles are reversed. The body becomes parasite to the host of the drug itself. Whoever I give love to, I steal from. Losing and finding, the guest and the enemy, sacrifice and salvation become exact equivalents, as in the Christian injunction.

Huncke finds his 'home' in the tawdry, commercial brilliance of Times Square, at the heart of the intersections of the twenty-four hour city, where the square and hip world meet, where everyone is on display, where products become pure electronic signs and the tourist-freak couple perform their arhythmic dances of self-congratulation. The noisiest, the loudest, the most spectacular win a fleeting attention. Yet his role is paradoxically modest, even self-effacing, curiously detached in his manner with a touch of the nostalgia for the good old values, where carnival was something *worth* watching, and to be a junkie made you different, exotic, someone who took their freedom on their own terms and lived by it, who preferred personal individualised danger to mass murder, lived by their own code rather than participating as a 'normal' human being in the mass-madness that will destroy the planet. In that sense he is paradoxically close in character to Chandler's detective, Philip Marlowe.

The photographs tell a great deal. The clean, pressed white shirt, the transparent delicacy of the post-addiction facial skin against the irreducible context of a New York that still appears to have its soul in the movies of the 1930s. His is the ravaged city face that sometimes seems bemused at the attention of the famous and, at other times, half drawn in and out of memories, animated in the company of the young, but always in place with a sense of attention.

If Huncke was the passive angel, Cassady was the reluctant angel. There are at least two possible approaches to Cassady: as envisioned by others, and envisioned by himself in the vision of his own more crafted work.

As envisioned by others, he is variously: 'the American person that Whitman sought to adore';[63] 'Mailer's White Negro raised exponentially';[64] 'cocksman and Adonis of Denver';[65] 'a natural Buddhist';[66] 'a provincial Mouth shooting naif';[67] and 'a Billy Budd'.[68]

The mythic figure as such was calculated to offend positivist (rightwing) criminologist and old-fashioned liberal equally. The actual ritual breakout of young men usually ends by their early twenties and is ritualistic to the extent of engaging in a pattern of denunciation and retribution by society. However the 'Delinquent is casually, intermittently, and transiently immersed in a pattern of illegal action.'[69] Prolonged into adulthood, beyond the socio-biological cycle, this activity creates a new meaning rather than predictable behaviour. In Goodman's words, referring to Dostoevsky's characters, they were 'adult delinquents' and he added, 'In our time Genet has made of the doomed delinquent culture a powerful thought and poetry.'[70]

In real life, in the 'dominant culture of modern America – ranging in its portrayal from ascetic puritanism to the oath of boy scouts ... delinquency is mandatory'.[71] As such, it threatens no one, except the poor. Breakout, containment and punishment follow in a dreary cycle. Cassady will not fit Goodman's category of 'old fashioned poor',[72] except in his capacity to survive.

The greatest mythicisation of Cassady was of course Kerouac's. What is at issue here is not the 'truth' of the real life/myth opposition, but the construction of the myth within differing discourses.

Kerouac's mythicising was of a different order, and the figure that emerged was not homogeneous or simple. Gerald Nicosia is perhaps right to say that : 'Jack promoted Neal as a myth figure, just as Allen had done for Jack; in effect, Jack and Neal's relationship became a mirror image of the intense, almost priestly bond between Jack and Allen.'[73]

In *On The Road*, as well as holy fool and angel, Dean Moriarty (Cassady) is perhaps most of all the scapegoat. As well as being an embodiment of social and individual energy in Dionysian form, close to the ecstasy of the jazz rhythms, articulating the sacredness of sexual exchange, the eternal hope of renewal after divorce, and the hope of the eternal return itself, he is also the sacrificial victim. Here the sainthood of the beautiful man confronts the sainthood of the mother. Destiny is confirmed in the rejection of the one by the other. Pietà: the dead Christ in the arms of the holy mother: the nihilistic centre of the sacred.

The reverse and complementary figure of the sacrificial victim is the betrayer: two modes of the pseudo-passivity of evil. Genet embraces the role of betrayer consciously; Dean Moriarty, in his dual role as scapegoat and betrayer, unconsciously and furtively, protests his innocence. In that sense, Dean Moriarty is less evil than Genet for he lacks shrewdness. In the same way the women who represent the 'social good' indicate no more than a crude economic utilitarianism accompanied by piety:

the Carolyn Cassady who in real life did not like the naughty words in McClure's 'Fuck Ode'.

In *Visions of Cody*, Cassady, as Holmes once observed, is a more monumental than a dramatic figure.[74] Here, the ambiguity of the presentation in *On The Road* moves into obsessive contradiction. Cassady is at once devil and angel.The street speech and style that works its way from Cassady's into Kerouac's prose is clearly an occasion of guilt. The debt is reversed in the quasi-paranoid perception. 'Cody' is a 'devil, an old witch, even an old bitch form the start ... he can read my thoughts, and interpret them on purpose so I'll look on the world as he does'.[75] As *The Vision of Cody* progresses, so the dream vision of Cassady as Cody himself filters in. Here is one moment:

> It is a face that's so suspicious, so energetically upward-looking like people in passport or police line up photos, so rigidly itself, looking like it's about to do anything unspeakably enthusiastic, in fact so much the opposite of the rosy coke-drinking boy in the Scandinavian ski sweater ad, that in front of a brick wall where it says *Post no Bills* and it's too dirty for a rosy boy ad you can imagine Cody standing there in the raw gray flesh manacled between sheriffs and Assistant D.A.s and you wouldn't have to ask yourself which is the culprit and which is the law. He looked like that, and God bless him he looked like the Hollywood stunt man who is fist-fighting in place of the hero and has such a remote, furious, anonymous viciousness (one of the loveliest things in the world to see and we've all seen it a thousand times in a thousand B-movies) that everybody begins to be suspicious because they know the hero wouldn't act like that in a real unreality. If you've been a boy and played on dumps you've seen Cody, all crazy, excited and full of glee and power, giggling with the pimply girls in back of fenders and weeds till some vocational school swallows his ragged blisses and that strange American iron which later is used to mold the suffering man-face is now employed to straighten and quell the long wavering spermy disorderliness of the boy. Nevertheless the face of a great hero – a face to remind you that the great Assyrian bush of a man, not from an eye, an ear or a forehead – the face of a Simon Bolivar, Robert E. Lee, young Whitman, young Melville, a statue in the park, rough and free.[76]

This passage is in a tradition of the portrait of the American hero as composite myth. Melville had done the same for Billy Budd in his posthumously published story, particularly in the opening sequences. Read carefully, this passage shows Kerouac, too, building a pattern of conflicting characterisations from innocent hoodlum to the petrified hero of history. In terms of the American fictional hero, he is Leslie Fiedler's good bad boy, opposed for ever to the blond, good boy. He is also the Whitmanian average man transposed, via the movies, to the twentieth century. There is a grand binary allegory of order and disorder here which is the passage's strength and weakness. Its strength is its clear will to be on the side of the too-soon-crushed discarded young. The weakness is in the very need to create that Manichean world between 'nature' and 'iron' which recalls the psychological naturalism of the early part of the century, and between the opppositional types which merely play the system as carnival.

Turning now to Cassady's own account of himself, several things becomes clear at once. The first is that it is Cassady's the language whose diction and rhythms Ginsberg and Kerouac worked into their own different synthetic styles to an astonishing extent. Robert Stone, a friend of Kesey's described it as 1940s stuff: 'old time jail and musician and street patter ... American-Denver talk, what Kerouac liked to think of as Okie drawl, but with free-lancing Proustian detail'.[77] Yet the inventiveness goes beyond street talk with its buzz words, repetitions and proverbial variations. The language of the earlier part of the Prologue is quite different in its brilliant crispness and artful simplicity from the longer more 'Proustian' sentences it develops into later. There is, in fact, more than a touch of West, imitating Voltaire, in the piling up of incidents of woe in the earlier pages. It is Defoe with a hint of mockery in the narrative voice at its own omnipotence. Here, Neal describes his father with affectionate humour and with the authority of absolute historical statement:

> Anyway, he enlarged his social life immeasurably, and if one can point to a period in Neal's lifetime that was most balanced and contentedly full, it must be in the year or eighteen months following the mutilation of his nose. He was literally at his peak and the happiest he ever was to be.[78]

In short, there is artfulness in the style which gives the lie to Ferlinghetti's 'homespun, primitive prose', and a different slant to Carolyn Cassady's remark that 'he knew he was neither trained nor equipped to think of writing in terms of literary merit'. Kerouac, of course, admired his prose intensely, and neither he nor Ginsberg spared their efforts to encourage him.[79] That his radical nervousness and lack of intellectual self-discipline (almost an impossibility in any case, given the extraordinary disorder of his early life) frustrated his clear promise does not alter the case.

There is an epic quality of entry into the story, the journey to settlement of the days of the pioneers. It signals that sense of movement, once a historic fact, now a psychological restlessness, which will structure the movement throughout the work's compellingly irreducible and discrete details. But the epic requires that those details become enlarged into representative moments of archetypal conflict. The fight of the good and evil brothers, with the acquittal by jury of the good killer (the grandfather), who is victor points to a major American obsession with personal justice and law. Neal (the father), himself sixth and last child, is bullied by his brothers and partially protected by his sister. In a recurring pattern of small-town violence, and persecuted and humiliated by his sadistic school-teaching brother, Neal Sr makes the first of his attempts to flee from home.

In this intitial section, the language has a decorum which fits the subject matter precisely. The stubborn and empirical detail is often placed alongside a qualified abstraction, which might be taken as an inexperienced writer's search after authoritative literariness, but in fact, given the way Cassady handles it, manages to sidestep the danger to create a strangely haunting cadence, which mingles a tone of nervousness with elusive authority, and makes narrative itself the servant of mood: nostalgia, fear, and the shocks of accident.

Neal Jr, whose affection for his father seems to have been the one steadfast love of his life, went, as he lugubriously puts it, at six years old with 'his wino father into the lowest slums of Denver' to become the 'natural son of a few score beaten men' (pp.46–7). The resultant 'freedom' is a freedom from that experience of the internalised emotional and physical violence of the American family under economic pressure, and rightwing imperatives to consider the family a holy site of bio-sociality. The father provided a role model of the life of absolute failure which, given the American context in which economic failure is sign of a moral and spiritual degeneracy, has a particular poignancy. The father is the unconscious, will-less, speechless version of Genet's articulate saint:

> In his weakness, Father accepted complete subjugation to the power of his vice and, thus gripped by its onslaught, his unrebelling slavery to drink produced the sustaining force for a saint-like gentleness always displayed when he was sober. Deeply penetrated by the destroying excess of an uncontrolled flaw, his soul assumed the guilt which made unquestionable the right of his suffering, and without evident bitterness he would innocently accept the torment administered, as though unaware that he could protest. In him this Christian virtue of 'turning the cheek' was no pretension ... (p.77)

Cassady reacted to the helpless and beloved father with the only response he could draw on: *speed* – of both mind and body. It was the *slowness* of the father, his endless still passion which formed such a powerful antithesis to the American Way. For Cassady needed movement and noise against the immobility and dumbness of the father. But he also internalised that furious speed that America's own commitment to its futuristic destiny, its competitive restlessness, seemed to require. Virilio speaking of the futurists once declared: 'In fact the human body huddling in the "steel alcove" is not that of the bellicose dandy seeking

the rare sensations of war, but of the doubly-unable body of the pro-
letarian soldier.'[80]

In her magnificent essay, 'Must we Burn Sade?', Simone de Beauvoir
declared herself tempted to make 'a very cautious comparison between
this conception of perpetual motion [the exhaustion of Sade's repetitive
excursions into dissolution exhaustion and annihilation] and the Hindu
doctrine of *samsara*':

> Nature's aspiration to escape from herself in order to recover an uncondi-
> tioned state would seem to be a dream much like that proposed by the
> notion of Nirvana – at least to the extent that a Western man has a capacity
> for such dreams. Sade, rather than setting off on the path which Schopenhauer
> searched for, thrashes out the one Nietzsche was to follow: the acceptance
> of *samsara*, the *eternal return of the same thing*.[81]

Certainly that erotic movement and the spiritual existence have their
repetitive convergences in their search for innocence.

The young Cassady's movement has not yet obtained the yo-yo-like
self-hypnosis of petrochemical-injected movements across the continent.
The journeyings are journeyings of marvellously told, youthful nostalgias
on foot, where the poor could still *walk* through the city in the sun
without harassment on quiet Sundays, through the deserted business
warehouses whose Christian owners resisted capitalism's final speeding
up of commercial life into twenty-four-hour business, seven days a
week. Without the family, notoriously quarrelsome because taken off
the labour fix for a day, Neal Sr and Neal Jr could make something of
the 'sabbath-deserted street'. No less than for Melville's Ishmael, the
Sabbath streets lead to water, to where 'the South Platte River passes
beneath the 15th Street bridge of angle-iron and wood that squeaked
aloud in protest as autos pass over its rapidly deteriorating surface ...'
(p.82). The Platte provided the 'flexuous corridor for my travels', a
difference in tone and emphasis from Kerouac's description of Riverside
Street in *Dr Sax*, which leads to a more transcendent Merrimac and to
a more cosmic sea.[82] Though geographically far away, technologically
the world is that of Williams' *Paterson*: an industrial world of iron, mill,
brick, steam, country viaducts which provided superb climbing frames
for boys. The still places are the factories and schools which crush the
spirit. They exist at the nexus of intersecting points of movement.

With its echoes of Proust the walk to school is one of the virtuoso
passages in the book. There is a visionary quality to these pages where
mastery over self-initiated movement is developed in the long run to
the schoolhouse: dribbling the tennis balls, avoiding pavement cracks,
creating a zig-zag route to save time, skirting banks whose 'enormous

bronze doors of scrolled bas-relief (featuring charioteered archers, mostly) were never opened'. Each detail has the quality of a sign which moves beyond its immediate meaning, like the fleeting glimpses of a city which become dream icons of consciousness in a French *nouvelle vague* movie.[83] Or, perhaps, details are closer to images – the same quality to be found in Ginsberg's poetry which he took in turn from Whitman's 'haiku' style.[84]

The zig-zag route is the enforced penitents' journey through the maze – here recaptured for the authority of the self. The cracks in the pavement are ancient signs of taboo and superstition. In the words of the Opies, when the child walks to school, the 'day ahead looms large and endless in front of him, and his eyes are wide open for the prognostics which will tell him his fortune'.[85] The same authors also report that, in the United States, 'pavement lore' is more uniform than in Britain. In Illinois, Iowa, New Jersey, Louisiana, New York State, Ohio, and Texas, the child says 'Step on a crack' and continues 'You'll break your mother's back' or 'You'll break your grandmother's back' or 'Break the devil's back'.[86]

'The block of Arapahoe Street whorehouses' speaks of more adult matters, and of more than one social rape. The 'mighty colonnaded Post Office' hanging over the cheap stores of Curtis street is a rival for that scrolled bas-relief of the bank's doors. Its neo-classical style, in the tradition of American architecture and once signifying the democracy of Athens, is now a sign of power whose presence intimidates the shopkeepers and bums of the poor city streets. There's humour here, too, as he hears in his swift journey 'from the depths of musty second hand clothing stores, screech sounds of serious adolescent violin lessons'. Again, tone and meaning hesitate between endorsement and rejection.

Indeed, many of the fleeting images point to a sense of potential entrapment which the boy's run circumvents by skill and speed. The image of the public fountain flowing through winter and sometimes choked by ice, the movement of the young boy on to it to drink before getting his feet wet, and the sententious motto inscribed on its base, 'Desire rest but desire not too much', all indicate the potential for being trapped between the stern authoritarian and therefore contradictory commands of simultaneous movement and stasis. The 'weaving run' moves between the colonnaded Stout street, along the tightrope of the 'angled top of a half-foot high sidewalk border' of the Federal Building. But all the self-testing is on his own terms. Crossing spaces without taking breath in long takes is a favourite activity, and is linked with his later car escapades. First and foremost, said Huizinga, 'play is a voluntary activity'.[87]

Here, that voluntary activity is set within the shadow of its opposite: the unfulfilling labour America offers to the young and poor. Unlike Huizinga's 1940s anthropological and structuralist self-balancing universe of adaptive play, there is a strange sense of menace in Cassady's run to school. The boy's feat of leaping from the top of a swing's arch onto the iron pipe guardrail of the playground, not only suggests obvious lurking danger but a kind of Gothic potential of escape from the prison by exceptional feats of daring. The Denver business school nestles between a Catholic church with 'matching slender spires of rough stone' and the Denver Bible Insitute, 'whose odd belfry was a squat clapboard affair of afterthought'. It's business as usual between the Catholic senses and the Protestant spirit.

The threat to the body and soul is about equal. This Wordsworthian education by beauty and fear is even captured in the deliberately archaic phrase – 'often the chase led upwards' (on the homeward run) – but it ends on arrival at school with the shades of the prison house: 'Around the entire block-square schoolyard ran a seven foot woven wire fence that enclosed all and was made by a U.S. Steel subsidiary, as a metal tag attached every few yards testified.' The sign attached to fences seems magically to invest the very patrolling of borders with the public product's privatised name. It is indeed a man's retrospective dream of a boy's freedom in a world of slavery but it is placed within a prosody which indicates full consciousness of the fact in every image.

It is speed which holds the whole thing together. And finally it is not enough. It moves toward the vertiginous melancholy of its own solip-sistic centre. As early as 1948, Cassady was writing to Ginsberg about his 'periods of semi-consciousness', where he speaks of the conjuncture of marijuana and psychology as seeming to open possibilities of both freedom and imprisonment. The passage in this letter of 1948 describes a condition which seems to lead to that more productive, more poten-tially creative foreground, which Bachelard would call *reverie* – 'not dreams, nor guilt nightmares, but, are great impressions of things'.[88]

It is clear that Cassady has great difficulty in distinguishing the poetics of reverie from the troubling nightmares of guilt, frustration and wish-fulfilment, and it is also clear, particularly in the letter, that Bachelard's words, 'Writing a book is always a hard job. One is always tempted to limit himself to dreaming it', are all too appropriate.[89] In *The First Third*, however, Cassady's speculations on consciousness are more complexly thematised. His perpetual fear of suffocation, though he gives the actual origins of the fear, has the quality of psychological exemplar and, as written, joins an American theme which goes back to Poe, and to the intense examination of dream, drug, and religious vision in William James.[90] Characteristically, in the following example, he speaks of the sensation of speed, of spinning sensations, the acceleration of time:

> But the prime requisite – to hold still as death and listen intently for the inner ear to speed up its buzz until, with regular leverlike flips, my mind's gears were shifted by unknown mechanism to an increase of time's torrent that received in kaleidoscopic change searing images, clear as the hurry of thought could make them, rushing so quickly by that all I could do was barely catch the imagery of one before another crowded ... I failed to match these mental eruptions firmly enough to any reasonable explanations in reality, so that the cause, cure or real workings of these singularly fresh and concise visions were forever beyond my diagnosis, in fact beyond my remembering, except as residue, almost every flashing scene once it had spun by. (p.113)

The passage can be read in many different ways, as a 'romantic' attempt, neo-Platonically, to describe the threshold and absence of original vision; as a reworking of the thematics of the book in relation to memory, speed, and failure; and as a description of the drug experience. In fact, however, the general argument is sadly predicated not on the poet's confidence in reverie, but on the failure of the ordinary world to validate the experience, thus producing a general sense of impotence. Time is drugged, not suspended in the magic of the imagination's ability to close down the world of anxiety. It perhaps sums up Cassady's relation to the more disciplined writers of the circle. He internalises their more articulate, diagnostic and memory-rich sense of himself, he becomes the object of their dreams and is robbed of that *reverie œuvrant*, the reverie that prepares books – except, paradoxically, in this one instant, where he records the failure of speed to produce that tranquillity which would make him the author of his own solitude.[91] For, finally, it is just in that record of failure that the stories of Huncke and Cassady are most moving. They turn failure into celebration in the face of a society which denies that very possibility.

NOTES

1. The question is Kerouac's. Ginsberg to Cassady, quoting Kerouac, 4 September 1953 in *As Ever: The Collected Correspondence of Allen Ginsberg & Neal Cassady*, Foreword by Carolyn Cassady, Afterword by Allen Ginsberg, ed. and introd. Barry Gifford (Berkeley, California: Creative Arts Book Company, 1977), p.153. This work will be referred to hereafter as *The Collected Correspondence*.
2. Ginsberg to Cassady, [n.d., Sept] 1948 in *The Collected Correspondence*, p.51.
3. William Burroughs, *Queer* (London: Pan Books, 1986), p.49.

4. John Milton, *Areopagitica; a Speech of Mr John Milton For the Liberty of Unlicenc'd Printing* (London, 1644) p.12.
5. Philip Thody, ed. and trans., *Albert Camus: Selected Essays and Notebooks* (Harmondsworth: Penguin Books, 1970) p.271.
6. Ted Morgan, *Literary Outlaw, the Life and Times of William S. Burroughs* (New York: Henry Holt and Company, 1988) p.487.
7. Carolyn Cassady, *Off the Road: Twenty Years with Cassady, Kerouac and Ginsberg* (1990; rpt London: Flamingo, 1991) p.313.
8. George Butterick (ed.), *Charles Olson & Robert Creeley: The Complete Correspondence*, Vol. 1 (Santa Barbara: Black Sparrow Press, 1980) p.47.
9. Norman Mailer, 'The White Negro: Superficial Reflections on the Hipster', *Dissent* (Summer, 1957) pp.276–93, rpt in *Advertisements for Myself* (New York: Putnam, 1957).
10. Carolyn Cassady, *Off the Road: Twenty Years with Cassady, Kerouac and Ginsberg* (London: Flamingo, 1991) p.166.
11. Tom Clark, *Jack Kerouac: A Biography* (1984; rpt New York: Paragon House, 1990) p.5.
12. Jack Kerouac, *Visions of Cody*, introd. Allen Ginsberg (London: André Deutsch, 1973) p.xi.
13. Louis Zukofsky, '*A*' 4 in '*A*' (Berkeley, Los Angeles and London: University of California Press, 1928) p.32.
14. Cassady to Ginsberg, 4 September 1953 in *The Collected Correspondence*, p.153
15. Jean-Paul Sartre, *Saint Genet, actor and martyr*, trans. Bernard Frechtman (New York: Pantheon Books, 1963), p.5.
16. Robert Duncan, *The Truth and Life of Myth: An Essay in Essential Autobiography* (Fremont, Michigan: The Sumac Press, 1968) p.8.
17. Ibid., p.14.
18. William Plummer, *The Holy Goof: A Biography of Neal Cassady* (New York: Paragon House, 1990) p.98.
19. Sartre, *Saint Genet*, p.195.
20. Ibid., p.200.
21. Paul Goodman, *Growing Up Absurd: Problems of Youth in the Organized Society* (New York: Vintage Books, 1960) p.189.
22. William Plummer, *Holy Goof*, p.101.
23. 'John Tytell Talks with Carl Solomon', in Arthur and Kit Knight (eds), *The Beat Vision: A Primary Sourcebook* (New York: Paragon House, 1987) p.242. Hereafter referred to as *The Beat Vision*.
24. Carolyn Cassady, *Off the Road*, p.222.
25. Barry Miles, *Ginsberg: A Biography* (London: Viking, 1990), p.127.
26. Eric Mottram, *Allen Ginsberg in the Sixties* (Brighton: Unicorn, 1972) pp.15.
27. See Eric Mottram, 'The Wild Good and the Heart Ultimately: Ginsberg's Art of Persuasion', *Spanner*, Vol. II, No. 5 (July 1978).
28. Interview with Gary Snyder by James McKenzie in *The Beat Vision*, p.10.
29. Goodman, *Growing Up Absurd*, p.187.
30. Gerald Nicosia, *Memory Babe: A Critical Biography of Jack Kerouac* (Harmondsworth: Penguin Books, 1986) p.146.
31. Plummer, *Holy Goof*, p.35.

32. Allen Ginsberg and Allan Temko respectively in Barry Gifford and Lawrence Lee, *Jack's Book: An Oral Biography of Jack Kerouac*, pp.42–3, 66.
33. Nicosia, *Memory Base*, p.139.
34. James McKenzie, 'An Interview with Allen Ginsberg', in Arthur and Kit Knight, *Kerouac and the Beats: A Primary Sourcebook*, Foreword by John Tytell (New York: Paragon House, 1987) p.254.
35. Quoted by Wolf Lepenies, *Between Literature and Science: the Rise of Sociology*, trans. R.J. Hollingdale (Cambridge: Cambridge University Press, 1988) p.255.
36. Hayden White citing 'The Use and Abuse of History' in *Metahistory: The Historical Imagination in Nineteenth-Century Europe* (Baltimore and London: The Johns Hopkins University Press, 1973) p.355.
37. Jack Kerouac, *On The Road* (London: Pan Books, 1961) p.12.
38. White, *Metahistory*, p.361.
39. Stuart H. Hughes, *Consciousness and Society: The Reorientation of European Social Thought 1890–1930* (New York: Vintage Books, 1977) p.105.
40. Fyodor Dostoevsky, *The Idiot*, trans. and introd. David Margashack (Harmondsworth: Penguin Books, 1955) p.97.
41. Mottram, 'The Wild Good', p.71.
42. Neal Cassady to Allen Ginsberg, 3 August 1948 in *The Collected Correspondence*, p.38. Cassady remarks in the next paragraph: 'of course we've all been long familiar with Dost.'s work The Idiot. Personally, I first read it in 1943 in a reform school on the pacific coast …'.
43. Neal Cassady to Allen Ginsberg, [August 1948] in *The Collected Correspondence*, p.43.
44. Neal Cassady to Allen Ginsberg, 25 November 1950 in *The Collected Correspondence*, p.86.
45. Roland Barthes, *Writing Degree Zero*, trans. Annette Lavers and Colin Smith (New York: Hill and Wang, 1967) p.20.
46. Walter Benjamin, 'Karl Kraus' in *One Way Street and Other Writings*, trans. Edmund Jephcott and Kingsley Shorter (London: New Left Books, 1979) pp.282–4.
47. Simone de Beauvoir, 'Must we burn Sade?', introd. to The Marquis de Sade, *The 120 Days of Sodom and Other Writings*, compiled and translated by Austryn Wainhouse and Richard Seaver (New York: Grove Press, 1966) p.7.
48. Beauvoir, 'Must we Burn Sade?', p.29.
49. Allen Ginsberg to Neal Cassady, 14 May 1953, *The Collected Correspondence*, p.144.
50. Nicosia, *Memory Babe*, p.253.
51. Jean Genet, *The Thief's Journal*, trans. Bernard Frechtman (Harmondsworth: Penguin Books, 1967) p.13. Further references follow in the text.
52. Sartre, *Saint Genet: actor and martyr*, trans. Bernard Frechtman (New York: Pantheon Books, 1963) pp.379–80.
53. Georges Bataille, 'Genet and Sartre's Study' in *Literature and Evil*, trans. Alastair Hamilton (London, New York: Marion Boyars, 1985) pp.173–208.
54. Norman O. Brown, *Love's Body* (New York: Vintage Books, 1968) p.132.

55. Herbert Huncke, *Huncke's Journal, Drawings by Erin Matson* (New York City: The Poet's Press, 1965) p.1.
56. Ibid., pp.9–10.
57. Ibid., p.27.
58. Herbert Huncke, *Guilty of Everything, the Autobiography of Herbert Huncke*, Foreword by William S. Burroughs (New York: Paragon House, 1990) p.207. Further references to this work follow in the text.
59. Miles, *Ginsberg*, pp.105–16.
60. Ibid., p.119.
61. Thomas S. Szasz, *Psychiatric Justice* (New York: The Macmillan Company, 1965) p.11.
62. Thomas S. Szasz, *The Myth of Mental Illness,* rev. edn (New York: Harper and Row, 1974) p.69.
63. Jack Kerouac, *Visions of Cody*, p.xi. Allen Ginsberg commented on Neal's relation with Jack Kerouac: 'Whitman's adhesiveness! Sociability without genital sexuality between them.' See Allen Ginsberg: *The Visions of the Great Rememberer: with Letters by Neal Cassady and Drawings by Basil King* (Amherst, Mass.: Mulch Press, 1974) p.27.
64. Plummer, *Holy Goof*, p.9.
65. Allen Ginsberg, 'Howl' in *Collected Poems, 1947–1980*, p.128.
66. Jim Holms in *Jack's Book*, p.94.
67. Nicosia, *Memory Babe*, p.175. This was a general reaction of Ginsberg's group when Cassady first appeared in New York.
68. Pierre Delattre in *The Beat Vision*, p.59.
69. David Matza, *Delinquency and Drift* (New York, London and Sydney: John Wiley, 1964) p.28. Matza distinguishes the culture of delinquency sharply from 'the radical or bohemian tradition', p.37. I am most grateful to Dr S. Groarke for drawing my attention both to this and to other works of criminology on delinquency.
70. Goodman, *Growing Up Absurd*, p.197.
71. Matza, *Becoming Deviant* (Englewood Cliffs: Prentice Hall, 1969) p.19.
72. Goodman, *Growing Up Absurd*, pp.64, 168, 185.
73. Nicosia, *Memory Babe*, p.250.
74. Knight, *Kerouac and the Beats*, p.154.
75. Kerouac, *Visions of Cody*, p.298.
76. Ibid., p.48.
77. Cited in Plummer, *Holy Goof*, p.129.
78. Neal Cassady, *The First Third, & Other Writings*, rev. and expanded edn, with a new Prologue (San Francisco: City Lights, 1981) p.26.
79. Lawrence Ferlinghetti, editor's note to *The First Third*, and Carolyn Cassady, *The First Third*, p.140. Further references to this work follow in the text.
80. Paul Virilio, *Speed and Politics*, trans. Mark Polizzotti(New York: Semiotext, 1986) p.62.
81. Simone de Beauvoir, 'Must we Burn Sade?', p.79.
82. Jack Kerouac, *Dr Sax* (1959; rpt New York: Grove Weidenfeld, 1987) pp.7–9.
83. I am especially thinking of Agnes Varda's *Cleo from 5 to 7* (1961).

84. Ginsberg in conversation with author, at Warwick University, 1983, spoke of the phrasal image in Whitman's poetry as 'haiku'.
85. Iona and Peter Opie, *The Lore and Language of School Children* (London: Paladin, 1977) p.233.
86. Ibid., p.242.
87. Johan Huizinga, *Homo Ludens: A Study of the Play-Element in Culture*, author's translation (Boston: The Beacon Press, 1955) p.7.
88. Neal Cassady to Allen Ginsberg, 4 August 1948, in *The Collected Correspondence*, p.41.
89. Gaston Bachelard, *The Poetics of Reverie: Childhood, Language and the Cosmos*, trans. Daniel Russell (Boston: Beacon Press, 1969) p.66.
90. See the author's study of James' hypnogogic vision in *Halfway to Revolution: Investigation and Crisis in the Work of Henry Adams, William James and Gertrude Stein* (New Haven and London: Yale University Press, 1991) pp.249–58.
91. The phrases used here are Bachelard's. See *The Poetics of Reverie*, pp.173, 182.

8

Black Beats: The Signifying Poetry of LeRoi Jones/ Amiri Baraka, Ted Joans and Bob Kaufman

A. Robert Lee

Already well known and virtually revered in ultrahip literary circles, Roi had become by then a Greenwich village luminary. Along with New York's Ted Joans and San Francisco's Bob Kaufman, he was among a handful of mid-century African American poets whose early reputations are identified with the Beat Generation. We're talking here of course about a literary movement shaped, loosely speaking, by Whitmanesque confessionalism, the modernist iconoclasm of Ezra Pound, T.S. Eliot and William Carlos Williams, as well as by abstract expressionist painting, Eastern mysticism, drug culture and jazz.

> Al Young: 'Amiri Baraka (LeRoi Jones)', in J.J. Phillips,
> Ishmael Reed, Gundars Strads and Shawn Wong (eds.):
> *The Before Columbus Foundation Poetry Anthology* (1992)[1]

Williams was a common denominator because he wanted American Speech, a mixed foot, a variable measure. He knew American life had out-distanced the English rhythms and their formal meters. The language of this multi-national land, of mixed ancestry, where war dances and salsa combine with country and Western, all framed by African rhythm-and-blues confessional.

> *The Autobiography of LeRoi Jones/Amiri Baraka* (1984)[2]

I cannot deny that I am Ted Joans Afro American negro colored spade spook mau mau soul-brother coon jig darkie, etc.

> Ted Joans: *Tape Recording at the Five Spot* (1960)[3]

Let us blow African jazz in Alabama jungles and wail
savage lovesongs of unchained fire.

> Bob Kaufman: 'Jazz *Te Deum* for Inhaling at Mexican Bonfires',
> *Solitudes Crowded With Loneliness* (1959)[4]

I

Allen Ginsberg's 'Howl' (1955–56), the Grand Anthem of Beat poetry, has 'the best minds of my generation ... dragging themselves through the negro streets at dawn'. In *On The Road* (1957), Jack Kerouac invokes Harlem as quintessential 'Jazz America' while his narrator in *The Subterraneans* (1958) recalls 'wishing I were a Negro' when in Denver's 'colored section'. In 'The Philosophy of The Beat Generation', a key manifesto first published in *Esquire* in 1958, John Clellon Holmes eulogises Charlie Parker ('Bird') as black godfather to the movement. Gregory Corso, for his part, puts him alongside Miles Davis in 'For Miles' (*Gasoline*, 1958), recalling a set 'when you & bird/wailed five in the morning some wondrous/yet unimaginable score'. Norman Mailer, whose 'The White Negro' (1957) served as apologia for Beat and Hipster alike, found himself arguing that 'the Negro's equality would tear a profound shift into the psychology, the sexuality, and the moral imagination of every White alive'. Could it ever be doubted that in virtually all white-written Beat poetry and fiction, or associated polemic, Afro-America supplies a touchstone, a necessary black vein of reference and inspiration?[5]

Yet black Beat writers themselves might well be thought to have gone missing in action. Only LeRoi Jones, still to metamorphise into Imamu Amiri Baraka, got reported in dispatches. That, however, had as much to do with his Greenwich Village 'bohemianism' – and the small magazine publication of his 'projective' early verse – as with a life begun in black Newark, New Jersey, and continued at Howard University and in the airforce. He thus seemed caught in the shadow of an already senior Beat pantheon of Kerouac, Ginsberg, Burroughs, Corso, Ferlinghetti, Clellon Holmes, Di Prima and the rest. Jones/Baraka, in fact, did have company: Ted Joans, the self-styled 'Afro-American surrealist', and Bob Kaufman, the Jewish-black and Zen-inclined 'Abomunist', to cite from his several manifestos,[6] and, among yet others, a painter-poet like A.B. Spellman or a verse-writing jazzman like Archie Shepp. But black writers or not, and whatever the borrowings from blues and black 'cool' and speech, Beat even so rarely seemed to speak other than from, or to, white America.

Jones hardly failed to acknowledge, at the time any more than later, this oversight towards his black fellow-writers. Thinking back on his co-editorship (with Hettie Jones) of the journal *Yugen* (1952–62), a major literary forum not only for the Beat but 'Black Mountaineers' like Charles Olson and Robert Creeley and 'New York School' virtuosi like Frank O'Hara and Kenneth Koch, he would recall in his *Autobiography*:

I was 'open' to all schools within the circle of white poets of all faiths and flags. But what had happened to the blacks? What had happened to me? How is it that only the one colored guy?[7]

The same held not only for *Yugen* but the host of other magazines which printed his early work, whether *Floating Bear, Kulchur, Penny Poems, Locus-Solus, Nomad/New York, Fuck You: A Magazine of the Arts, Naked Ear, Quicksilver, Combustion*, or *Red Clay Reader*.[8] It was no doubt further symptomatic, or at least some continuance of the assumed status quo, that he made himself the only black contributor to his own anthology of 'popular modernism', *The Moderns* (1963).[9]

This 'white social focus', however, as he calls it, and which included his marriage to Hettie Jones in 1958 and their shared participation in *Yugen*, would move quickly enough to a close.[10] First came his transforming visit to Cuba in 1960, about which, in 'Cuba Libre', he would write against the Cold War grain: 'the Cubans, and the other *new* peoples (in Asia, Africa, South America) don't need us, and we had better stay out of their way'.[11] Then, in quick order, came a politics of black nationalism, which also lay behind 1960s poems like 'BLACK DADA NIHILISMUS' – 'may a lost god damballah, rest or save us/against the murders we intend/against his lost white children/black dada nihilismus' – and his adversarial, myth-laden theatre one-acter, *Dutchman* (1964).[12] Almost all these transpositions and shifts of allegiance, too, had their foreshadowings in his voluminous essay work, later collected as *Blues People: Negro Music in White America* (1963), *Home: Social Essays* (1966) and *Black Music* (1967).[13]

His personal life took its own symbolic turn when he moved from Greenwich Village to Harlem, breaking not only with white bohemia but with Hettie Jones and their daughters. Suddenly he became news, a black figure of controversy. In the white media, his politics immediately typecast him as a voice of race-hatred. His literary work routinely attracted charges of anti-Semitism and a paranoia towards all of white America. In 1965, the proof seemed conclusive. Had not the FBI been called in to investigate his Harlem theatre-work and its funding through the *HARYOU-ACT*, arrested him and, among other things, accused him of building a gun arsenal? In other words, he and his Black Arts Movement had become part of a feared, insurrectionary impetus for which 'Black Power' served as the banner.

In fact he belonged to a far larger canvas.[14] In the South, that meant events like the Birmingham school bombings (1963), the Selma March (1965), and the desegregationist sit-ins at lunch counters and other 'Colored Only' facilities. It called up the 1950s white supremacism of Dixiecrats like Senator James Eastland of Mississippi, Governor Orval

Faubus of Arkansas, and Police Commissioner 'Bull' Connor of Birmingham, Alabama, with George Wallace and Lester Maddox waiting in the wings. More ominously still, it brought to mind the cross-burnings and violence of a revived Ku Klu Klan, aided at every turn by the South's White Citizens Councils (first established in Mississippi in 1954) and their camouflage of 'States Rights' and 'law and order'. In the North it increasingly meant 'long hot summers', the inner-city riots which burned from Watts, in 1962, to South Side Chicago, Harlem and Bedford-Stuyvesant, in 1964, and thereafter for much of the decade. By the end of the 1960s, in fact, no less than 150 American cities would have been enflamed. Nationally, America would be obliged to deal with the assassinations of John F. Kennedy in 1963, Malcolm X in 1965, and Martin Luther King in 1968.

Racially, the 1950s thus supply a series of preludes, especially for the key Civil Rights and Voter Registration bills of 1964 and 1965 passed by the Kennedy–Johnson congress: typically *Brown v. Board of Education of Topeka* (1954) which outlawed 'separate but equal' schooling; the Rosa Parks bus protest and ensuing economic boycott in Montgomery, Alabama (1955); and the court-ordered desegregation of Central High School in Little Rock, Arkansas (1957). Still to emerge, too, was a militant leadership beyond anything seen in the NAACP (National Association for the Advancement of Colored People) or Urban League, from King's Christian-pacifist SCLC (Southern Christian Leadership Conference founded in 1957), John Lewis' and then Stokely Carmichael's SNCC (Student Nonviolent Coordinating Committee founded in 1960), and Bobby Seale's and Huey Newton's Black Panthers (founded 1960) – with Eldridge Cleaver as its best known voice – to Elijah Muhammad's Nation of Islam as embodied in the charismatic Malcolm X and its warrior convert from boxing, Muhammad Ali. A change of consciousness, and beyond it a politics of strategic racial turnabout, South and North, indeed had been launched.

Even the Beats, bohemian and dissident as they may well have seemed to a white middle America which twice had voted in Eisenhower (in 1952 and 1956) and which had become gridlocked in consumerism and Cold War ideology, could not have anticipated 'black' as the force for change it was shortly to become. Not without cause had Robert Lowell, in his WASP confessional poem, 'Memories of Lepke', called the 1950s 'tranquillized',[15] or J.D. Salinger, in *The Catcher in The Rye* (1951), supplied Holden's 'phony' as the *mot clé* for generational ennui.[16] Among other complacencies, it was an age, after all, which still assumed 'Negro' or (as was still used) 'Colored', to be terms of acquiescence – no matter the bitter, exploitative history they encoded.

Which is not to suggest that rising black awareness lacked serious literary markers. Rarely, for instance, had 'witness' read more passionately, or with greater authority, than in the Harlem-driven, prophetic essays eventually to become James Baldwin's landmark trilogy, *Notes of a Native Son* (1955), *Nobody Knows My Name* (1955) and *The Fire Next Time* (1963).[17] If virtuosity were the touchstone, then that could be found in Ralph Ellison's bluesy, yet dazzlingly modernist, *Invisible Man* (1952),[18] or in the ongoing poetry of, say, Langston Hughes, Gwendolyn Brooks or Robert Hayden. 'Black', even so, had not yet become 'Beautiful'; exotic maybe, beginning to vaunt Afros and dashikis maybe, but still a minority America kept to the racial margins.

For Jones/Baraka, too, although he would soon go on to Africanise his name and indeed become a founding energy in the Black Arts Movement, the pathway to Black Power, first through community activism (initially in Harlem, then Newark) and, from 1974 onwards, through 'Third World Marxism', still lay some distance ahead. 'Black', at this stage, signified more a call to consciousness and culture. Equally, for Joans and Kaufman, however frequent their barbs at American racism or strong their belief in 'those TWO/beautiful words BLACKPOWER' (from Joans' poem, 'TWO WORDS'), theirs were literary black-resistance voices rather than allied to a specific politics.

In this connection, for instance, all three typically took up the Beat interests in Zen and Eastern-transcendental spirituality but frequently linked it to the blues – with Africa as a prime source of reference and imagery. Similarly, if their poetry could be sexually celebratory and playful, à la Ginsberg, it could also broach the racial taboos of sex, a Beat articulation (long continued in Joans and Kaufman) of the 'black' senses. Given, overall, then, a heritage 'up from slavery' and formed as much by jazz or spiritual or rap as by Blake and Whitman, Williams and Pound, who better to have adapted Beat to a black dispensation, or in an honoured African-American usage, to have made it signify?[19]

II

A number of linked references-back help situate Baraka as Beat poet. First, in the *LeRoi Jones/Amiri Baraka Reader* (1991), he and his co-editor, William J. Harris, supply precise dates for his Beat phase, namely 1957–62.[20] These constitute 'bohemian' years before 'ethnic consciousness' gave way to 'political consciousness'. The *Autobiography*, however, gives the circumstances and flavour of his relationship to the movement:

I'd come into the Village *looking*, trying to 'check,' being open to all flags. Allen Ginsberg's *Howl* was the first thing to open my nose, as opposed to, say, instructions I was given, directions, guidance. I dug *Howl* myself, in fact many of the people I'd known at the time warned me off it and thought the whole Beat phenomenon a passing fad of little relevance. I'd investigated further because I was looking for something. I was precisely open to its force as the statement of a new generation. As a line of demarcation from 'the silent generation' and the man with the ... grey flannel skin, half brother to the one with the grey flannel suit. I took up with the Beats because that's what I saw taking off and flying somewhere resembling myself. The open and implied rebellion – of form and content. Aesthetic as well as social and political. But I saw most of it as Art, and the social statement as merely our lives as dropouts from the mainstream. I could see the young white boys and girls in their pronouncements of disillusion with and 'removal' from society as related to the black experience. That made us colleagues of the spirit.[21]

A 1980s interview sets these remembrances within a wider historical perspective:

Beat came out of the whole dead Eisenhower period, the whole of the McCarthy Era, the Eisenhower blandness, the whole reactionary period of the 50s. The Beat Generation was a distinct reaction to that, a reaction not only to reactionary politics, reactionary life style of American ruling class and sections of the middle class, reaction to conservatism and McCarthyism of that period. Also reaction to the kind of academic poetry and academic literature that was being pushed as great works by the American establishment. So it was a complete reaction: socially, politically, and of course artistically to what the 50s represented. That whole opening and transformation of course had its fullest kind of expression in the 60s in the Black Liberation Movement.[22]

There also remains to hand the Beat aesthetic as Baraka fashioned it in the late 1950s, published under the rubric 'How Do You Sound?' in 'The Statements on Poetics' section of Donald Allen's *The New American Poetry* (1960).[23] Revealingly, Black Power – cultural nationalism at least – nowhere features in any explicit way. Rather Baraka takes aim at New Critical academicism, advocating open forms and fields of expression. The formulation (right down to the abbreviations and punctuation) shows the residual impress of Charles Olson, together with a Ginsbergian, and behind that a Whitmanesque, will to inclusiveness:

'HOW DO YOU SOUND??' is what we recent fellows are up to. How *we* sound; our peculiar grasp on, say: a. Melican speech, b. Poetries of the world, c. Our selves (which is attitudes, logics, theories, jumbles of our lives, & all that),

d. And the final ... The Totality Of Mind: Spiritual ... God?? (or you name it): Social (zeitgeist): or Heideggerian *umwelt*.

MY POETRY is anything I think I am. (Can I be light & weightless as a sail?? Heavy & clunking like 8 black boots.) I CAN BE ANYTHING I CAN. I make a poetry with what I feel is useful & can be saved out of all the garbage of our lives. What I see, am touched by (CAN HEAR) ... wives, gardens, jobs, cement yards where cats pee, all my interminable artifacts ... ALL are a poetry, & nothing moves (with any grace) pried apart from all these things. There cannot be closet poetry. Unless the closet be wide as God's eye.

And all that means that I *must* be completely free to do just what I want, in the poem.[24]

Given the self-liberative urgings, the affirmations and the learning lightly worn and, as it were, spoken, this might be thought virtually a Beat poem in its own imaginative right, or at least some prose equivalent. Certainly, it links directly to the twenty-plus poems which make up his *Preface to a Twenty Volume Suicide Note* (1961), the volume which taken in retrospect has most become associated with his part in the Beat movement.[25]

'You are/as any other sad man here/american' Jones has his speaker confide in 'Notes for a Speech', the collection's closing poem which pointedly echoes Countee Cullen's 'Heritage', a New Negro classic from the 1920s ('What is Africa to me ... *One three centuries removed/From the scenes his fathers loved,/Spicy grove, cinnamon tree,/What is Africa to me?*'). Jones' black bohemian would seem to have lost touch not only with Africa but African-American life and origins. Yet even as he considers that double deracination, the measure of his lament sounds blues-like and drawn from the most intimate repertoire of his own blackness. This applies, too, in the title poem, which opens proceedings on a note of generalised alienation ('Nobody sings anymore'), only to give that same alienation the lie by the sight of his young, cross-racial daughter, Kellie Jones, at prayer.[26]

Other poems in *Preface* likewise do double duty. In 'For Hettie', his affectionate, roistering mock-complaint at his pregnant wife's 'left-handedness' points obliquely to other (for example, racial) styles of 'difference'. In 'For Hettie in Her Fifth Month' he attempts, with just a hint of William Carlos Williams, to catch both the otherness of pregnancy itself and of the unborn child – the latter as 'one of Kafka's hipsters,/parked there/with a wheelbarrow'. Even lyrical vignettes like 'Symphony Sid' or 'Theory of Art' hint of a racialised sexuality. At yet another reach are the poems dedicated to his co-Beats. 'One Night Stand', for Ginsberg, teases the triumphalist fervour of the New Bohemia ('We entered the city at noon! The radio on ...'), a funny-wry vision of Beat's legions as dressed out in motley and full of pose:

We *are* foreign seeming persons, Hats flopped so the sun can't scald
our beards; odd shoes, bags of books & chicken. We have come a long
way, & are uncertain which of the masks
is cool.

'Way Out West', for Gary Snyder, explores perceptual process from 'As
simple an act/as opening the eyes' to 'Closing the eyes. As/Simple an
act. You float' – as if, whether in an America of Sheridan Square or a
Greece of Tiresias, to emphasise how the poet's vision must always be
as inner as it is outer. Snyder's Zen affinities undoubtedly had aroused
an answering note in Jones.

Probably the most Beat-cum-projective composition in *Preface*,
however, is to be found in 'Look For You Yesterday, Here You Come
Today', its title taken from an old blues line, as if to give added emphasis
to the memories of an American childhood fast giving way to a meaner,
tougher, 'adult' human order. The note is nostalgic, yet a nostalgia itself
chastised and mocked. 'I have to trim my beard in solitude./I try to hum
lines from "The Poet in New York"', confides the speaker, a kind of
latterday Prufrock, unable to seize a true direction for his life. 'It's so
diffuse being alive', the speaker continues, juxtaposing an existence in
which 'terrible poems come in the mail', a dark Strindbergian feeling
comes over him at his wife's pregnancy, a Frank O'Hara prefers silence
to 'Jack's incessant yatter', and his own thoughts, in a nice put-down
of literary self-consciousness, have become 'Flowers of Evil/cold &
lifeless/as subway rails'.

Only 'dopey mythic worlds hold', a childhood pop-culture arcade
which includes Tom Mix (now 'dead in a Boston Nightclub/before I
realized what happened'), Dickie Dare, Captain Midnight, Superman
and the Lone Ranger ('THERE *MUST* BE A LONE RANGER!!!'). These
stalwarts (they have company in the Hammett title-figure reference of
'The Death of Nick Charles' and the broadcaster references to Lamont
Cranston and The Shadow of 'In Memory of Radio') thus lie behind in
time and place, tokens of a pristine order. The loss is palpable – 'My
silver bullets all gone/My black mask trampled in the dust … & Tonto
way off in the hills/moaning like Bessie Smith'. One just about hears a
LeRoi Jones ready to move on from Beat self-absorption into politici-
sation, with Bessie Smith, as much as other black touchstones, likely
to be invoked for altogether more committed ends and purposes.

In this respect few poems in *Preface to a Twenty Volume Suicide Note*
assume a 'blacker' animus than 'Hymn for Lanie Poo' (the nickname
of his sister, Sandra Elaine). Freely associative in range, it develops a
montage of skilfully parodic, if at times rueful, slaps at white social norms
and their emulation by America's black middle class. Rimbaud's *Vous*

êtes de faux Nègres offers the point of departure, with sequences to follow indicting white America's taste for primitivising superstitions about sunburnt black skin, Lanie's Gatsbyesque 'coming-out party/with 3000 guests/from all parts of the country' and the typical superficiality of most culture-talk about race. Jones' ending takes especial aim at black-bourgeois assimilationism and, as he sees it, the inevitable outcome of so obviously wrong a cultural turning:

> Smiling & glad/in
> the huge & loveless
> white-anglo sun/of
> benevolent step
> mother America

If the form (and tone) can be said to be Beat, it rests in the poem's spontaneous voices and transitions. Certainly, the playful iconoclasm can scarely be missed ('The god I pray to/got black boobies/got steatopygia ... '), any more than the self-ironising cliché ('it's impossible/to be an artist and bread/winner at the same time') or, with a perhaps irreverent eye (and ear) to Ginsberg and Snyder, the show of dubious 'oceanic' feeling ('Each morning/I go down/to Gansevoort St./and stand on the docks./I stare out/at the horizon/until it gets up/and comes to embrace/me. I/make believe it is my father./This is known/as genealogy.'). Throughout, and not least in its touches of phantasmagoria, ('A white hunter, very unkempt,/with long hair,/whizzed in on the end of a vine./spoke perfect english too.), 'Hymn for Lanie Poo' yields nothing less than a kind of flyting, an indictment at once regretful and angrily comic at how an American blackness can be made false to itself, even eviscerated.

From the start, therefore, and some time ahead of the Black-Nationalist and Marxist phases, Jones' poetry clearly involved a subtle overlap of both a personal and more inclusive racial feeling. 'Beat', as brief an affiliation as it may have been for the then LeRoi Jones, had, in other words, assumed its own mediating black textures.

III

Black Beat yields no more companionable a presence than Ted Joans. A self-pronounced Afro-surrealist, jazz adept, trumpeter, painter by early training, and lifelong performance poet, even into his sixties he continues to maintain the role of international stroller-player with alternating bases in Manhattan, Paris and Mali. His insistence has always been upon an oral poetry, a 'talking' blues or jazz – by his own count, one of 'funk' and 'afrodisia'. The connection to the Beat movement begins with his arrival in New York City in 1951, from Indiana, and an early link-up with Jack Kerouac. Their friendship, evidently full of warmth an unhampered by racial lines, is recalled by Joans in 'The Wild Spirit of Kicks', written to commemorate Kerouac's death in October 1969, and marked out by allusions to blues and jazz (including Kerouac's own 'Mexico City Blues'), on the one side, and to the Beat icon of 'the road', on the other:

JACK IN RED AND BLACK MAC
RUSHING THROUGH DERELICT STREWN
    STREETS OF NORTH AMERICA
JACK IN WELLWORN BLUE JEANS AND
    DROOPYSWEATER OF SMILES
RUNNING ACROSS THE COUNTRY LIKE A
    RAZOR BLADE GONE MAD
JACK IN FLOPPY SHIRT AND JACKET
    LOADED WITH JOKES
OLE ANGEL MIDNIGHT SINGING MEXICO
    CITY BLUES
IN THE MIDST OF BLACK HIPSTERS AND
    MUSICIANS
FOLLOWED BY A WHITE LEGION OF COOL
    KICK SEEKERS
POETRY LIVERS AND POEM GIVERS
PALE FACED CHIEFTAIN TEARING PAST

THE FUEL OF A GENERATION

AT REST   AT LAST

JK SAYS HELLO TO JC
JOHN COLTRANE, THAT IS[27]

Joans' prolific output, almost thirty titles in all – from *Funky Jazz Poems* (1959), *Beat Jazz Poems* (1960) and *All Of Ted Joans And No More Poems* (1960) and running through to *Wow: Selected Poems of Ted Joans* (1991) – perhaps met its greatest success in two late-1960s (and still available) collections, *Black Pow-Wow: Jazz Poems* (1969) and *Afrodisia* (1970).[28] Both exhibit Joan's laconic wit and wordplay at strength, a largely freeform, 'spoken' poetry in which blues, jazz, sex, Black Power, Africa and surrealist motif (his debt to André Breton is acknowledged in 'Nadja

Rendezvous') plait one into another.[29] His own working credo especially shows through in 'Passed on Blues: Homage To A Poet', a celebration of Langston Hughes, which opens affectingly on the following note:

> the sound of black music
> the sad soft low moan of jazz ROUND ABOUT MIDNIGHT
> the glad heavy fat screaming song of happy blues
> That was the world of Langston Hughes.

As it works its way through a montage of reference to Harlem nights, Jesse Simple bars, downhome food (whether 'pinto beans', 'Hamhocks In The Dark', 'grits' or 'spareribs'), the A-Train, 'the dozens', 'the rumping blues', 'migrated Dixieland', the Jitterbug, rent parties, 'Ain't misbehavin'' and 'sweaty, hard-working muscle' – all, as he says, 'THE WORLD OF THE POET LANGSTON HUGHES/BLACK DUES!/BLACK BLUES!/BLACK NEWS!' – the poem becomes both a homage to Hughes' lyric genius and to Afro-America's First City, a 'sonata of Harlem'. It also bespeaks Joans' own considerable inventive talent, his ventriloquist fusion of Beat and jazz.

This fusion extends throughout most of *Black Pow-Wow* and *Afrodisia*. In the former, in 'O Great Black Masque', for instance, he invokes a negritude embracing Bouake and Alabama, Mali and Manhattan, which suggests at one and the same time the cadences of the Black Spiritual and of Whitman. In 'For the Viet Congo', an indictment of black Third World exploitation set out in capitalised typescript, he simulates what might be a newspaper 'Report From The Front' made over into verse form. The comic, teasing side to Joans comes through in his 'No Mo' Kneegrow', written while flying over Dixie ('I'M FLYING OVER ALABAMA/WITH BLACK POWER IN MY LAP') and which, according to his own gloss, 'can be sung to the tune of "Oh! Susannah"', a short but infinitely to the point piece of satiric wordplay on the price of racial deference; or 'Uh Huh', a line-up of seemingly muttered banalities from behind which he takes aim at 'THE COLORED WAITING ROOM'; or 'Santa Claws' which opens with 'IF THAT WHITE MOTHER HUBBARD COMES DOWN MY BLACK CHIMNEY ...' and goes on to lampoon Santa as some white patriarchal 'CON MAN'. Nor can there be any mistaking the angrier Joans, as in his well-known 'The Nice Colored Man', which offers a column of therapeutic, iconclastic variations on the word 'nigger', beginning from 'Nice Nigger Educated Nigger Never Nigger Southern Nigger' and working through to

> Eeny Meeny Minee Mo
> Catch Whitey By His Throat
> If He Says – Nigger   CUT IT!

This gathers yet greater authority from the fact that Joans' own father was killed by whites in a 1943 Detroit race riot.

Similarly, the poems which invoke jazz very much become the thing they honour, as in 'They forget too fast', written in memory of Charlie Parker, 'Jazz Is My Religion' ('it alone do I dig') and 'Jazz Must Be A Woman', a sound poem made up of the accumulating and run-on names of jazz's greats. One hears, too, a near perfect blues sense of pitch in the carefully interspaced 'True Blues for Dues Payer', his elegy to Malcolm X written in North Africa:

> As I blew   the second chorus   of Old Man River
> (on an old gold trumpet loaded with blackass jazz)
> a shy   world traveling   white Englishman   pushed a
>   French-Moroccan
> newspaper   under my   Afroamerican eyes
> there it said   that you were dead   killed by   a group
> of black assassins   in black Harlem   in the black of night
> As I read   the second page   of bluesgiving news
> (with wet eyes and trembling cold hands)
> I stood   facing east   under quiet & bright   African sky
> I didn't cry   but inside   said goodbye   to you whom
>   I confess
> I loved   Malcolm X

Afrodisia reflects more of Joans' African sojourns and his resolve to link Afro-America back to the mother continent (his opening poem, 'Africa', envisions Africa as 'Land of my mothers, where a black god made me/My Africa, your Africa, a free continent to be'). 'Afrique Accidentale', another Hughes-like montage which parallels the Mississippi with the Niger, Greenwich Village with the Sudan, re-enacts his own African *Wanderjahr*, that of a 'jiving AfroAmerican' in search of the half-mythic (and cleverly multi-spelt) Timbuctoo. 'I have traveled a long way on the Beat bread I made/now I'm deep in the heart of Africa, the only Afroamerican spade', he says teasingly, yet pointedly, of his own true, black homecoming. The concluding lines make the point even more emphatic:

> so now lay me down to sleep
> to count black rhinos, not white sheep
> Timbukto, Timbucktoo, Thymbaktou!
> I do dig you!
> Timbuctu, Timbouctou
> I finally made you
> Timbuctoo
> Yeah!!

Throughout, too, Joans', surrealism shows its paces. In 'No Mo Space For Toms' he takes an absurdist bead on colonialism; in 'The Night of The Shark', he concocts a priapic mock creation-parable; and in 'Harlem to Picasso' he lowers a satiric eye on Euro-American artistic 'borrowings' from Africa with all the accompanying talk of 'primitivism' ('Hey PICASSO why'd you drop Greco-Roman &/other academic slop then picked up on my black ancestors sculptural bebop?'). In 'Jazz Anatomy', the poem itself becomes surreal while invoking surrealism in painting and music. The body, Magritte-like, turns into a combo, a line-up:

> my head is a trumpet
> my heart is a drum
> both arms are pianos
> both legs are bass viols
> my stomach the trombone
> my nose the saxophone
> both lungs are flutes
> both ears are clarinets
> my penis is a violin
> my chest is a guitar
> vibes are my ribs
> my mouth is the score
> and my soul is where the music lies

Taken with the plentiful erotica, at its best in poems like 'I Am The Lover' and 'Sweet Potato Pie' (and at its quasi-sexist, dated worst in a poem like 'Cuntinent'), Joans has long earned his corner. 'Whenever I read a poem of my own creation', he has written, 'I intentionally lift it off the page and "blow it" just as I would when I was a jazz trumpeter'. Veteran of both Beat and Blues, friend to Kerouac and Ginsberg as to 'Bird', 'Dizzy' and 'Monk', black surrealist and longtime Euro and Africa hand, his continues to be a truly ongoing and live performance.

IV

Though born in New Orleans of a Catholic black mother and Jewish father, raised in the Lower East Side (whose human variety he warms to while condemning its squalor and poverty as in pieces like 'East Fifth St. (N.Y.)' and 'TeeVeePeople'), and with twenty years in the Merchant Marine to follow, Bob Kaufman has long been best known as a controversial, drugs-and-poetry doyen of San Francisco. Despite the drug habits which led to several jail terms, or the self-denying and Buddhist ten-year vow of silence from 1963–73 taken to protest John Kennedy's assassination, his adopted city, on his death in January 1986, appointed 18 April 'Bob Kaufman Day' as well as naming a street after him. It was Kaufman, too, no doubt appropriately for the counterculture voice which in 'Benediction' had once told America – 'Everyday your people get more and more/Cars, television, sickness death dreams./You must have been great/alive' – who had a shaping part in creating with the journalist Herb Caen the term 'beatnik'.

Throughout the 1950s and early West Coast 1960s (if less so afterwards), when *Beatitude*, and then Lawrence Ferlinghetti in City Lights, first published his 'Abomunist' poems and broadsides, his often Jazz-accompanied, Dadaist poetry readings and legendary 'happenings' won him the reputation of a Beat irregular, San Francisco's own one-off bohemian. His different 'Abomunist' papers (*Abomunist Manifesto*, *Second April* and *Does the Secret Mind Whisper?*),[30] each an anarcho-surreal parody of all 'isms' and issued under the name 'Bomkauf', argue for a Beat-derived 'rejectionary philosophy'. As he puts matters in 'Abomunist Manifesto':

ABOMUNIST POETS CONFIDENT THAT THE NEW LITERARY FORM "FOOT-PRINTISM" HAS FREED THE ARTIST OF OUTMODED RESTRICTIONS SUCH AS: THE ABILITY TO READ AND WRITE, OR THE DESIRE TO COMMUNI-CATE, MUST BE PREPARED TO READ THEIR WORK AT DENTAL COLLEGES, EMBALMING SCHOOLS, HOMES FOR UNWED MOTHERS, HOMES FOR WED MOTHERS, INSANE ASYLUMS, USO CANTEENS, KINDERGARTENS, AND COUNTY JAILS. ABOMUNISTS NEVER COMPROMISE THEIR REJECTIONARY PHILOSOPHY.

Yet amid the noise, the heat, the often dire turns in his life, Kaufman managed poetry of genuine distinction as born out in his three principal collections, *Solitudes Crowded With Loneliness* (1959), *Golden Sardine* (1960) and *The Ancient Rain: Poems 1956–1978* (1981).[31]

In *Solitudes*, Kaufman strikes his own Beat affinity in 'Afterwards, They Shall Dance', a poem in which he claims a lineage with Dylan Thomas ('Wales-bird'), Billie Holiday ('Lost on the subway and stayed there/forever'), Poe ('died translated, in unpressed pants') and, for him, the *symboliste* master of all, Baudelaire. Only a dues-paying black Beat, one suspects, would end in terms which resemble both Ginsberg's 'sunflower Sutra' and a dreamy, flighted blues:

> Whether I am a poet or not, I use fifty dollars' worth
>   of air every day, cool.
> In order to exist I hide behind stacks of red and blue poems
> And open little sensuous parasols, stinging the nail-in-
> the foot-song, drinking cool beatitudes.

Nor can the Beat connection be missed in 'West Coast Sounds –
1956', one of his best-known 'Frisco' compositions, in which he identifies
Ginsberg, Corso, Rexroth, Ferlinghetti, Kerouac and Cassady and himself
as co-spirits for a changed America, even to the point of crowding the
East Coast. Jazz and 'hip', 'swinging' and 'cool' make inevitable touchstones:

> San Fran, hipster land,
> Jazz sounds, wig sounds,
> Earthquake sounds, others,
> Allen on Chesnutt Street,
> Giving poetry to squares
> Corso on knees, pleading,
> God eyes.
> Rexroth, Ferlinghetti,
> Swinging, in cellars,
> Kerouac at Locke's,
> Writing Neil
> on high typewriter,
> Neil, booting a choo-choo,
> on zigzag tracks.
> Now, many cats
> Falling in,
> New York cats,
> Too many cats,
> Monterey scene cooler,
> San Franers, falling down.
> Canneries closing.
> Sardines splitting,
> For Mexico.
> Me too.

This, too, has to be sited alongside poems like 'Ginsberg (for Allen)',
his surreal, larky homage to the author of 'Howl' ('I have proof that he
was Gertrude Stein's medicine chest', 'I love him because his eyes leak');
like 'Jazz *Te Deum* for Inhaling at Mexican Bonfires', hymn to the possibilities of human exuberance ('Let us walk naked in radiant glacial rains
and cool morphic thunderstorms'); like 'A Remembered Beat', with its
play of opposites, to the one side Charlie Parker as 'a poet in jazz', Mexico
and the 'hidden Pacific', and to the other, coercive 'organization men'
and 'television love'; like 'War Memoir', his contemplative, Hiroshima-
haunted lament at nuclear folly; and like 'Jail Poems', his 34-part,
moving, self-inquisitorial lyric sequence ('I sit here writing, not daring

to stop./For fear of seeing what's outside my head'). *Solitudes Crowded With Loneliness* made for an auspicious debut.

Though far less even – a suspicion arises that some of the poems were either unfinished or too hasty – *Golden Sardine* has its own triumphs. The untitled opening poem, a bitter, vivid dream sequence based on Carl Chessman in death-row (which oddly anticipates the execution of Gary Gilmore as told by Norman Mailer in *The Executioner's Song*), exudes a fierce compassion. The jazz poems, whether 'Round About Midnight', 'Tequila Jazz', 'His Horn' or 'Blue O'Clock', might all have been written by the Beat voice of 'Night Sung Sailor's Prayer'. There, America's 'born losers, decaying in sorry jails', find redemption (as they do in Ginsberg's 'Footnote to Howl') through the poet's own life-affirming articulacy:

> Sing love and life and love
> All that lives is Holy,
> The unholiest, most holy of all.

But the presiding note in *Golden Sardine* is one of angry, sad revolt at American venality, materialism and 'ritual lies', a revolt, however, redeemed from solemnity or mere complaint by Kaufman's linguistic energy and flair. His poem, 'On', set out in serial form, envisages an America of disjunctures and fracture, beginning, 'On yardbird corners of embryonic hopes, drowned in a heroin tear' and moving through to 'On lonely poet corners of low lying leaves & moist prophet eyes'. The view is one from the Beat or Hipster margins, appalled at American conformity, the 'comic-book seduction', the 'motion picture corners of lassie & other symbols'. It is, too, a view unmistakably Kaufman's own.

In his Introduction to *The Ancient Rain: Poems 1956–1978*, Kaufman's editor, Raymond Foye, rightly characterises the later work as 'some of the finest ... of his career – simple, lofty, resplendent'. Two poems especially do service. In 'War Memoir: Jazz, Don't Listen To At Your own Risk', he makes jazz a counterweight, a moral balance, to war and rapacity ('While Jazz blew in the night/suddenly we were too busy to hear a sound'). He also focuses on the memory of Hiroshima and Nagasaki ('busy humans were/Busy burning Japanese in atomicolor-cinescope/With stereophonic screams,/What one-hundred-percent red-blooded savage would waste time/Listening to Jazz, with so many important things going on ...'). For Kaufman, jazz, 'living sound', so restores and harmonizes, a (Beat?) act of life over death. Or as he himself puts it: 'Jazz, scratching, digging, bluing, swinging jazz,/And we listen/And we feel/And live'.

In 'Like Father, Like Sun', with Lorca as tutelary spirit, he again invokes an America of life – from New Orleans to the Mississippi to the 'Apache, Kiowa, and Sioux ranges' – against a 'rainless', 'fungus' America. But his ending looks even further, to a pluralised, uncoercive, universal nation – to, as it were, Emerson's 'poem' America:[32]

> The poem comes
> Across centuries of holy lies, and weeping heaven's eyes,
> Africa's black handkerchief, washed clean by her children's honor,
> As cruelly designed anniversaries spin in my mind,
> Airy voice of all those fires of love I burn in memory of.
> America is a promised land, a garden torn from naked stone,
> A place where the losers in earth's conflicts can enjoy their triumph.
> All losers, brown, red, black, and white; the colors from the
> Master Palette.

Kaufman's 'Like Father, Like Sun' no doubt bespeaks his own pains, his own will to redemption. But as in the poems of Jones/Baraka and Joans, it equally seeks to 'signify' at a wider level: nothing other than the exposure of America and beyond to a black beatitude.

NOTES

1. J.J. Phillips, Ishmael Reed, Gundars Strads and Shawn Wong (eds), *The Before Columbus Foundation Poetry Anthology* (New York: W.W. Norton, 1992).

2. Imamu Amiri Baraka, *The Autobiography of LeRoi Jones/Amiri Baraka* (New York: Freundlich Books, 1984) p.159.

3. Ted Joans: *Tape Recording at the Five Spot*, reprinted in Seymour Krim (ed.):,*The Beats* (Greenwich, Connecticut: Fawcett World Library, 1960) pp.211–13.

4. Bob Kaufman: *Solitudes Crowded With Loneliness* (New York: New Directions, 1965).

5. References are as follows: Allen Ginsberg, *Howl and other Poems* (San Francisco: City Lights Books, 1956); Jack Kerouac, *On The Road* (New York: Viking, 1957) and *The Subterraneans* (New York: Grove, 1958); John Clellon Holmes, 'The Philosophy of the Beat Generation', reprinted, together with his two other key Beat essays, 'This is the Beat Generation' and 'The Game of the Name', in *Nothing More to Declare* (New York: Dutton, 1967); Gregory Corso, *Gasoline* (San Francisco: City Lights Books, 1958); and Norman Mailer, *The White Negro* (San Francisco: City Lights Books, 1956).

6. Reprinted in *Solitudes Crowded With Loneliness*, pp.77–86.

7. *The Autobiography of LeRoi Jones/Amiri Baraka*, p.157.

8. A full list of these early magazine publications is to be found in Werner Sollers, *Amiri Baraka/LeRoi Jones: The Quest for a 'Populist Modernism'* (New York: Columbia University Press, 1978) pp.301–28.

9. LeRoi Jones (ed.), *The Moderns: an Anthology of New Writing in America* (New York: Corinth Books, 1963).

10. For a true insider's account of these years, see the early chapters of Hettie Jones, *How I Became Hettie Jones* (New York: E.P. Dutton, 1990).

11. 'Cuba Libre' first appeared in *Evergreen Review* and was republished in *Home: Social Essays* (New York: William Morrow & Co., 1966).

12. 'BLACK DADA NIHILISMUS' appeared in *The Dead Lecturer* (New York: Grove Press, 1964), *Dutchman* in *Dutchman and The Slave* (New York: William Morrow & Co., 1964).

13. *Blues People: Negro Music in White America* (New York: William Morrow & Co., 1963), *Home: Social Essays* (1966), and *Black Music* (New York: William Morrow & Co., 1967).

14. For general historical accounts see: Thomas R. Brooks, *Walls Come Tumbling Down, 1940–70* (Englewood Cliffs, New Jersey: Prentice-Hall, 1974); Sar A. Levitan et al. (eds), *Still A Dream: The Changing Status of Blacks Since 1960* (Cambridge, Massachusetts: Harvard University Press, 1975); August Meier and Eliott Rudwick, *Along the Color Line* (Urbana, Illinois: Illinois University Press, 1975); Harvey Sitkoff, *The Struggle For Black Equality, 1954–1980* (New York: Hill and Wang, 1981); and Juan William, *Eyes on The Prize: America's Civil Rights Years 1954–1965* (New York: Viking Penguin, 1987).

15. Robert Lowell, 'Memories of Wast Street and Lepke', In *Life Studies* (New York: Farrar, Straus & Cudahy, 1959).

16. J.D. Salinger, *The Catcher in The Rye* (Boston: Little, 1951).

17. James Baldwin, *Notes of a Native Son* (Boston: Beacon Press, 1955); *Nobody Knows My Name: More Notes of a Native Son* (New York: Dial Press, 1961); and *The Fire Next Time* (New York: Dial Press, 1963).

18. Ralph Ellison, *Invisible Man* (New York: Random House, 1952).

19. Full-length general contextual anthologies, studies and memoirs include: Gene Feldman and Max Gartenberg (eds), *The Beat Generation and the Angry Young Men* (New York: Citadel, 1958); Lawrence Lipton, *The Holy Barbarians* (New York: Julian Messner, 1959); Lawrence Ferlinghetti (ed.), *Beatitude Anthology* (San Francisco: City Lights Books, 1960); Seymour Krim (ed.), *The Beats* (1960); Donald M. Allen (ed.), *The New American Poetry: 1945–60* (New York: Grove Press, 1960); Elias Wilentz (ed.), *The Beat Scene* (New York: Corinth, 1960); Gene Baro (ed.), *'Beat' Poets* (London: Vista, 1961); Thomas A. Parkinson (ed.), *A Casebook on the Beat* (New York: Crowell, 1961); LeRoi Jones (ed.), *The Moderns* (New York: Corinth, 1961); Richard Seaver, Terry Southern and Alexander Trocchi (eds), *Writers in Revolt* (New York: Frederick Fells, 1963); *Wholly Communion* (London: Lorrimer Films, 1965); *Astronauts of Inner Space: An International Collection of Avant-Garde Activity* (San Francisco: Stolen Paper Review, 1966); Leslie Garrett, *The Beats* (New York: Scribner's, 1966); John Clellon Holmes, *Nothing More to Declare* (1967); Tina Morris and Dave Cunliffe (eds), *Thunderbolts of Peace and Liberation* (Blackburn, England: BB Books, 1967); M.L. Rosenthal,

The New Modern Poetry (New York: Macmillian, 1967); David Kherdian, *Six Poets of the San Francisco Renaissance* (Fresno, California: Giligia Press, 1967); Diane Di Prima, *Memoirs of a Beatnik* (New York: Olympia Press, 1969); David Meltzer (ed.), *The San Francisco Poets* (New York: Ballantine, 1971); Nick Harvey (ed.), *Mark in Time: Portraits & Poetry/San Francisco* (San Francisco: Glide, 1971); Bruce Cook, *The Beat Generation* (New York: Scribner's, 1971); Laurence James (ed.), *Electric Underground: A City Lights Reader* (London: New English Library, 1973); Yves Le Pellec (ed.), *Beat Generation* (Rodez, France: Entretiens, 1973); John Tytell, *Naked Angels: The Lives & Literature of the Beat Generation* (New York: McGraw Hill, 1976); Ed Sanders, *Tales of Beatnik Glory* (New York: Stonehill, 1975); David S. Wirshup (ed.), *The Beat Generation & Other Avant-garde Writers* (Santa Barbara, California: Anacapa Books, 1977); Lee Bartlett (ed.), *The Beats: Essays in Criticism* (Jefferson, North Carolina: McFarland, 1981); Arthur and Kit Knight (eds), *The Beat Vision: A Primary Sourcebook* (New York: Paragon House Publishers, 1987).

20. Amiri Baraka, *The LeRoi Jones/Amiri Baraka Reader*, edited by William J. Harris (New York: Thunder's Mouth Press, 1991).

21. *The Autobiography of LeRoi Jones/Amiri Baraka*, p.156.

22. Arthur and Kit Knight (eds), *The Beat Vision: A Primary Sourcebook*, p.131.

23. Donald Allen (ed.), *The New American Poetry*.

24. Donald Allen (ed.), *The New American Poetry*, p.424.

25. LeRoi Jones, *Preface to a Twenty Volume Suicide Note* (New York: Totem Press/Corinth, 1961).

26. A considerable critical bibliography has now built up around Jones/Baraka. See: Donald B. Gibson (ed.), *Five Black Writers* (New York: New York University Press, 1970); Letitia Dace, *LeRoi Jones: A Checklist of Works By and About Him* (London: Nether Press, 1971); Theodore Hudson, *From LeRoi Jones to Amiri Baraka: The Literary Works* (Durham, North Carolina: Duke University Press, 1973); Stephen Henderson, *Understanding/The New Black Poetry: Black Speech and Black Music as Poetic References* (New York: Morrow, 1973); Donald B. Gibson (ed.), *Modern Black Poets: A Collection of Critical Essays* (Englewood Cliffs, New Jersey: Prentice Hall, 1973); Esther M. Jackson, 'LeRoi Jones (Imamu Amiri Baraka): Form and Progression of Consciousness', *College Language Association Journal*, Vol. 17, No. 1 (September 1973); Kemberley Benston, *Baraka: The Renegade and the Mask* (New Haven: Yale University Press, 1976); Kemberley Benston (ed.), *Imamu Amiri Baraka (LeRoi Jones): A Collection of Critical Essays* (Englewood Cliffs, New Jersey: Prentice-Hall, 1978); Werner Sollers, *Amiri Baraka/LeRoi Jones: The Quest for a 'Populist Modernism'* (1978); Thomas M. Inge et al. (eds), *Black American Writers: Bibliographical Essays, Volume 2: Richard Wright, Ralph Ellison, James Baldwin, and Amiri Baraka* (New York: St. Martin's Press, 1978); Lloyd W. Brown, *Amiri Baraka* (Boston: Twayne Publishers, 1980); Henry C. Lacey, *To Raise, Destroy, and Create: The Poetry, Drama, and Fiction of Imamu Amiri Baraka (LeRoi Jones)* (Troy, New York: The Whitson Publishing Company, 1981); William J. Harris, *The Poetry and Poetics of Amiri Baraka: the Jazz Aesthetic* (Columbia: University of Missouri Press, 1985).

27. Reprinted in Arthur and Kit Knight (eds), *The Beat Vision: A Primary Sourcebook* (1987), p.269. His connection with Kerouac and the Beats generally is set out in the interview which follows with Gerald Nicosia, pp.270–83.
28. *Black Pow-Wow: Jazz Poems* (New York: Hill and Wang, 1969) and *Afrodisia* (New York: Hill and Wang, 1970).
29. Ted Joans, 'The Beat Generation and Afro-American Culture', *Beat Scene Magazine*, No. 13 (December 1991) pp.22–3. The same issue, p.13, contains a brief profile, 'Ted Joans in Paris', by Jim Burns.
30. All three of these manifestos, the originals now collector's items, are republished in Bob Kaufman, *Solitudes Crowded With Loneliness* (New York: New Directions, 1959).
31. *Solitudes Crowded With Loneliness* (1959); *Golden Sardine* (San Francisco: City Lights Books, 1967); and *The Ancient Rain: Poems 1956–1978* (New York: New Directions, 1981). For bearings on Kaufman, see: Barbara Christian, 'Whatever Happened to Bob Kaufman', pp.107–14, in Lee Bartlett, *The Beats: Essays in Criticism* (1981); Ellen Kaufman, 'Laughter Sounds Orange at Night', pp.259–67, in Arthur and Kit Knight (eds), *The Beat Vision: A Primary Sourcebook* (1987); and Ted Joans, 'The Beat Generation and Afro-American Culture', in *Beat Scene Magazine*, No. 13 (December 1991) pp.22–3.
32. As given in Emerson's 'The Poet': 'America is a poem in our eyes; its ample geography dazzles the imagination ...'.

9

The Archaeology of Gender in the Beat Movement

Helen McNeil

In her memoir *Minor Characters*, Joyce Johnson took a comment Allen Ginsberg once made and tried it out with the gender changed: 'The social organization which is most true of itself to the artist is the girl gang.'[1] Doesn't sound quite right, does it? Johnson thought so too.

Were the Beats a 'boy gang'? Is the boy gang, as Ginsberg had originally said, the ideal model for creativity? The Beats were certainly a boy gang: Kerouac, Ginsberg, Burroughs and the Beat 'saint' Neal Cassady, were all friends; Ginsberg and Cassady had been lovers. In a larger circle were Gregory Corso, John Clellon Holmes, Charles Bukowski, the San Francisco poets Lawrence Ferlinghetti, Gary Snyder, Philip Whalen, Lew Welch and the circle around Robert Duncan and Jack Spicer.

The discourse, the definition and the often punishing lifestyle of the Beat generation were set by the men, even more markedly than in other literary avant gardes, because the men tended to share lives and to support each other actively. There were a couple of woman poets such as Diane Di Prima and Denise Levertov (Levertov worked separately from the Beats but was admired). Later came Anne Waldman. Some poets were known to a small circle, often by association with men, such as the San Francisco poets Joanne Kyger, Lenore Kandel, the older Helen Adams. Later came the memoirists: Joyce Johnson, Carolyn Cassady, Bonnie Bremser, Janine Pommy Vega. But the Beats have never been seen as a movement engaging with women or responsive to feminist critique; even revisionist literary history has had little to say about gender and the Beats. To put it bluntly, everyone knows they were sexist, so why bother?

The moment when 'everyone knows' what a given group of writers had to say is, however, the moment when the questions and contradictions come most valuably into play. If the Beats were a boy gang, what are the consequences for the 'boy' or for the 'girl' – the woman artist or would-be artist? The answers to such questions are likely to be revealing not only about the Beats but also about the construction and cultural appropriation of avant garde or 'outlaw' art. On a larger scale an answer may offer a model of how the cultural discourse of gender affects the real political subject – the woman, the man. What did it feel like *then* to be a man? To be a woman? How did 1950s American society construct and maintain the ways the sexes were supposed to define themselves? Did the Beats participate in that construction or challenge it? Was life in and around 'the gang' different?

Answers to such questions cannot, in my view, be derived wholly or even mainly from the interpretation of Beat writing. The recuperation of texts and what is in them is a limited tool, though I shall be using it. What is in the texts is itself connected to other texts, discourses and institutions of power. Answers about the constitution and effects of discursive fields are also not available to a history, either as a history of continuity or a history of rupture.

The discourse about gender among the Beats can arguably be traced back historically to the American mythos of the frontier or of the 'bad boy', or seen as a continuation of the romantic topos of the quest-romance.[2] Those origins are, however, themselves ideological, as culturally and academically agreed discourses about what happened. A reading of the Beats as rupture may seem to work better, since the Beats did break with the establishment line of American literature. Kerouac was unable to get his novels published from 1951 to 1957, Ginsberg and Burroughs were prosecuted for obscenity, and much Beat writing, male and female, was (and still is) published by small presses and largely excluded from the academic canon. Yet even such a classic avant garde as the Beats displays neither a single shared attitude towards gender nor a consistent separation from other cultural discourses about it. The stance of literary avant-gardism is no guarantee of a break from a dominant discourse.

Taking the reception of the Beats as a guide, and using the moment of publication of *On The Road* as the core, I would like to see how and where the Beat discourse entered the prevailing American cultural discourses about gender. Those larger framing discourses will be my first concern, since they both shape the real institutions of power and offer a language to culture. This chapter, then, is an 'archaeology' in Michel Foucault's sense: a synchronic study which places content, context and discursive terminology equal to any unity of genre, author or movement. Initially at least I shall take remarks about gender as material 'in its raw neutral state'.[3] No matter what the source, I shall be looking at it in the first instance as 'a population of events in the space of discourse in general'. My comments then temporarily become, as Foucault remarked of the work of the archaeologist, *'a pure description of discursive events'*. My description does not assume unities but should ideally act as a 'horizon for the search for the unities that form within it'.[4]

Foucault's model in *The Archaeology of Knowledge* has its own limitations: his effort to deconstruct conventions of personality and text can tend to render the individual subject powerless and render all works equal and typical. Additionally, the condition of women and the discourses constituting sexual difference were not of interest to him. But when the question at issue is precisely how to re-enter the Beat moment without reimposing a received history of continuities or rupture, then he offers a radical, and valuable, set of warnings for the archaeologist to take on the road.

When Gilbert Millstein's rave review of *On The Road* in the *New York Times* of 5 September 1957 catapulted Kerouac into the national spotlight, women were a major topic of discourse in that newspaper (hereafter referred to as the *Times*). Then, as now, the *Times* acted self-consciously as cultural arbiter for educated middle-class America. Since it represents the cultural frame into which 'the literary' was supposed to fit, its discourses deserve a closer look. The women at issue in the pages of the 1957 *Times* were not, as today, remarked upon for their demands and activities, or for their difficulties as members of racial or ethnic minorities, but for their role as wives and 'homemakers' – the use of a euphemism for housewife is significant. (Attention to women celebrities remains interestingly constant.)

A cultural snapshot may serve to illustrate the field of discourse in which gender is an object: in Foucault's terms, a formulation with known bounds. On 9 September 1957, a full page *Times* advertisement for *Good Housekeeping* magazine[5] assured potential advertisers that theirs is the magazine the contemporary homemaker 'learns by, lives by', and spends by: *Good Housekeeping* is, it claims, 'the buying guide of 31,000,000 women' seeking 'gracious living'. The accompanying two-thirds page photograph of an immaculately coiffured homemaker and daughter setting the table looks like one of Esther Greenwood's nightmare images in Sylvia Plath's *The Bell Jar*, which looks back from 1963 at the meagre choices available to the young woman of the 1950s. The ad's discourse is, however, male-directed, to advertisers targeting the housewife-consumer. Mother is both consumer and maid, literally setting the place which the male wage-earner will soon enter to make the picture complete.

In fact, during the 1950s, employment by married women rose slightly but steadily in the United States, recovering from the postwar enforced return to domesticity, though not returning to its wartime high.[6]

New York, as the national corporate capital, employed disproportion-
ate numbers of both unmarried and married female clerical workers.
Yet these women appear only peripherally in the discourse of advertising[7] in spite of the fact that a two-income household would have
purchased more of the consumer goods which were flooding the postwar
economy. Some discursive force stronger than economic advantage
must have been operating to generate this oversight. There was, as it
were, no space in the field of discourse for such a practice or concept.

Are all 1950s women either girls or mothers? On the same day in the
Times, TWA airlines advertised its new Jetstream service with a photograph
of Jayne Mansfield, smiling at a faceless male TWA employee whose back
is to the camera, standing in for the reader. Mansfield is wearing a tight
dress with a low, square-cut bodice and rows of ruching over her large
breasts. She also wears ladylike gloves. Overhead is the phrase 'quiet ...
roomy ... perfect', attributed to the star but referring to those pleasur-
able qualities she ostensibly shares with jet planes. To the left of this
ad is another, for the rival *New York Post* newspaper, whose columnist
Mike Wallace will be interviewing that week, among others, Senator
McClellan on the senate racketeering hearings, Elia Kazan on movie
censorship, Zsa Zsa Gabor on 'What are clothes for?' and Jayne Mansfield
on 'What do you think about everything?'

So, at the discursive level, there are some females who are neither girls
or wives; these are the sex objects, bodies processed by a commodity
culture into movie stars so that they are available to all as image without
commitment. In Billy Wilder's 1955 film comedy *The Seven-Year Itch*,
the most famous sex object, Marilyn Monroe, the nameless 'girl upstairs',
is an unmarried but sexually provocative woman. Since the film assumes
that sexual desire occurs by definition only outside marriage (and
marriage is the male condition), Monroe is the 'other woman', bad by
function even if she is too dumb to realise her effect.[8] I am speaking
here less of a concept of gender embodied by Monroe, more of the rules
which permit such a concept to appear. Wilder's confident collusion
with his audience, the riot of visual and verbal double-entendres,
Monroe's 'fit' as the dumb blonde, a fit so perfect she never escaped
from it: all these display a directorial knowingness about the rules
governing the field, and a sense that these rules – and therefore their
verbal formulations – are limited.

Because it relies on an internalisation of rules about what practices
and phrases are conventional or transgressive, humour can serve the
most delicate measure of the field of a discourse. The 1950s in America
were indeed a great age of humour whose butt was the woman-
as-housewife. A James Thurber *New Yorker* cartoon depicting a little man
hesitating in front of a huge house which merges into a glowering woman

decorates a light *Times* essay, 'War of the Sexes in Cartoonland'.[9] Thurber has beautifully illustrated the guiding metonymic shift by which the woman in the house becomes the house-wife or home-maker; she makes the home and is then indistinguishable from her setting. The article's summary says that 'the US male, pictured as a second-class citizen in a matriarchy' is such a favourite subject for humour 'because we recognize him'.[10] It is a moot point whether the discourse here is of gender, family, power or politics: to use Foucault's terms again, there seems rather to be a discursive field in which these terms operate as forces perceived as consistent, converging.

In a feature article published the same week as *On The Road*, a European pundit 'sees our [American] men as an "oppressed minority" – but the girls' victory is Pyrrhic'.[11] Amaury de Riencourt considers that 'the American woman is a major problem today'. 'The alarming ascendency of the female sex' is occurring because American women, their lives eased by labour-saving devices in the home, 'have real freedom while their mates are more than ever tied to their business. Surplus time, energy and freedom amount to a surplus of power.' De Riencourt uses the term 'power' dissociated from political, economic or institutional power, just as he separates the term 'freedom' from its political correlative in the Cold War era, namely the Free World or a free (non-communist) people.[12]

The article's conclusion brings unconscious Cold War and con-sciously essentialist gender discourses to bear on the issue of the contemporary American woman. Using language usually applied to the communist threat, de Riencourt finds woman an 'internal threat to freedom, worming its very way into the heart of our society'. The implication is that society is male, and woman, like communism, threatens to subvert it from the inside. The 'overspecialized' man of today has been tricked into believing that 'to give and to give endlessly without expecting anything in return is a sign of masculinity'. He is lost: 'he can no longer develop that most masculine of qualities, mental creation (the natural counterpart of women's physical conception) in an atmosphere of complete freedom'. Freedom means not being interfered with by women.[13]

While the housewife 'has usually trained her husband to wash dishes and change diapers', middle age is 'when feminine ascendency really starts'.[14] De Riencourt's emphasis on middle age here continues the 'momism' which shaped the gender discourse of the 1940s, expressed most extremely in the misogynist assault on the menopausal woman in Philip Wylie's *Generation of Vipers* (1942);[15] while the homemaker typically appears in the 1950s discourse as a (demographically accurate) late-twentyish mother of two or more young baby-boom children, and the man is positioned as working commuter husband, the shadow of 'mom' still falls on the scene.

Even such a feminist icon as anthropologist Margaret Mead let herself become part of the woman-blaming discourse. Writing in the *Times Magazine* on 10 February 1957 in an essay titled 'American Man in a Woman's World', Mead points out crisply that American women have not in fact improved their position since the 1930s. Anticipating (and, I suspect, influencing) Betty Friedan's arguments in *The Feminine Mystique*, she argues that middle-class American women also suffer from the unique paradox that they are offered education but discouraged from using it after marriage.[16]

Appealing to what seems to be an assumed male audience, Mead points out that in suppressing women 'we set up a situation whereby men also become less than full human beings and more narrowly domestic'. The radical solution Mead proposes is that society should include among its ideals a degendered model of people who are utterly dedicated to their work: 'People, not just men.' Mead is using what I would term a discourse of responsibility, but one in which the highest responsibility is to one's own gifts rather than to society.[17]

By targeting domesticity, Mead breaks out of the house/wife metonymic bind, but she operates well within the dominant formation through her devaluing of all domestic activity. By projecting a degendered goal for a few superior talents, she is by definition relegating the mass of women to an unanalysed housewifery. Mead's target may well have been the sentimentalising of the family as a democratic ('free world') force, anti-creative in its conservativism. To give one example, perhaps the most effective sentimentalisation in the artistic field was the famous 1955 Museum of Modern Art photography show *The Family of Man*, curated by Edward Steichen. Impressively selected and presented, this show functioned both as a representationalist rebuttal of artistic avant-gardism and as an explicit propaganda tool when it was sent around the world by the United States Information Agency; Mead is thus addressing an immediate issue in American social and cultural discourse.[18] Because of the absence of a gender-based critique in her argument, however, Mead's article was readily repackaged so that it became *men* who were presented as most endangered by the domestic. As the article's large-type summary notes, by keeping all women home, 'we have hamstrung the men, too, says an expert. The result is a new breed of men, subservient and narrowly domestic.'[19]

How did gender intersect the discursive field of the writer in the 1950s? There were established women writers, such as Lillian Hellman, Mary McCarthy and Eudora Welty, and recognised younger novelists such as Carson McCullers and Flannery O'Connor. Gwendolyn Brooks was not visible despite the publication of *Maud Martha* in 1953.[20] For six months preceding the publication of *On The Road* the number one bestseller in the US was Grace Metalious' steamy suburban saga *Peyton Place*. But the women were operating in a ladies' annexe; the definition of the literary was established and maintained by men, and women writers had to enter that discourse to be recognised.

On its fourth page, the *Sunday Times* Book Review of 8 September 1957 printed reviews of May Sarton's *The Birth of a Grandfather* and Josephine Carson's *Drives my Green Age*. Elizabeth Janeway, reviewing Sarton, writes that she misses 'force', as in 'John P. Marquand [or] the brilliant unravelling of social relations of a James Gould Cozzens'. Janeway is relieved that this is 'not a "woman's novel"' but 'it is limited to much the same material as these contrivances, the feminine world of family and home'. What is worse than this limitation is that Sarton refuses 'to try to see' her male characters 'in male terms'. Janeway feels that although women novelists, 'must begin by seeing the world through a woman's eyes', later they have a 'duty' to represent the male in his own terms. 'Family' is a feminised term here, and the discourse of responsibility takes the form of the woman writer also being responsible for the masculine point of view.

In the next review, William Goyen expresses relief that although 'it has been hard to find a first-class woman novelist these days who also writes well about childhood', Carson is that rarity, showing 'gentle order' and conveying a 'tranquillizing and heartening' mood rather than a 'bizarre and bedevilled' one, like other unnamed women writers (McCullers? O'Connor?). Here the woman writer is rewarded for remaining in her traditionally limited and meliorist role.

On the same page appears a review of Kerouac's *On The Road* by David Dempsey. Writing from an authoritative distance established by repeated use of the canonical 'we' and the abstract 'one', Dempsey begins by remarking sarcastically that while being 'lost' was enough for Fitzgerald, today 'in order to remain uncommitted one must at least flirt with depravity'. Unaware that Kerouac invented the term 'Beat', Dempsey assumes Kerouac is also writing at a distance, 'inspired by the so-called "beat" generation'.

Dempsey does not criticise Kerouac for failing to represent his women characters through a woman's eyes, nor for the restriction of his subject matter to car rides with stops in between. He mentions with high praise the book's sexual adventures; 'the hot pursuit of pleasure' enables Kerouac, in the reviewer's meat-market image ,'to serve up' to the reader 'great, raw slices of America'. The novel is 'a stunning achievement' but Kerouac, in Dempsey's view, has also failed because 'having absolved his characters of all responsibility, he can absolve himself of the writer's customary attention to motivation and credibility'.

The male novelist, then, is also implicated in a discourse of responsibility, but his obligation is to convey realistic motivation, society as it actually is. This is seen as involving the creation of socially responsible characters. Irresponsible characters seem to infect the writer retroactively, permitting him to evade his responsibility for realism. Dempsey does not apply his discourse of responsibility to *On The Road*'s treatment of women, which is hypostatised as male sensation: 'hedonism' and 'hot pursuit' (though hedonism refers to drugs, jazz and fast cars as well as to sex). The reduction of women to sex is neither a negative element, nor it is neutral; it is seen as a positive aspect of the novel's appeal.

The female readers at Viking Press, where Malcolm Cowley had been campaigning for the publication of *On The Road* for some years, shared the conceptual and semantic shifts and gaps of Dempsey's review. Senior editor Helen K. Taylor, who was the in-house editor for *On The Road*, agreed in a memo to Cowley that 'this is a "classic of our times"'. She finds it a novel about evil, though all the characters appear to her to be victims, 'a bunch of young people who are irretrievably gone in the literal sense of the word'. Her empathy goes to the male travellers, with Dean Moriarty seen as 'a gargantuan but believably pitiable "hero"'. Women are covered under sex, and possible legal problems. Taylor is, she writes, 'not much worried about the obscenity. I'm sure the whorehouse scene can get by practically in toto. Not that people won't think it's a dirty book. It's a question of publishing it quietly for the discerning few.'[21]

In a second internal memo, junior editor Evelyn Levine sees *On The Road* as being about 'young people trying to find their identity'. Levine is aware that she has been referring to male characters when she has written 'young people': 'All the male characters are for me – very well drawn ... I dug 'em all [but] ... The girls in the story – are another thing – almost none of them are real.' Levine then reverts to the use of male as synecdoche for human: 'So here are these characters – in search of their identity.' Defending *On The Road* against possible 'immorality', she notes: 'In the search for their identity, they're also trying to live life to the fullest; protesting against the older generation's and society's rules.' Levine continues, subsuming woman under the functions of 'sex' and 'promiscuity' or the legal category of 'obscenity'. Neither woman editor uses a discourse of responsibility, whether for praise or blame.[22]

Gilbert Millstein's 5 September 1957 *Times* review uses a new set of discursive terms to celebrate *On The Road*. Millstein boldly uses Kerouac's novel to define a generation: not 'lost' or 'depression' but 'beat'. Its publication is 'a historic occasion in so far as the exposure of an authentic work is of any great moment'.[23] Troping the Beat generation as 'the' generation, Millstein is attempting to seize the 1950s on behalf of the Beats. When his argument is considered as description, however, it becomes clear that Millstein is also saying that 'Beat' means '1950s'. Although Kerouac's text indicates that the events described are taking place around 1950, Millstein, like other reviewers, takes the novel as exemplifying the spirit of the mid to late 1950s present.

For Millstein the core of *On The Road* is a quest for belief. He locates the novel's 'freedom' in a refusal of dominant discourses; the Beat hero 'takes for granted the imminence of war, the barrenness of politics and the hostility of the rest of society. Only in that condition can the quest be undertaken.' The 'frenzied pursuit of every possible sensory impression ... is the external manifestation of the inner search'. Like Kerouac, Millstein doesn't comment on the fact that, due to its terms, this quest can only be male, and that the female, again hypostatised as sex, is only a small part of the 'frenzied pursuit'. Because the pursuit is rebellious it is seen positively. In her domestic maternal role, woman is a small part of the intermittently visible apparatus of containment and control which Sal and Dean escape by staying on the road. Millstein's review valorises the views of the novel by reproducing them in his critical discourse as philosophy of life.

The confidence with which Millstein centralised the Beat hero implies that the views in his piece are not exclusively those of the nascent Beat movement or even of American literary culture but part of a larger social discourse whose central issues had to do with the masculine need for freedom, however defined, in relation to assaults on it. Culturally this is one of the discourses of existentialism; John Clellon Holmes emphasised the connection, and the popularity of Camus' works shows them intersecting American concerns about the nature of the hero and of freedom (Camus was awarded the Nobel Prize in December 1957).[24] In terms of social formation, American 1950s discourses tended to see individualism as the freedom being assaulted. The masculine is individual rather than social. When *On The Road* came out, Vance Packard's *The Hidden Persuaders* had been topping the non-fiction bestseller lists for several months with its argument that the individual's freedom of choice was being undermined by advertising, especially subliminal sexual messages. C. Wright Mills' *The Power Elite* had recently been published (1956). Mills notes that 'the mass has no autonomy from institutions'. Contemporary man loses not only his independence, but 'the will to be independent: in fact, he does not have hold of the idea of being an individual with his own mind'. With less social theory and more anecdote, William H.Whyte, Jr's *The Organization Man* (1956) also decried loss of individualism through grey flannel corporatism, as the Protestant ethic annihilates the individual, and individualism, which it had first created.[25]

For the postwar writers, corporate power impinges upon the artist through the lure of the sell-out. In Norman Mailer's *The Deer Park* (1957), Sergius O'Shaughnessy, the artistically and sexually potent hero, is tempted by a Hollywood studio head who tells him: 'This is your opportunity for the big money, kiddo, and dignity and importance.'[26] For Mailer, government power further erodes individuality by threatening assault on the body; the blacklisted character Charlie Gitel is forced to testify to 'the committee' (on Un-American activities) or be jailed.

The reception of Kerouac indicates that the Beat discourse on gender was perceived as fitting into the discursive formations which were already in place rather than challenging them, as they arguably did challenge some aspects of the discourse of responsibility. But were these contemporary views fair readings? What was happening in the Beat texts about gender and (as far as it can be recovered) what was happening in the lives of the Beat writers?

The Beats wrote in an era in which masculinity had been defined explicitly by war service, with either the Second World War or the Korean War imposing military discipline and putting the body of the man directly at risk. The Cold War maintained the posture of male preparedness. However, the Beats tended not to have served, or to have been promptly discharged: Kerouac, Ginsberg, Burroughs, Corso, also Cassady.[27] So male gendering of the man among his male peers is likely to have been defined in their work by other means. Ginsberg's 'boy gang' and the text of *On The Road* offer an alternative model of the man among men: freedom for the quest must be absolute; the Beat hero is responsible only to that quest and sometimes to his friends; the 'gang' is held together by ties of love. The Beat model shares with the dominant model the view of the masculine as individual rather than social. In the dominant model, however, the individual must endure the contradiction between individualism and responsibility. When this contradiction was enacted in the narratives of the postwar group of writers such as Mailer, Nelson Algren, Herman Wouk and Saul Bellow, it produced plots in which both historical women and institutions (military, political, corporate, religious, communal) play a much larger and often more positive role than in the Beats. Whatever the conclusion, these 'real' elements and their discourses must be encountered in the course of masculine self-definition.

It is where the discourse of responsibility engages the definition of the masculine among men that the Beats were most severely criticised. Interviewed for the *Detroit News* in 1958, Kerouac was careful to dissociate his writing from juvenile delinquency, denying 'suggestions that his writing encourages juvenile immorality or defiance of law'.[28] Criminals, he said, 'may be using the "beat generation" tag as an excuse for their actions, but the term as I meant it has nothing to do with crime'. Kerouac briefly explains beatitude, notes that he is an avid baseball fan and then tries to rescue rock 'n' roll from accusations that it causes delinquency, as in a recent 'rock 'n' roll riot in Boston'. In Britain, where Kerouac was not available for placatory interviews, the causal link between the Beats, rock 'n' roll and (male) juvenile delinquency was taken as proven: 'BLAME THESE 4 MEN FOR THE BEATNIK HORROR', cried a headline in *The People* in 1960.[29] 'Their cult of despair is driving the teenagers to violence', the story continued, blaming 'the outbreak of teenage violence that wrecked Lord Montagu's jazz festival' on the teachings of Kerouac, Corso, Burroughs and Ginsberg. The clincher about the Beatniks is: 'They despised work. They didn't wash.' Fears of a postwar breakdown in the Protestant ethic are offloaded on to the foreign Beats.

On The Road is a love story, but it is about love between two men, both of them meanwhile being in love with the womanly body of America. Dean is the antitype of the controlled 'responsible' man; indeed, he sees responsibility *as* control. He leads the quest because his freedom is absolute, though it is freedom *from* as much as freedom *for*. While Dean is more 'mad' than Sal, he may also be the more old-fashioned of the two; his love for the continent is adulterous, since he meanwhile feels obliged to marry various actual women prior to leaving them for the road. Dean's ecstatic sweating body, in jeans, 'T-shirted and joyous', or 'stark naked', receiving 'the world in the raw', makes him the priapic spirit of the road. In the novel's central epiphany, Dean becomes for Sal 'the HOLY GOOF', a prophetic saint of Beatitude, because he totally refuses the rhetoric of responsibility, which both he and Sal read as feminine. Accused by a woman of lacking 'any sense of responsibility' for years, Dean simply giggles and starts a Dionysiac dance as his wounded thumb appropriately works its way out of its wrapping and sticks up in the air.[30]

The body of America is not penetrated by the Beat travellers, as by a pioneer or warrior. Instead it is lovingly criss-crossed as each new turn promises ecstasy. As Sal and Dean head towards New Orleans, 'He and I suddenly saw the whole country like an oyster for us to open; and the pearl was there, the pearl was there'(p.131). Capacious and unfathomable, the continent can never be possessed because man is mortal and can't take every road at the same time. This means the nation's body can never control the traveller because it is already always and everywhere his infinitely flexible setting, ready to respond to his every desire and whim.

Actual historical women encountered along the road are puny avatars of this great continental body, having only its sex functions, displayed by their bodies. When Sal first sees Terry, 'the cutest little Mexican girl ... Her breasts stuck out straight and true; her little flanks looked delicious' (p.78). To the extent that women show volition, they are dangerous. Marylou, Dean's first wife, travels in the car for a while, but she is sullen, plotting, vengeful, finally 'a whore' because she sleeps with other men, as the men sleep with other women.

In other words, in terms of gender, the novelty of the Beat movement for American culture was the insertion into its discourse of the 'chick', the attractive, young, sexually available and above all silent ('dumb') female. Even safer is the 'fellahin' woman, with few expectations, lower on the social scale than even the automotive hoboes Sal and Dean (Sal is presented as a college boy, Dean is working class). Often the fellahin woman does not speak English, or only barely.

What Sal likes about Terry is not the woman herself but her proximity, as purported earth woman, to the American earth: 'I felt like a million dollars; I was adventuring in the crazy American night' (p.96). After a few weeks, having had his touristic experience, 'I could feel the pull of my own life calling me back' (p.94). Sal's aunt (a mother figure without maternal responsibility) sends money, as always, and Sal departs for the road. Near the end of the novel, the economic imperialism which creates fellahin sexual acquiescence is half acknowledged as the Yanqui heroes work their way through the wretched inhabitants of a Mexican whorehouse. 'I was trying to break loose to get at a sixteen-year-old coloured girl ... It was mad', says Sal (p.271). Flashes of guilt and pity surface but are not acted upon: 'It never, never occurred to me just to approach her and give her some money' (p.273).

The insertion of the chick category does not violate any existing gender codes, rather it opens new opportunities for sex without responsibility (for there is no marriage, or marriage – as with Dean – is not taken seriously). It is sex without guilt (for the true chick never complains). And it is sex without financial cost (because the chick is not a professional prostitute). And it is sex with those who will – mostly – not tell their side of the story. 'Here a chick, there a chick, everywhere a chick-chick', comments Alix Kates Shulman sardonically, noting how few chicks are ever named.[31] Even amidst this apparent discursive shift, the closeness of the old discourse of the 'bad' sexually independent single sexual woman is revealed in *On The Road* when Sal, sleeping with Terry less than a day after he has met her, fears 'she was a common little hustler'. (p.80).

'I realized what a rat he was', Sal finally says of Dean, but this refers not to Dean's efforts to set up his first wife Marylou as mistress while moving in with his second, Camille, nor to Dean's two abandonments of Camille and his children, nor to his abandonment of Inez, his third wife, the moment he marries her, in order to return to Camille. It refers to Dean leaving Sal ill in Mexico City because he has got the divorce he came for. In the same sentence Sal forgives Dean (p.285).

If only wives could be like chicks! After an ecstatic jazz session in San Francisco Sal and Dean go on to the home of Walter, a black man they met at the bar. They wake up his wife, 'the sweetest woman in the world ... she never asked Walter where he'd been, what time it was, nothing ... . She never said a word.' Dean is genuinely impressed: 'There's a *real* woman for you ... her old man can come in any hour of the night with anybody ... and leave any old time' (p.192). In a spring 1952 letter, inviting Kerouac to visit, Neal Cassady presented his wife Carolyn as this ideal: 'freedom, man, freedom, no bull, Carolyn loves you, be like your mama without you having any need to cater like to her, and coffee, gobs of expensive coffee, and clothes washed free, and your portrait painted'.[32] Cassady then notoriously offered Kerouac his wife as a means of cementing the bond between the men; as Carolyn recounts it in *Heart Beat*, she accepted being traded for quite other motives, as a means of keeping her husband interested in her.

Within less than three months of publication, the literariness of *On The Road* – Kerouac's dancing, jazzy prose style and his loose, apparently semi-improvised narrative structure – ceased to be the main issue as the media seized upon the lifestyle of the Beats and their sexy chicks. So-called 'men's magazines' were the most avid promoters, featuring the Beats as audience draws in their circulation and status wars. *Playboy*, founded at the end of 1953 as a coarser porn rival to the men's magazine *Esquire*, immediately bought a Kerouac piece, 'The Rumbling, Rambling Blues', for its January 1958 issue. *Esquire* itself, which traditionally paid 'serious' writers high fees to place their works next to girlie pictures, commissioned John Clellon Holmes to write 'The Philosophy of the Beat Generation' for February 1958, followed by Kerouac (same title) in the March issue and again in May.[33] *Playboy* struck back with Kerouac's rather serious piece 'The Origins of the Beat Generation' (June 1959, pp.31–2, 42, 79, followed by letters September 1959), and two more pieces by Kerouac in its December 1959 issue. *Life* magazine, having briefly covered Ginsberg's pornography trial in 1957, added its middlebrow weight to the trend with a disapproving 1959 cover story on the Beats, which, however, promoted the novelty of the 'beatnik' lifestyle.[34]

In *The Hearts of Men* Barbara Ehrenreich points out that the way *Playboy* 'joined the battle of the sexes'[35] was by promising the American man that he could have sex without marriage, indeed without any relationship at all. No guilt, no responsibility, no paying a prostitute. It is small wonder that the publishers of *Playboy* recognised gender role models in the Beats, despite their anti-consumer stance and occasional wish for spiritual accord with the chick. The 'playmate' exists for play only. In the notorious centrefold nude photo, she looks neither good nor wicked, only inviting. Her apparent stupidity and willingness are signalled by her large bared breasts, impersonally airbrushed body and fixed smile.

Centrefold woman is only another object which can be purchased and disposed of in the consumer culture. The discourse of responsibility promoted by the discourses of the 1950s (and later satirised by Philip Roth through the rampant immaturity of *Portnoy's Complaint* [1966]) involved commitment by the male to a mature relationship. *Playboy* offered pleasure in sex without recognition of the presence of the partner as human. Release from guilt over sexual desire was linked with denial of the woman, as if recognising her could only mean being controlled by her. It is useful to remember the parallels between the Beats and *Playboy* as twin sources of the sexual revolution of the 1960s.

One striking innovation of *On The Road* was its refusal to join in the dominant psychoanalytic discourse of the day. By not writing a psychological novel, Kerouac successfully externalized patriarchal power and its Freudian discourse; in *On The Road* there is no regularly functioning superego 'above' to repress and regulate the libido below. There is, however, a discourse of control and power, functioning as a critique of both the discourse and the practice of male responsibility. Once 'responsible' self-control has been externalised it is revealed as mere control, and negative. The Beat hero experiences it as a source of fear rather than as a reward for maturity. Marginalised by the free zone of the Road, the law and its agent, the cop-force, still lurch into view now and then, attempting to control, to locate transgression, and to punish. The journeyers refuse the discourse. Beatitude is the absence of guilt over sex, over treatment of women, over property.

When Kerouac did use the psychoanalytic discourse in *The Subterraneans*, his 'confessional' novel, the consequence is an upwelling of sexual and racial fear, denial and guilt. It seems that all that is needed to deny the liberation of *On The Road* is a shift in the discourse. The psychoanalytic topography of above and below gives space to those repressed fears which *On The Road* exists to deny.

Kerouac's of course, was not the only Beat discourse about gender, though his was the most available to the mass heterosexual audience, and so the most influential. Allen Ginsberg and William Burroughs have their own gender discourses. In 'Howl' Ginsberg seeks to redeem the ecstatic body, defined as male, from Moloch and from female control figures such as the 'one eyed shrew/of the heterosexual dollar the one eyed shrew that winks out of the/womb'. Someday there will be release, 'with mother finally ******', but not yet.[36] In the great lament of 'Kaddish' he confronts the disgusting and alluring maternal body; the mad, ugly, frightening and dead Naomi remains horribly dead, but also becomes the archetypal mother and a sacrifice, ultimately one of the six million.

Burroughs founded some of his paranoid visions on the paradox that woman, whom he considered to be a biological mistake, has somehow achieved the ultimate monoploy, that of monopolosing fecundity. Although Burroughs' misogyny is startling even as part of a woman-blaming discourse of the 1950s, it has tended not to be seen as a major issue in his work, perhaps because it is part of a stance against control in general. The larger frame of paranoid revolt may also permit misogyny to slip in, almost as a comfortingly recognisable element in otherwise alien fictive worlds.

In noting that there are internal coherences between the textual, personal, cultural, economic and political discourses of gender in the 1950s, I am not claiming any architectonic unity, 'the same thing' occurring at different levels. Nor does use of the same terminology, such as 'responsibility', or even having the feminine as shared object of discourse prove a homology of discourse. There is *not* one unified or pervasive cross-cultural discourse of sexism or misogyny. What we have found, I think, is that for men in 1950s America, woman is located in the discursive formation of threat. Like the self-conscious cultural discourses in the *Times*, much of the Beat rebellion against authority displaced male power on to the maternal/domestic, blaming the woman for controlling what she did not and could not control. As in the cartoon war between the sexes, the less real social and economic power woman had, the more she was perceived to have.

But amidst this, what was it like for the woman? Did she have her own beat? This must be the work of another essay, but I shall offer some brief indications.

As we have seen, the Beat movement's amplification of dominant cultural discourses about women closed off the movement as a ready ideological escape route for the would-be female rebel. But even before ideological debate could ensue, the Beat life had to be lived. Many would-be women writers simply could not transfer the Beat lifestyle across gender lines and survive in a society that had gendered female behaviour much more conventionally. In a 1978 interview Anne Waldman asked Diane Di Prima about other women Beat writers:

I can't say a lot of really great women writers were ignored in my time, but I can say a lot of potentially great women writers wound up dead or crazy. I think of the women on the Beat scene with me in the early '50s, where are they now? ... I know some of them ODed [overdosed] and some of them got nuts, and one woman that I was running round the Village with in '53 was killed by her parents putting her in a shock treatment place.... I don't want to rant on about individual cases, but the threat of incarceration or early death in one form or other was very real ... I was a brash little brat. Probably why I'm still alive![37]

There were no female Kerouacs because external social controls of the woman functioned as silencer even before the rhetoric of the chick could function. Of the eight women writers out of 67 Beat writers covered in Ann Charters' 1979 bibliographical compilation,[38] Bonnie Bremser and Carolyn Cassady were autobiographical memoirists, Janine Pommy Vega a memoirist and poet; Joyce Johnson should be added to the list for her memoir *Minor Characters*. The other women writers were poets: Di Prima, Lenore Kandel, Joanne Kyger and Anne Waldman. (Janine Pommy Vega and Anne Waldman, born 1942 and 1945, are a generation younger than the others.)

There were also no female Kerouacs because to go on the road did bring the 'chick' rhetoric into play, and ruinously. The effort to be chick, mother and creative artist led down a spiral towards madness and death. For this reason almost no record survives; the one essential text, by Bonnie Bremser, has been out of print for many years, but it is worth a long look. At the opening of her devastating existential narrative, *For Love of Ray*, Bonnie Bremser represents herself on the road, riding southwards in a bus from Matamoros to Mexico City, with her husband, poet Ray Bremser, and with their blonde baby Rachel on her lap. She is overwhelmed by a highly specific fear:

Was my fear at this time all composed of not being able to handle external circumstances, afraid I would not be able to keep Rachel healthy, or at least not crying, (and that was a feat, I didn't often succeed in) and not to be able to satisfy Ray – what was happening in his head, something similar? And it all was so extremely personal, this service of responsibility, that the failure of it and maybe the success I have not had much chance to experience up to this point was a very lonely thing.[39]

In spite of her felt obligation to carry through this cultural 'service of responsibility' she shared with other 1950s mothers and wives, Bonnie keeps 'trying to groove, trying to groove under the circumstances' (p.13). Soon they find a 'hip food stand' where they smoke some marijuana along with the kind of all-American food they and Kerouac favoured: 'hamburgers and apple pie with ice cream and coffee'. For the moment, this is the promised joy of the Beat way:

It is one of those great pot feasts that are always for all time remembered like some memorial along the road of our beautiful experiences. God praise marijuana, yes, my baby, I will never put you down. A few things stay close to our hearts, definitive, a happy to have habit thing with no pain, no remorse, no sickness ... Ray was perhaps responding to the illusion of everything being beautiful. He was always ahead of me in that respect, and I do respect, although it in fact leaves me behind. (pp.55, 57)

Bonnie feels it part of her failure that she is slower than Ray to believe in 'everything being beautiful'.

For Love of Ray is written retrospectively, but while Joyce Johnson's narrative of her affair with Kerouac is written from a calm distance, Bonnie Bremser's is violently immediate, written while still in the contradictory coils of guilt, shame and unrepentant desire. In her prefatory comments she says: 'I have got plenty of nothing' (p.7). Enjoying her nakedness, she takes her pleasure away from herself: 'the afternoon sun I while away thus with my dirty mind' (p.8). She is like a mummy : 'My soul is black to its depth and the heart shines through like a beacon.' 'Within the pyramid' of herself, what she declares to be a 'pacified ghost' roams endlessly, sending out a black light, itself 'its own sphinx' (p.10).

In Mexico, when the money runs out and there is no family to send more, Ray decides to solve the problem by putting his beautiful wife on the street. As Bonnie literally prostitutes herself so Ray can write and groove, she becomes a prostitute in her own eyes and his: 'He has told me with no hesitation that I am a whore, emphatically, he loves my whoreness – so fuck!' Hustling money to get it to Ray, who has been busted and is in jail in Veracruz, she reads de Sade's *Juliette*, 'a story of a whore, like me' (p.55).

Through incredible scenes of degradation and disillusion punctuated by uplifts of getting stoned and being back with Ray, Bonnie comes to want to die; she loses her daughter, taken away for adoption, and she loses Ray, only to have the narrative circle round again as, back in New York, Ray reappears and introduces Bonnie to amphetamine, the latest promise of happiness: 'his face came up looking so strong, like voyages down under in those few seconds of complete introspection with the needle going in, and I knew it was good, and let myself be talked into it, and truly my eyes were opened' (p.192). Masochism was part of the definition of the chick who follows her man on the road. Today Bonnie Bremser has changed her name and does not participate in events such as the one at the New York University Conference on the Beats in May 1994, where women were placed on the same panel because of who they slept with or who fathered them.[40]

Some of the discourse of the Beat women writers continued the male discourse, but from the female position, sometimes taken literally, as in Lenore Kandel's *The Love Book* (1966) or Di Prima's written-for-money porn sections of *Memoirs of a Beatnik*. Di Prima, aware that her (male) audience wants more porn per page, at one point tries out two versions of the group-sex-in-a-bed trope. In the first version, 'A Night By The Fire: What You Would Like To Hear', all sexes and orifices are put to work; in the second version, 'A Night By The Fire: What Actually Happened', there is no sex and everyone is freezing cold in the unheated apartment.[41] Since the woman is the narrator, the lighthearted joke is on the reader. When, at the end of the memoir, Di Prima decides to have a baby, she also decides to leave the pad and find a more stable situation. The sensible and robust Di Prima has survived, written and developed because she did not follow a Beat lover.

A more enduring route out of immediate discursive positioning has been to transcend it through religious belief: Kyger, Di Prima and Waldman have all been deeply involved in Buddhism. For Waldman, a practising Buddhist, 'Bad moods never seemed a place for writing. I usually write out of some concentrated high energy place.'[42] Although Waldman does not feel that Buddhism, as a personal religion, can be summarised as dogma, for her it is 'about becoming a warrior, making yourself impeccable'.[43]

In their poetry, many women Beat writers sought to remove their gender positioning as female from the immediate 1950s discourse while still accepting the feminine as an essentialist archetype. Even if this was a lesser position, it was at least their own. Then it could grow. Kyger played with rewriting the Penelope myth in *The Tapestry and the Web*.[44] Di Prima has generated her own woman-as-animal-and-goddess archetype in the long series called *Loba*.[45] Writing at a time when women poets such as Adrianne Rich and, in the 1960s, Anne Sexton, had been questioning received myths and tales, Di Prima re-creates an archetype from its avatars. In these fierce and powerful poems, Loba is the fellahin woman, the mad Beat Woman, the goddess Kali, the aborter, the crone, the proud natural predator, the mother eternally renewed as virgin: 'I slough off this pain which is claim/to womanhood',[46] says the Loba. The Loba has a lot to say about herself. But that is another chapter, another story.[47]

NOTES

1. Joyce Johnson, *Minor Characters* (New York: Simon and Schuster, 1983), p.85.
2. In 'The Quest and the Question: Cosmology and Myth in the Work of William S. Burroughs, 1953–1960', in Lee Bartlett (ed.), *The Beats: Essays*

in Criticism (Jefferson, NC and London: McFarland, 1981), William L. Stull
makes a convincing case for the quest archetype in *The Naked Lunch*. Leslie
Fiedler's *Love and Death in the American Novel* (New York: Criterion Books,
1960) fits in well with the image of the Beat men without women heading
for the territories. At the time, however, Fiedler did not acknowledge the
Beats as part of the tradition he established: see his *Waiting for the End* (New
York: Stein and Day, 1964), pp.138–78.

3. Michel Foucault, *The Archaeology of Knowledge* (London: Tavistock Press,
    1972), p.27. I am bearing in mind that discourses referring to given objects
    – here, women, male–female relations, male–male relations, femininity,
    masculinity and sexuality – do not necessarily constitute a unity of
    discourse. The connection may lie in the interconnection of rules about
    the self, or sexuality, or the man in society, or power and the body (to name
    a few likely candidates). Any map that emerges may have gaps, since the
    discourse may leave free points of choice. It may also reanimate or change
    perspectives on existing discourses; seeing culture as 'always the same' except
    for details is yet another trap to avoid.

4. Foucault, *Archaeology*, p.27.

5. The advertisement appeared on the last page of Section I.

6. Suzanne M. Bianchi and Daphne Spain, *American Women in Transition* (New
    York: Russell Sage Foundation for the National Committee for Research
    on the 1980 Census), Figure 5.1, p.144, text pp.148–9, 225–6.

7. Department store advertisements for crisp blouses and dark skirts, evidently
    for office use, do appear, clustered in the second, metropolitan section of
    the paper. The images are not signposted as business wear.

8. In *The Seven-Year Itch* Monroe dubiously 'works' as a photographer's model;
    it is unimaginable that she could be employed at anything but displaying
    her body. There appears not to be a natural female body in the physical
    discourse of the era. One striking feature of fashion advertising is the
    number of ads for corsets. As *The Corsetorium* noted, promoting its Lili
    Marlene range: 'you need them all to wear the latest fashions ... all with
    built-in contours for added lift' (*Times*, 8 September 1957). The antitype
    of Monroe, the slender and agile Audrey Hepburn, passes directly from
    girlhood to Electral marriage with a much older man in her 1950s romantic
    comedy vehicles.

9. *Times* Magazine Section, 1 September 1957.

10. Ibid., p.18.

11. *Times* Magazine Section, 8 September 1957.

12. Ibid., p.32.

13. Ibid., p.99.

14. Ibid., p.32.

15. Philip Wylie, *Generation of Vipers* (New York: Rinehart, 1942), pp.184–204.

16. Betty Friedan, *The Feminine Mystique* (New York: Norton, 1963).

17. *Times* Magazine Section, 10 February 1957, p.23.

18. Allan Sekula, 'The Traffic in Photographs', in Benjamin Buchloh, Serge
    Guibaut and David Solkin (eds), *Modernism and Modernity* (Halifax: Press
    of the Nova Scotia College of Art and Design, 1983), cited in W.W. Lhamon,

Jr, *Deliberate Speed: The Origins of a Cultural Style in the American 1950s* (Washington and London: Smithsonian Institution Press, 1990), p.137.

19. A cartoon illustrating Mead's article shows a triumphant wife, arms akimbo, standing by as her seated husband holds the baby. The prevalence of such imagery indicated that 1950s society believed fathers were being asked to undertake an unprecedented responsibility for child-rearing. For men, marital sex meant being left holding the baby.

20. Writing by African–Americans seemed to have been allotted only one spokesman and until the publication of Ralph Ellison's *Invisible Man* the post was still held by Richard Wright. The positive reception to the beatnik image must have owed something to the fact that the Beat hero was paradigmatically white, while the similar 'hipster' was either black or clearly derived his lifestyle from black jazzmen.

21. Robert J. Milewski, *Jack Kerouac: An Annotated Bibliography of Secondary Sources 1944–1979* (Metuchen, NJ and London: Scarecrow Press, 1981), p.179. The memos are on file in the Malcolm Cowley archives at the Newberry Library, Chicago.

22. Milewski, *Jack Kerouac*, pp.180–1.

23. *Times*, Section I, 5 September 1957, p.27.

24. The parallelism of a stance of resistance does not hold in other areas. Camus stresses the need for lucidity in the creator, and the necessity for struggle; if life is worth continuing in the face of the silence of the world, it is only through facing it totally. Although Camus' anti-communism in *L'homme révolté* contributed to his American reputation, he had always been well received in the United States; as early as his visit in March 1946 Justin O'Brien wrote a full-page article in the *NY Herald Tribune* Book review and *L'étranger* was published as *The Stranger* in the US in April 1946. See Herbert R. Lottman, *Albert Camus* (London: Weidenfeld and Nicolson, 1979), pp.379–95.

25. C. Wright Mills, *The Power Elite* (New York and London: Oxford University Press, 1956), pp.304, 323. William H. Whyte, Jr, *The Organization Man* (New York: Simon and Schuster, 1956).

26. Norman Mailer, *The Deer Park* (London: Allen Wingate, 1957), p.217.

27. Kerouac enlisted in the US Navy after dropping out of Columbia, but he was hospitalised for psychiatric observation after walking off duty during boot camp, and discharged soon after. San Francisco poet Robert Duncan was drafted in April 1941 but soon discharged following psychiatric hospitalisation after declaring his homosexuality. Burroughs was also in the army only briefly. Poet Philip Whalen served three years and mentions it in his biographical note for *The New American Poetry*. None of the Beats dramatises the masculine by having an individual hero triumph through conflict despite controlling institutions. If Mailer, who emphasises such conflicts, is any marker, this structure owes much to the experience of war service. In *The Organization Man*, Whyte also notes the structuring of power and conflict in Herman Wouk.

28. UPI press release printed in *Detroit News*, 24 August 1958, reprinted in *The Kerouac Connection*, 4 (1985), p.13.

29. *The People*, 7 August 1960, reprinted in *The Kerouac Connection* 2 (1984), pp.6–7.
30. Jack Kerouac, *On The Road* (Harmondsworth: Penguin, 1972), pp.212, 172, 183, 182.
31. Alix Kates Shulman, 'The Beat Queens: Boho Chicks Stand By Their Men', *Village Voice Literary Supplement*, June 1989. Admiring Diane Di Prima and critiqueing the memoirs of Johnson, Bremser and Cassady, Shulman notes that even Ronald Sukenick's memoir of literary bohemia, *Down and In*, names very few of the 'chicks'. Upon sharing a panel with Alix Kates Shulman at the May 1994 New York University conference on the Beats, I found that many of my ideas converged with hers, and I have benefited from conversations with her.
32. *Heart Beat*, p.4.
33. *Esquire*, February 1958, pp.35–8; March 1958, pp.24, 26; May 1958, pp.87–8.
34. *Playboy*, June 1959, pp.31–2, 42, 79 followed by letters, September 1959; *Life*, 30 November 1959, 'The Only Rebellion Around', cover and pp.114–16, 119–20, 123–4, 126, 129–30.
35. Barbara Ehrenreich, *The Hearts of Men: American Dreams and the Flight from Commitment* (London: Pluto Press, 1983), p.42. Ch. 5 brilliantly traces media appreciation of beatniks and chicks and sees their contribution to the flight from responsibility as the identification of the normal with the 'square'.
36. Allen Ginsberg, *Collected Poems 1947–1980* (New York: Harper and Row, 1984), pp.128, 130. Asterisks in the original.
37. Arthur Knight and Kit Knight (eds), *The Beat Vision* (New York: Paragon, 1987), pp.144–5.
38. Ann Charters (ed.), *The Beats: Literary Bohemians in Postwar America, Dictionary of Literary Biography*, Vol. 16, Pts I and II (Detroit: Gale Research Publications, 1983). Nine women's names are mentioned, but Fran Landesman, mentioned in a joint entry with her husband Jay, was an editor.
39. Bonnie Bremser, *For Love of Ray* (London: London Magazine Editions, 1971), p.13.
40. The panel in question featured Joyce Johnson, Carolyn Cassady, Hettie Jones and Jan Kerouac, and was chaired by Anne Waldman. In fact the women generally took their being lumped together with good humour, though their reactions to what they felt they should say differed. Hettie Jones gave a fresh and vigorous account of the tragicomedy of bohemian life, Joyce Johnson and Carolyn Cassady defended their published memoirs, and Jan Kerouac read some passages from her fiction but appeared to be ill or stoned.
41. Diane Di Prima, *Memoirs of a Beatnik* (San Francisco: Last Gasp, 1988), pp.104–106; first published Paris: Olympia Press, 1969.
42. Anne Waldman, 'My Life a List', in Anne Waldman and Marilyn Webb (eds), *Talking Poetics from the Naropa Institute*, Vol. II (Boulder, CO and London: Shambhala, 1978), p.310.
43. *Talking Poetics* II, p.318.
44. Joanne Kyger, *The Tapestry and the Web* (San Francisco: Four Seasons Foundation, 1965). See especially 'The Long Poem', 'The Dance' and the

untitled poem beginning with the epigraph 'Somewhere you can find
reference to the fact that PAN was the/son of PENELOPE' (p.29).

45. Diane Di Prima, *Loba: Parts I–VII* (Berkeley, CA: Wingbow Press, 1978).

46. Ibid., p.180.

47. A shorter version of this essay appeared in the University of East Anglia
American Studies journal *Signifying Us*, I (1995).

10

'I say my new name':
Women Writers of the
Beat Generation

Amy L. Friedman

'A few of the newer beat women are worn-out ex-prostitutes from the Times
Square area, in their early twenties, who realized they had nothing to show
for several years of hustling – no love, no money, no friendships. They want
to escape the hustling scene but of course have difficulty adjusting to the
square scene, and hence are attracted to the beats, toward whom they are
motherly.'

'The Village Beat Scene: Summer 1960'[1]

'Shortly after Ray Bremser's release from prison in May 1966, he brought the
manuscript of a long poem called *Angel* to Tompkins Square Press, on New
York's Lower East Side. The poem, about his wife, Bonnie [who to support
him and their child while on the run in Mexico had worked as a prostitute],
had been written, according to Bremser, during one night in solitary con-
finement at Trenton State Prison.

Ann Charters, *The Beats: Literary Bohemians in Postwar America*[2]

With their flair for frankness and for lending crudity an air of ineluctable
charm, the male Beat Generation writers succeeded in refocusing the
age-old female paradigm of Virgin Mother. As the above passages
indicate, the Beats' blunt, paradoxical reconfiguring of the female fixes
upon an axis of Angel–Prostitute. Cast in the impossible role of the beatific
whore, it comes as no surprise that women writers of the Beat generation
presage some of the later agendas of the feminist movement. The work
of Bonnie Bremser (Brenda Frazer), Diane Di Prima, Anne Waldman and
Joanne Kyger constructs a radical proto-feminist poetic in its shared investigation of what it means to be female and a writer.

The writers selected here have all appeared in Beat anthologies and
bibliographies, and all have artistic or publishing connections, as well
as personal associations, with 'core' Beat writers: Waldman, for example,

as co-founder with Allen Ginsberg of the Jack Kerouac School of Disembodied Poetics in 1974 at the Buddhist Naropa Institute; and Diane Di Prima as founder of Poets Press, where she published, among other things, Herbert Huncke's *Huncke's Journal* in 1965. Di Prima also helped establish the school at Naropa, and with LeRoi Jones (Amiri Baraka) she also co-edited the little magazine, *Floating Bear*, from 1961 to 1969.[3] Novelist Joyce Johnson, also referred to in this chapter, was involved with Kerouac at the time *On The Road* was published, and is a Beat memoirist.

The women writers of the Beat generation share the writerly attributes which Berkeley's Thomas Parkinson accorded the men when distinguishing Beat writers from the generally louche, unproductive beatniks: 'The beat writer ... is serious and ambitious. He is usually well-educated and always a student of his craft.'[4] A number of women writers have sustained lengthy literary careers which grew out of their participation in the Beat movement, with its opportunities for lively artistic exchanges, and its generation of artistic material which challenged the strictures of civilised society.

But while both men and women were writing, reading aloud, editing and publishing, the Beat milieu was male-dominated, with patriarchal attitudes and an overwhelmingly male orientation. The Beats 'idealized defiant masculinity', Barbara Ehrenreich has written, assessing the Beat phenomenon as male rebellion.[5]

> [...] their adventure did not include women, except, perhaps, as 'experiences' that men might have. And in their vision, which found its way into the utopian hopes of the counterculture, the ideal of personal freedom shaded over into an almost vicious irresponsibility to the women who passed through their lives. (p.171)

Beat angst was male angst: 'It seems we are all inadequate for this world, no one is brave enough, strong enough, happy enough, man enough', Jack Micheline wrote in the characteristically titled 'Whores, Streets, Saints and Dreams'.[6]

The epiphanies belonged to men, 'who copulated ecstatic and insatiate with a bottle of beer a sweetheart/a package of cigarettes a candle and fell off the bed', while the women were interchangeable, any one of 'a million girls trembling in the sunset', in a vast landscape determined by memories of sites of 'innumerable lays of girls'.[7]

Meanwhile, in Greenwich Village, Joyce Johnson bravely found her own apartment and began tentative work on a first novel, socialising with Beat artists and writers despite the fact that her neighbours spied through their doors to see who she was bringing home, the caretaker banged on her door demanding admittance at 3 a.m., and his wife harangued her from the landing as 'Kurva! Kurva!' (Polish for whore).[8]

Of the Beat literature about and produced by women, the material around Bonnie Bremser embodies the impossible axis most acutely. Her literary historical existence is circumscribed by two Beat memoirs: her husband Ray's prose poem about her and their life together, entitled *Angel*, and her own memoir, first published as *Troia: Mexican Memoirs* in 1969 and in London as *For Love of Ray* in 1971. Bremser, Ann Charters records, was incensed that the publishers 'sensationalised' her record of her life with Ray among the Beats and in Mexico by using 'troia', which means adventuress or whore.[9] In attempting to create her own record, Bonnie Bremser was participating in the Beats' undeniable democratisation of the scope and authorship of the literary memoir. However, having been written into Beat history by Ray, she is exhibited only in the single, fixed context of available and exploited sexuality. He writes: 'I shaped her, limned her, limbed her, trimmed her,/blued her, grew & sylphed & hoped to God &/prophecied her nightly & by darkness everywhere.'[10]

Ray's documentation of Bonnie as Angel is a register of his own sexual concerns and his jealousies and urge to possess. The idea of his wife's sexual availability to others torments him. He is conflicted in his desires, ordering her to get dressed and undressed, weighing his dependence on her against her unworthiness, insinuating a note of aversion in his attraction when he writes that 'angels aren't always worthy of what large love a man can sometimes offer up to them' (p.56).

Bonnie Bremser elaborates Beat themes in celebrating the eschewal of material possessions for the freedom and endless possibilities of travel in both 'I Hear a Trane, I Hear You',[11] and in *Troia/For Love of Ray*.[12] She develops a rhythmic, flowing poetic prose, meditating on love, nature and the abstract qualities of human relationships. It is significant that while developing her own voice she none the less articulates many of the extant mysogynistic perceptions towards women prevalent in male Beat writing. She consistently juxtaposes her growing self-awareness with acknowledgement of her vulnerabilities and weaknesses. When Ray tells of her of his infidelities, she briefly blames him and then absorbs the blame for his betrayals: 'I still blamed him for it, even though his right of beauty and spirit was undeniable and my inferiority and contentedness were established in a stroke within an hour after I knew.'[13]

In Bonnie Bremser's texts it is only the ascendant poetic voice that runs counter to the increasing sublimation of self. *For Love of Ray* is a detailed account of her work as a prostitute in Mexico, a narrative which includes harrowing episodes of violence, Ray's imprisonment, and the loss of the Bremser baby to adoption. But it is foremost a literary document, a reworking of the past to assess meaning and intent, and to ascribe presence and consideration to actions which could have been 'read' as meaningless:

> So build more on it, keep writing; yesterday at the Sunday visit with Ray I took him more news of the world as it truly is now. He has told me with no hesitation that I am a whore, emphatically, he loves my whoreness ... this weekend I picked up a man on 42nd Street who could have supplied me with rent money I need now, but I let him drift away. My eye is on visions of writing it instead.[14]

She almost undergoes a renaming in her claiming of the words which describe her work, status and motivations. Initially she says, 'I am going to have trouble with how to call this hustling' (p.31) but later states, 'I embrace my prostitution' (p.51), underscoring her importance as the 'breadwinner' (p.53) as a challenge to delineated gender roles and notions of female economic passivity.

The ascendant poetic voice also flourishes in the work of Beat writer Diane Di Prima, an artist recognised for the strength of her convictions. Di Prima is the most frequently mentioned female Beat writer, known for her associations with Beat writers and artists, her involvement in New York readings and publishing, and later in similar ventures on the West Coast. She is the author of a body of inspired, visionary writing encompassing poetry, translations, drama, prose and a memoir, some of which are ground-breaking, imaginative works. A look at a single issue of the Beat-orientated journal *Yugen* (no. 7, 1961), gives a snapshot of a prolific, productive writer: in addition to Di Prima's poem 'The Jungle', there is an advert for her first poetry collection, *This Kind of Bird Flies Backward*. Two further adverts for publications list her as a contributor: the 'comment and criticism' quarterly *Kulchur*, and *Beat Coast East, An Anthology of Rebellion*, edited by Stanley Fisher. Jack Kerouac, recommending writers in 1963 for a 'very selective' Beat anthology to be published in Italy, identified only four women on his list of 27 writers: Denise Levertov, Lois Sorrells, Barbara Moraff as 'best girl poet' and Diane Di Prima as 'other best girl poet'.[15]

The male bias of the Beat literary scene and of New York publishing generally was not 'an issue' for Di Prima when she was establishing herself as a writer, but she has acknowledged retrospectively that the prevalent attitudes could have been more encouraging:

> It's only more recently I've come to spend any time realizing or thinking about the fact that if the body of work I had done by '63 ... had been done by any of the male writers on that scene at that point, who were my close friends,

I think the acknowledgement that a body of work was in progress would have been much greater.[16]

The value Di Prima articulates with regard to literature is that of the visionary role of the poet, 'the last person who is still speaking the truth when no one else dares to ... the first person to begin the shaping and visioning of the new forms and the new consciousness when no one else has begun to sense it' (p.31). Increasingly she explores the experiential overlap between visionary and female, questioning with escalating intensity male resistance to women's rarefied insights.

There are in Di Prima's work echoes of the agenda the critic Linda A. Kinnahan has explored in the work of William Carlos Williams and Denise Levertov, particularly the drive to 'question the cultural meanings of the masculine, feminine, and maternal, further deconstructing patriarchal definitions of gender'.

Although both Levertov and Di Prima were published in Lawrence Ferlinghetti's City Lights poetry book series, Levertov's poetry has no explicit connection with Beat themes. But there are parallels in each having been, at times, the lone female voice in a group of important male poets, and of having been oblivious at the time to this singularity. Having been 'selected' in this way but unaware of it, Levertov assessed later that she had been positioned as 'the exception that proved the rule – the rule that poetry was a masculine perogative and that women were, by and large, either muses or servants'.[17]

In Di Prima's work this translates into the quest for self-definition and for a clear expression of feminine poetics. Her poetry explores female perspectives of bohemian life, love, motherhood, community and independence. Her poetic voice is variously iconoclastic, wry and meditative. She introduces strategies that involve parody and satire of the communications misfires between men and women as a means of interrogating gender difference. To borrow Kinnahan's terms, in Di Prima's work these approaches allow 'the feminine and the maternal [to] become important figures for alternative authority' (p.125).

Through comic and ironic inversions Di Prima eviscerates the myth of female domesticity. In her 'Nightmare' series cockroaches rule, the bed is 'bug-jumping' (p.4), she uses the vegetable brush on her face and it starts turning vegetables 'kinda strange' (p.7), the cat eats her dinner and she bludgeons it to death.[18] Reference to the beatnik milieu is usual in Beat writing but, like a palimpsest, Di Prima superimposes the experiences of female creativity and fertility, and of motherhood, as themes in her work. The expectant poet-mother in 'Song for Baby-O, Unborn' focuses on poetic gifts she has to offer her child over material ones:

> When you break thru
> you'll find
> a poet here
> not quite what one would choose
> ...
> but I can show you
> baby
> enough to love
> to break your heart (p.24).

'Lullaby' is sung to a child whose father is married to someone else:

> Rockabye
> baby-o
> nothing is strange
> your daddy cut
> for Baltimore
> your mommy's
> making
> songs' (p.27)

'Jeanne Poems', written about one of Di Prima's daughters, is rhapsodic about the arrival of a child in the midst of the usual bohemian disorder:

> Say Baby-O
> how the hell did you come to join me
> with my dirty drawing table
> and my two hundred records
> all stolen (p.29)

Alicia Suskin Ostriker has located in this poem a 'maternal euphoria' embedded as 'a form of cultural defiance' based on Di Prima's 'deliberate hyperbole'.[19] This is typical of the rebellion and lucid anarchy which obtain in Di Prima's work, which Michael Davidson has described as audacious intimations of feminine weakness which only underscore female resiliency. Female and maternal strengths also coexist with the poet's celebrations of an anti-establishment stance and the assertion of independence through creative expression.

The quest for naming forms a thread through Di Prima's *Selected Poems* and also gives a referencing narrative of Beat experience. 'Nightmare 1' is about living on a beach and writing poetry, and unsuccessfully trying to claim a parcel from the post office with no identification cards: 'A package I said a book my name is thus and they said identification please' (p.2). 'Nightmare 7' is about making a passionate advance towards a 'beautiful god' who assumes the next morning he has slept with a prostitute. A scheme to 'get even' with an errant lover involves the plan 'next bedtime/... to call your name wrong' in 'More or Less Love Poems' (p.9). She responds to Gary Snyder's 'Praise for Sick Women', which equates female fertility with illness, by stressing the unity of female creativity in 'The Practice of Magical Evolution': 'i am a woman and my poems/are woman's' (p.39). As with many other Beat writers, a burgeoning interest in Buddhism and Eastern mysticism is recorded as a literary influence: 'I say my new name/over and over/coming home from the temple' (p.270). Here Di Prima uses renaming in the context of a Buddhist consecration, as a rebirth, but I believe the trope is useful in understanding the way in which the work of women writers reflects the process of their participation in what Allen Ginsberg has termed 'the progressive literary explosion' of the Beats.

Powerful statements evolve over the course of her work. 'Brass Furnace Going Out: Song, after an Abortion' addresses some of the the concerns of Allen Ginsberg's 'Howl'. In Di Prima's work the lost generation is the aborted child, the sense of fury the product of the emotional aftermath:

what is it that I cannot bear to say?
that if you had turned out mad, a murderer
a junkie pimp hanged & burning in lime
        alone & filled w/the rotting dark
if you'd been frail and a little given to weirdness
or starved or been shot, or tortured in hunger camps
it wd have been frolic & triumph compared to this (p.92)

Both poems are enunciations of the torment of bearing witness, and of the desperation for spiritual purification, for 'holy forgiveness' (Ginsberg) and peace. Di Prima also shares Ginsberg's sense of polemic. Her 'Revolutionary Letter 40' is sibling to his 'America', adding ecological ruin to the themes of moral decay and personal displacement.

AMERICA, the wilderness is spreading from the parks you have
        fenced it into, already
desert blows through Las Vegas, the sea licks its chops
at the oily edges of Lost Angeles, the camels are breeding, the bears,
        the elk are increasing
so are the indians and the very poor
do you stir in your sleep, America, do you dream of your power
(p.211)

Di Prima and Ginsberg, along with the younger poet Anne Waldman, have also created a body of incantatory verse. Examples are the 'Moloch' section of Ginsberg's 'Howl', the HYMMNN to Naomi Ginsberg in 'Kaddish', Di Prima's 'No Problem Party Poem' and 'Ave', and Waldman's 'Fast Speaking Woman'.[20] Waldman introduces the latter as inspired by a Mazatec Indian Shamaness guide in Mexico to the magic mushroom ceremony. Ostriker has described the character of the 'fast-speaking woman' as an 'urban tribeswoman' (p.204).

> I'm the woman abashed ...
> the woman absorbed, the woman under tyranny
> the contemporary woman,
> the mocking woman
> the artist dreaming inside her house[21]

The incantation is a logical formal choice for Beat writing, with its rhythmic structure, repetition and potential for oral performance, evoking sacred and ancient rites of community. Incantation also evokes the 'songs' and 'chants' of Walt Whitman's *Leaves of Grass*, Dionysian precursor to the Beat sensibility. Di Prima writes of identification with the Dionysian spirit in 'Early Pot Notes', conjuring a poetic spirit which is both sacred and communal: 'Dionysius dismembered comes together again in my own body/rises from my flesh like from the earth–/= spring/giving birth to yes'.[22] She achieves both focus and sublime release in her evocation. Ostriker sees feminist incantatory verse as embodying recognition of the multiplicity of the female self, and Waldman's chants are indeed dizzying celebrations of myriad potentiality. They are also about defiance of fixed definitions: 'I'm a thought woman/I'm a creator woman/I'm a waiting woman/I'm a ready woman' (p.7). Waldman's introduction explains the piece itself as a continuous production which is further improvised during performance. The theme of the limitless expansion of the female spirit also arises in Waldman's later work, as in 'Iovis Omnia Plena', a Menippean mix of poetry, poetic prose, various letters including a satirical one to the President of the US, and a transcript of an interview between Waldman and artist Red Grooms in a New York City taxi cab. The title is from Virgil, 'all is full of Jove': 'in herself a turf of woman becoming Amazonian in proportions (I grow larger even as I write this) as she spans a continent takes on the wise mother as she dies'.[23] The text suggests cycles of suffering and spiritual restitution, against an ascendant axis of experience. Di Prima's search for an alternative creative power which can be configured as feminine and maternal is fulfilled in material such as the

Loba poems, her epic 'creation myth' which establishes the totem of the 'The Loba/mother wolf &/mistress/of many/dances':

> And we wear exhaustion like a painted robe
> I & my sisters
>   wresting the goods from the niggardly
>   dying fathers
> healing each other w/ water & bitter herbs[24]

The Loba merges ancient and contemporary spirits, bringing curative powers to the diseased city, and acclaiming a female sexual potency that resists being demeaned by male aggression. The Loba is fearless, athletic and creative. Her wild fur hidden by blue jeans, she dances with other women in a bar, an elemental force of joyous expression with hidden resources and strengths. She is impervious to male stares.

Di Prima's later works also explicitly construe this 'alternative creative power' as political, as in the *Revolutionary Letters*[25] and in poems such as 'To The Patriarchs':

> My body a weapon as yours is
> MY CHILDREN WEAPONS ETERNALLY
> My tits weapons against the immaterial (*Selected Poems*, p.317)

The critique of power and authority in Waldman's and Di Prima's work is overtly feminist. The ideology, to borrow Kinnahan's words again, 'provides a reference point for advancing ethical and political concerns, a reference point for beginning to remap the realm of authority within a world dominated by men' (pp.125–6). The fires of creativity burn just as fiercely in the Beat women writers as in the men, and the occurrence is just as much a natural phenomenon for both. While not all writing by Beat women refutes their objectification by male writers, resistance does evolve, and there are patterns of claiming territorial rights within the landscape of Beat creativity. Beat women writers have charged the female and the maternal with mystic power, and have illustrated that the necessities and realities of being female are not *de facto* incongruities or inconveniences in literary bohemia.

Diane Di Prima's *Memoirs of a Beatnik* recounts her first encounter with Ginsberg's *Howl and Other Poems*: 'I knew that this Allen Ginsberg, whoever he was, had been breaking ground for all of us.' Suddenly Di Prima was experiencing an immense sense of being part of a connected wave of writers, 'writing what they heard, living ... what they knew, hiding out here and there ... and now, suddenly about to speak out'.[26] Interestingly, *Memoirs* has achieved notoriety in the Beat 'canon' for its scene of an orgy involving Di Prima, several dancers, Kerouac and Ginsberg, and it is always in the context of this material, and other scenes of a sexual nature, that the book is mentioned, in the same way that the poetry of Bonnie Bremser's sexually explicit *Troia* is ignored. What has been overlooked is that *Memoirs* also includes statements about Di Prima's sense of evolving Beat poetics. *Memoirs* rather wryly begs the question of why shouldn't a book about Beat poetics have an orgy scene?

Joanne Kyger began writing poetry as part of the second wave of the San Francisco Renaissance, but her appearance on that literary scene overlaps with the later days of the Beats on the West Coast. Like Di Prima she left college before completing a degree to pursue her own writing, and like Di Prima she often lived with or near other poets, creating a sense of artistic community. She was married for four years to Beat poet Gary Snyder, and in 1957–58 shared the communal East-West House in North Beach with Philip Whalen, Lew Welch and, for a brief period, Jack Kerouac.

Kyger attended the poetry workshop grouped around San Francisco Renaissance poets Robert Duncan and Jack Spicer, and developed her own style in that particular hothouse atmosphere of poetry gurus and devout followers. Duncan, in a published essay called 'Testimony', which reads like a frenzied courtroom defence of poetics, records a 'furore' created at a reading on 23 February 1958 when Kyger read her poem 'The Maze'. He reproduces the poem, and describes Kyger in her habitual stance of kneeling to read it, the image reminding him of Edith Sitwell's comment on becoming a Catholic: 'I had to kneel to something.' His praise of Kyger in 'The Maze' as poet is oblique: 'Intellect then, if it does not kneel to us, can kneel to the poem.'[27]

> She tortures
>   the curtains of the window
>   shreds them
>   like some
>   insane insect
> creates a
>   demented web
>   from the thin folds
>   her possessed fingers
>   clawing
>   she
> thrusts them away with
> sharp jabs of long pins
>   to the walls (p.5)

Kyger's work is spontaneous and lyrical, both facets which were commented upon when *Going On, Selected Poems 1958–80* was selected by Robert Creeley as one of the winners of the US National Poetry Series competition in 1983.[28] Kyger demonstrates a wholly individual perspective, celebrating the independent stance. For example, she blithely tampers with Greek mythology, making Pan the son of Penelope, and Penelope's invented indiscretion the subject of gossip: '... no fantasy of small talk./More the result of BIG talk.'[29] The language is sometimes hermetic but often colloquial: Penelope 'must have had her hands full' (p.2). The lax Beat sense of time pervades many of her lyrics: 'I could use a little rest too/I only slept 11 hours last night.'[30] Her humour is ironic, and she repeatedly uses it to undermine the sacred connection between the feminine and the domestic:

> I don't believe in any
> of your gods or powers ...
>
> I don't even believe
> in My powers or gods
>
> Her dying words were
> Keep the house clean[31]

Or in the same context she enacts an ironic renaming:

> No one was watching the tortillas.
> You were
> That's my new name. No One.
> That's my new name. No One.[32]

Kyger actually sets herself up in opposition to those Beat pillars, Ginsberg and Gary Snyder, in 'October 29, Wednesday', experiencing, by comparison to their active rhetoric, calm enlightenment: 'In a crowd of people I am suddenly elevated' (p.34). In her poem, Ginsberg and Snyder lead 'a quick demonstration march' and a throng follows them. But Kyger suggests that both 'leaders' are taking their roles too seriously, and that the obsequious 'followers' are subscribing to po-faced cant.

> Mr. Ginsberg
> and Mr. Snyder frown, not so much? As they are on their busy way,
> as groups of people pour their respect and devotion to-
> wards them. Pour, pour – they're busy drinking it up all day
> in teacups. Do you think we've sent these young ladies and
> gentlemen in the right direction?

The poet orders her readers' attention to her otherwise ignored moment of perfection.

> With my back against a stone wall
> in a courtyard, I am closing my eyes and – Now if you will
> just observe me, I will move up off the ground, hopefully
> as much as a foot.

The imperative commands 'Silence' as her rise begins, and with it the exorcism of negative influences in the perfect elevation of capturing a moment of truth. Kyger weighs up the mass attention paid to these particular two men against the ignored verity of her own experience.

Beat chroniclers have tended to mythologise the spark of spontaneous intimacy among the central coterie of Beat writers, underscoring the group's awesome capacity for closeness, generally ignoring the complications of their intellectual, creative and sexual intersections.[33] Beat women have been considered as largely peripheral to the artistic and personal lives of Beat men, and likewise Beat women writers have been construed as marginal in their contributions. Against the phenomenon of foregrounded, idealised and highly idolised mothers – Naomi Ginsberg, 'Memere' Kerouac – the attitude of male Beat writers was to reify the abstract axis of female sexuality into a mode of expectation of the female which privileged her (sexual) subservience and silence.

This is Joyce Johnson's emphasis, in her Beat memoir *Minor Characters*, when she registers her exasperation with John Clellon Holmes' preface to a new edition of his Beat novel, *Go*. It had been 25 years since its original publication, she notes, but Holmes defies completely the influence of the women's movement when he 'scrupulously matches each of the male characters in his roman à clef to their originals' but identifies 'the "girls"' only as 'variously "amalgams of several people"; "accurate to the young women of the time"; "a type rather than an individual".'[34] It seems to Johnson that to Holmes the women 'were mere anonymous passengers on the big Greyhound bus of experience'. She comments ruefully: 'What they did, I guess, was fill up the seats' (p.79). And in their silence they epitomised beat 'cool', as Johnson's friend, poet Elise Cowen, appraised the beautiful black-clad subterranean women she admired in Fugazi's Bar on Sixth Avenue who 'never, never say a word; they are presences merely' (p.74).

Despite her explicit irony, Johnson's text and even her title have been subjected to misreadings which fail to register that she asserts the ignored presence, rather than the absence, of women among the Beat writers.

Her memoir concludes elegiacally for the overlooked women who shared the madness and excitement of Greenwich Village in the 1950s: for Elise Cowen, desperately in love with Allen Ginsberg, a suicide at 28; for Hettie Jones and her 'poems ... kept mute in boxes for too many years'; and for her own 22-year-old self:

> As a female, she's not quite part of this convergence. A fact she ignores, sitting by in her excitement as the voices of the men, always the men, passionately rise and fall and their beer glasses collect and the smoke of their cigarettes rises toward the ceiling and the dead culture is surely being wakened. Merely being here, she tells herself, is enough.
> What I refuse to relinquish is her expectancy.
> *It's only her silence that I wish to give up.* (pp.261–2; my italics)

The theme of wanting to be seen, heard and recognised runs consistently through the work of Beat women writers, as in Sally Stern's 'Wait, I've been This Way Before':

> I know that I shall be the sea
> And the mother
> And never me.
> Wait
> I am here
> Under the sea
> Recognize me.[35]

Di Prima iterates a similar concern in 'The Party': 'I NEED TO BE LOOKED AT/be seen/& not twice a week/I'm not a Brancusi bird' (*Selected Poems*, p.74). Ostriker identifies these imperatives as key terms in the poetics of intimacy (p.170), but this is incongruous in light of the Beat generation's incessant flaunting of intimacy. In the Beat context these literal requests to be recognised reshape the politics of intimacy between men and women. Di Prima sets down some basics for communication in 'Coscia's: November 1963 (Letter to John Wieners)':

> I expect a certain amount of
> respect
> yes I do
> as do you
> (don't like to be called 'girlie')
> a certain amount of deference
> stopping to listen
> when I pronounce
> an opinion. (p.119)

Both Johnson and Di Prima assess the precariousness of the lives women writers, and women generally, led in the Beat period, highlighting manifold threats that were legal, parental, economic and psychological. Simply gaining access to the male-dominated and often exclusive discussions about the craft of writing was a struggle. Di Prima has commented in interview that:

> I can't say a lot of really great women writers were ignored in my time, but I can say a lot of potentially great women writers wound up dead or crazy. I think of the women on the Beat scene with me in the early '50s, where are they now? ... I don't want to rant on about individual cases, but the threat of incarceration or early death in one form or another was very real.[36]

Di Prima alludes to extremely complicated, barbed politics between men and women writers, a complex scenario of attention-seeking and -avoidance by women writers. She confirms that she persevered, but has no explanation for her 'survival' as a writer other than the fact that she did survive: 'We wrote the way Virginia Woolf describes Jane Austen hiding her papers under the table cloth. We really wanted to stay inconspicuous. Most of us. I was a brash little brat. Probably why I'm still alive!' (p.31).

Di Prima's comments help to explain why a conventional assessment of what was good literature, which is to say published literature, doesn't necessarily obtain. Not getting published was 'traceable' to being female, but Di Prima indicates that she and her contemporaries weren't aware of it at the time. It is only later that they fully recorded the obstacles they faced, and were able to transmit 'the information that makes you a proficient writer' to a subsequent generation of women (p.31). Far more just to the women writers of the Beat generation would be to determine their merit by the sole criterion established by LeRoi Jones: did they 'extend and enliven the language'?[37]

What happens to the whole idea of Beat if we include these writers? Beat literature is then resoundingly reshaped and widened in its scope. The women writers are finally read in their own right as major rather than minor contributors, no longer just as reference material for accessing the men, and no longer as ciphers for the assumed profundity of transient male desires. As women they lose in symbolic status but as writers they gain in literary credibility. Even a 'strict' Beat canon that excluded, for example, post-1961 work as too diffuse, would have to contend with the existence of Di Prima, Kyger and Sally Stern, as well as other writers not included in this essay because of lack of space, such as Barbara Ellen (Moraff), Lenore Kandel and Brigid Murnaghan. A less rigid chronological formulation would also have to encompass West

Coast poets Janine Pommy Vega and Joanna McClure, New York poet Fran Landesman and the memoirists Carolyn Cassady, Eileen Kaufman, Hettie Jones and Jan Kerouac. Further attention to the memoirs will no doubt raise additional interpretive issues around the domestic nature of the women's concerns and contributions. Carolyn Cassady asserts that her interactions were mutual ones: 'I wasn't the poor little housewife ... that's not what we had. It was an intellectual interest' which formed the dynamic of her enduring Beat relationships.[38]

The women writers of the Beat generation, while enscribing their presence, were also shaping a political consciousness, embarking on visionary declarations and rewriting the rules of literary bohemian life. The visionary mode explicitly characterises the later work of Waldman, Di Prima and Kyger. Adrienne Rich has called Di Prima's *Loba* poems 'a great geography of the female imagination'. An apt tribute to Di Prima, it is also a description befitting the contributions of the women writers of the Beat generation, defining and marking the significance of their acts of testimony and creation.

NOTES

1. The Village Beat Scene: Summer 1960' in Ned Polsky, *Hustlers, Beats and Others* (Chicago: Aldine Press, 1967; Harmondsworth: Penguin, 1971), p.153.
2. Ann Charters (ed.), *The Beats: Literary Bohemians in Postwar America, Dictionary of Literary Biography*, Vol. 16, Pts I and II (Michigan: Gale Research Publications, 1983), p.34. *Angel* was published in 1967.
3. In April 1962, Di Prima and Jones were cleared of obscenity charges stemming from their publication in *Bear* of William Burroughs' satire 'The Routine', and of an excerpt from Jones' 'System of Dante's Hell'. This was announced in *Yugen* issue 8, the New York journal Jones edited with his wife Hettie, author of the Beat memoir *How I Became Hettie Jones*.
4. Thomas Parkinson (ed.), *A Casebook on the Beats* (New York: Crowell, 1961, pp.279–80, quoted in Warren French, *The San Francisco Poetry Renaissance, 1955–1960* (Boston, Massachusetts: Twayne Publishers, G.K. Hall, 1991), p.xx.
5. Barbara Ehrenreich, *The Hearts of Men: American Dreams and the Flight from Commitment* (London: Pluto Press, 1983), p.107.
6. In *The Beat Book*, Vol. 4 (1974) of *The unspeakable visions of the individual*, eds Arthur Knight and Glee Knight, Calif PA, p.64. Series of numbered books, Vol. 4.
7. Allen Ginsberg, 'Howl', in Ann Charters (ed.), *The Penguin Book of the Beats* (Harmondsworth: Penguin, 1992), p.64.
8. Joyce Johnson, *Minor Characters* (London: Harvill, 1983), p.209.
9. Charters (ed.), *Penguin Book of the Beats*, p.465.

10. Ray Bremser, *Angel* (New York: Tompkins Square, 1967), p.13.
11. Bonnie Bremser, 'I Hear a Trane, I Hear You: for John Coltrane (who's been dead for years)', in Arthur Knight and Kit Knight (eds), *unspeakable visions of the individual*, 1980 Vol. 10, California, PA, pp.93–4.
12. Bonnie Bremser, *For Love of Ray* (London: London Magazine Editions, 1971); first published as *Troia: Mexican Memoirs* (New York, Croton Press, 1969).
13. Bremser, 'I Hear a Trane', p.96.
14. Bremser, *For Love of Ray*, p.55.
15. Letter dated 18 April 1963 to Fernanda Pivano Sottsass, in Knight, ed., *The Beat Book*, 1974. Kerouac wrote 'Da Prima' on the list, but then he also included 'Ferlingretti'. 'Be sure not to leave out Miss Da Prima & Miss Moraff or Mrs. Sorrells – so you can have a representative anthologia', he specified. The anthology Pivano Sottsass eventually edited and published in Italy was *Poesia Degli Ultimi Americani* (1965). She also wrote the introduction to the Italian edition of Kerouac's *The Dharma Bums*.
16. *The Beat Road, unspeakable visions* vol 14, 1984 (California, Pennsylvania: Knight). Diane Di Prima interviewed by Anne Waldman in 1978, p.29.
17. Levertov's introduction to *Poems by Women*, quoted in Linda A. Kinnahan, *Poetics of the Feminine: Authority and Literary Tradition in William Carlos Williams, Mina Loy, Denise Levertov, and Kathleen Fraser* (Cambridge: Cambridge University Press, 1994), p.128.
18. Diane Di Prima, *Selected Poems 1956–1975* (Vermont: North Atlantic Books, 1975).
19. Alicia Suskin Ostriker, *Stealing the Language: The Emergence of Women's Poetry in America* (Boston: Beacon Press, 1986; London: Women's Press, 1987), p.180.
20. As mentioned above, all three have been involved with the Naropa Institute. See Anne Waldman and Marilyn Webb (eds), *Talking Poetics from the Naropa Institute* (Boulder, CO. and London: Shambhala, 1978), for discourses, transcripts of talks and so on by Di Prima, Waldman, Ginsberg, et al.
21. Anne Waldman, *Fast Speaking Woman and other chants* (San Francisco: City Lights, 1975), pp.3–4.
22. In *The Beat Book*, eds Arthur Knight and Glee Knight, Vol. 4 1974, *unspeakable visions of the individual*, California, PA 1974, p.118. The piece, a prose-poem, is dated Fall 1958.
23. Anne Waldman, 'Iovis Omnia Plena', in Lawrence Ferlinghetti and Nancy J. Peters (eds), *City Lights Review*, No. 2, 1988, p.192.
24. Diane Di Prima, *Loba: Parts I–VIII*, in Charters (ed.), *Penguin Book of the Beats*, pp.531, 534.
25. Diane Di Prima, *Revolutionary Letters* (San Francisco: City Lights, 1971).
26. Quoted in Bruce Cook, *The Beat Generation* (New York: Charles Scribner's Sons, 1971), p.66.
27. Robert Duncan, *As Testimony: The Poem & The Scene* (San Francisco: White Rabbit, 1964), p.14.
28. Joanne Kyger, *Going On, Selected Poems 1958–80* (New York: Dutton, 1983).
29. Kyger, 'Pan as the Son of Penelope', in *Going On*, p.2.

30. Kyger, 'Tuesday, October 28', in *Going On*, p.33.
31. Kyger, 'I don't believe in any', in *Going On*, p.49.
32. Kyger, 'No one was watching the tortillas' in *Going On*, p.41.
33. Explication of this area generally has been undertaken by the women memoirists, many of whom wrote and published their work well after the main period of the Beat generation.
34. Johnson, *Minor Characters*, p.79.
35. Elias Wilentz (ed.), *The Beat Scene* (New York: Corinth Books, 1960), p.96.
36. *The Beat Road*, 1984, p.31.
37. LeRoi Jones in letters debate in *Partisan Review* 25, Summer 1958.
38. In conversation with the author, September 1995.

Notes on Contributors

Clive Bush is Director of American Studies at King's College, London. In addition to many articles on American themes, he has written *The Dream of Reason: American Consciousness and Cultural Achievement from Independence to the Civil War* (1977) and *Halfway to Revolution: Investigation and Crisis in Henry Adams, William James and Gertrude Stein* (1991). He has also published three books of poetry, *clearing the distance* (1978), *the range taken* (1983) and *shifts in undreamt time* (1989).

R.J. Ellis is head of English at the Nottingham Trent University. Over the last twenty years he has written a number of pieces on Beat writing, including studies of *Evergreen Review*, *Yugen*, Ferlinghetti and Burroughs. *Science Fiction: Roots and Branches* (co-edited with G.R. Garnett) appeared in 1990.

Amy L. Friedman, AB, Bryn Mawr College, is a postgraduate research student at Goldsmith's College, London. Her thesis analyses postcolonial satire and has led to two recent essays, 'Postcolonial Satire and Narratives of Immigration by Three South Asian Women Writers' and 'Women and Satire: Too Juvenal For Words'.

Cynthia S. Hamilton currently chairs American Studies at the Crewe and Alsager Faculty of the Manchester Metropolitan University. She is the author of *Western and Hard-boiled Detective Fiction in America: From High Noon to Midnight* (1987) and a forthcoming book on literary responses to slavery, as well as other work on American genre fiction.

David Ingram teaches American Studies at Brunel University College. His research interests include technology and environmentalism in American culture.

A. Robert Lee is Reader in American Literature at the University of Kent at Canterbury. His publications include eleven volumes in the Vision Critical Series, from *Black Fiction: New Studies in The Afro-American Novel*

217

Since 1945 (1980) to *William Faulkner: The Yoknapatawpha Fiction* (1990); Everyman Editions of Melville's *Typee* (1993), *Moby-Dick* (1973, 1993) and *Billy Budd* (1993); essay-collections like *A Permanent Etcetera: Cross-Cultural Perspectives on Post-War America* (1993) and *Other Britain, Other British: Contemporary Multicultural Fiction* (1995); *Shadow Distance: A Gerald Vizenor Reader* (1994); and a wide range of essays on American and European mutliculturalism.

Helen McNeil teaches American literature and studies at the University of East Anglia, is the author of *Emily Dickinson* (1986), has been a frequent broadcaster with the BBC and elsewhere, and has published widely on the topics of women and modernism, including chapters on Elizabeth Bishop and Sylvia Plath in Helen Vendler (ed.): *Voices and Visions* (1987).

John Muckle was General Editor of *The New British Poetry* (1988), has published a book of stories, *The Cresta Run* (1987), and short prose in magazines and anthologies like *Seeing in the Dark* (1990) and *Brought to Book* (1995). He has reviewed poetry in *City Limits* and elsewhere and is co-editor of *Active in Airtime*, a magazine of contemporary poetry and fiction. He teaches at the University of Essex.

Jim Philip teaches in the Department of Literature at the University of Essex where he has also acted as the Director of the Centre of United Studies. He is the author of several articles on topics in American literature and contemporary travel writing.

Alistair Wisker is Deputy Director of the Extra Mural Board at the University of East Anglia. He is the author of many articles and essays as well as a full-length study, *The Writing of Nathaniel West*.

Index